Signs of Their Times

Signs of Their Times

History, Labor, and the Body in Cobbett, Carlyle, and Disraeli

JOHN M. ULRICH

Ohio University Press
Athens

Ohio University Press, Athens, Ohio 45701

Printed in the United States of America

Ohio University Press books are printed on acid-free paper ∞ ™

10 09 08 07 06 05 04 03 02   5 4 3 2 1

Library of Congress Cataloging-in-Publication Data

Ulrich, John McAllister.
Signs of their times : history, labor, and the body in Cobbett, Carlyle, and Disraeli / John M. Ulrich.
p. cm.
Includes bibliographical references and index.
ISBN 0-8214-1401-1 (alk. paper)
1. English prose literature—19th century—History and criticism. 2. Literature and history—Great Britain—History—19th century. 3. Literature and society—Great Britain—History—19th century. 4. Cobbett, William, 1763–1835. 5. Carlyle, Thomas, 1795–1881. Past and present. 6. Disraeli, Benjamin, Earl of Beaconsfield, 1804–1881. Sybil. 7. Historical fiction, English—History and criticism. 8. Body, Human, in literature. 9. History in literature. 10. Work in literature. I. Title

PR778.H5 U47 2001
809358—dc21

2001036002

for Lynn, Samantha Sage, and Adyn Sunn

Contents

Acknowledgments

For their guidance and encouragement as I prepared the initial version of this book, I am indebted to John Dings, Deidre Lynch, and William Warner. Their comments, suggestions, and criticisms always proved instructive and challenging, and I deeply appreciate the time they devoted to this project. I also thank Ben Agger for taking the time to respond to the whole of that first version. I thank my friend and colleague Larry K. Uffelman for his valuable comments on the published version of the Carlyle chapters, and for his generous support and encouragement of my work in general. I am grateful, in fact, to all the members of the Department of Languages and Literature at Mansfield University for their steadfast commitment to scholarship and their genuine interest in (and support for) the scholarly work of their colleagues, both within the department and across the university.

Portions of this book have been presented at several conferences, including meetings of the Modern Language Association, the Northeast Modern Language Association, the Victorian Work conference in Santa Cruz, and the Carlyle Bicentenary Conference in St. John's, Newfoundland. I am grateful to the organizers of these conferences (especially Mark Cumming, John O. Jordan, and Hilary Schor), the panel participants and chairs (particularly Gary Handwerk), and the audiences for the opportunity to present this work in a supportive, constructive context. An earlier version of chapter 3 was published as "'A Labor of Death and a Labor against Death': Translating the Corpse of History in Carlyle's *Past and Present*," in *Carlyle Studies Annual* 15 (1995): 33–46; and an earlier version of chapter 4 was published as

"The Reinscription of Labor in Carlyle's *Past and Present*," in *Criticism* 37 (summer 1995): 443–68. I am grateful to the publishers for permission to reprint material from these articles.

I am also grateful to the director of the Ohio University Press, David Sanders, for his support for this project, to Nancy Basmajian, for her editing expertise, and to the staff members for their assistance in bringing this book to print. I also thank the anonymous reader for the press, whose comments and suggestions were extremely helpful during the final revision of the manuscript.

My parents, Jack and Joan, and my sister, Julie, have provided me with invaluable support (both moral and material) since the very beginning, and to them I am deeply indebted. My greatest debt, though, is to Lynn Pifer, who has read and responded to this book at every stage of its progress with patience and wisdom. Without her love and her generosity, very little would be possible. And there is much I owe to my daughters Samantha Sage and Adyn Sunn, who cheerfully remind me that *work*—though weighted with moral, professional, and economic import—is no match for the disruptive and subversive pleasures of *play*.

Signs of Their Times

Introduction

Reading the Signs of the Times

Terms and Conditions

We were wise indeed, could we discern truly the
signs of our own time; and by knowledge of its wants and
advantages, wisely adjust our own position in it.
—Carlyle, "Signs of the Times"[1]

WITH HIS ESSAY "SIGNS OF THE TIMES" (1829), Thomas Carlyle first ventured into the field of social commentary, declaring his time to be a "Mechanical Age"—an age likely to produce "a mighty change in our whole manner of existence" (62). Arguing for the significance of "Signs of the Times" as central to Carlyle's subsequent body of work, and, indeed, as "a major element in the tradition of English social criticism," Raymond Williams claims:

> What is important in a thinker like Carlyle is the quality of his direct response: the terms, the formulations, the morphology of ideas, are properly a secondary matter. . . . Carlyle is in this essay stating a direct response to the England of his times: to Industrialism, which he was the first to name: to the feel, the quality, of men's general reactions—that structure of contemporary feeling which is only ever apprehended directly; as well as to the character and conflict of formal systems and points of view.[2]

In emphasizing "the quality of his direct response," Williams underscores the immediacy and clarity of Carlyle's essay, his ability to grasp and respond to what Williams famously terms the "structure of contemporary feeling." Carlyle himself, however, does not share Williams's absolute faith in the directness of such apprehension, and nowhere is this more evident than in the fact that Carlyle's "Signs of the Times" foregrounds the very "terms" and "formulations" that Williams deems secondary to the importance of that essay. In accentuating the *signs* of the times, Carlyle at once emphasizes the textual nature of any critical interrogation of the present, and further acknowledges that any apprehension of the present must necessarily proceed *indirectly*. It is this indirectness itself, ironically, that Carlyle ultimately designates as one of the primary characteristics of "the Age of Machinery," an era in which "nothing is done directly, or by hand" (59).

Carlyle's essay thus explicitly represents "the times" not only as a text to be read and deciphered, but also as a text marked by indirectness, by a profound mediation of all productive work, including the production of knowledge. Although the task Carlyle sets for himself, as formulated in the epigraph to this introduction, is to "discern truly the signs of our own time," that task, as Carlyle recognizes, remains problematized by its inescapable context—from within "the perplexed scene where we stand" (59). And it is precisely this context, of course, that serves as the object of Carlyle's "discernment." Carlyle indeed hopes that "on a more serious inspection, something of its perplexity will disappear," but that desire for a clear or direct apprehension can be pursued only through a mediated reading of the signs of the times. While Carlyle purports to come to some conclusion as to the true meanings of these signs (what he calls the "distinctive characteristics and deeper tendencies" of the present age), everywhere he represents the present as a time of perplexity, indirectness, and instability. If one of the "deeper tendencies" of the time is thus its tendency toward mediated indirectness—toward, one might say, a system of signification that appears to be organized arbitrarily, without a "natural" or guaranteed relation of reference—then any interrogation of such an age that seeks a deeper, fundamental structure can only be at odds with the age itself, engaged in a paradoxical attempt at defining and ordering that which has already, by its very "nature," rendered definition and coherence problematic and provisional.

It is no surprise, then, that Carlyle finds such indirectness not only in the increasingly automated modes of production, but also in the shifting focus of social discourse away from the inner "spiritual" truth and toward the outer, material world: "It is no longer the moral, religious, spiritual condition of the people that is our concern, but their physical, practical, economical condition, as regulated by public laws. Thus is the Body-politic more than ever worshipped and tendered; but the Soul-politic less than ever" (67). Such a shift, Carlyle goes on to argue, neglects the "true dignity of soul and character" (73) that gives meaning and coherence to human endeavor, producing instead a society of shallowness and contrivance.[3] As a result, Carlyle diagnoses the "condition" of England, borrowing Hamlet's familiar terms of ill health and disorder: "The time," he writes, "is sick and out of joint" (81).

A decade later, in *Chartism* (1839) and *Past and Present* (1843), Carlyle would have cause to reassess the need for attention to the material condition of the people of England. Indeed, by then Carlyle would find himself characterizing the everyday lives of the "Body-politic" in the terms he previously reserved for the "Soul-politic," with the generalized spiritual emptiness of the times now mirrored in the literal, physical emptiness of ordinary laborers suffering from inanition.[4] Although Carlyle thus modifies his position with respect to the material condition of the British and Irish workers, in his writing of the two decades following "Signs of the Times," his diagnosis does not change.[5] And this "diagnosis," I would argue, marks the beginning of Carlyle's engagement with the interrelation between representation (both textual and political) and the material condition of the people.

This interrelation lies at the heart of what Carlyle called the "Condition-of-England question," and any interrogation of this question necessarily requires both the "representation" of that condition and its remedy. Not surprisingly, the two are always interdependent; to argue that agrarian or urban workers are quite capable of improving their own condition on their own terms, for example, one also would have to represent that condition as allowing for the possibility of such improvement. Indeed, in advocating the restoration of a balance between the Body-politic and the Soul-politic as a way of "curing" the "sick and out of joint" condition of England, Carlyle's envisioning of such a balance, as Raymond Williams himself notes, can proceed only according to "the terms he [Carlyle] has set."[6] Ultimately, then, the condition-of-England discourse itself, though it takes up the matter of material conditions, does so only indirectly, as a matter of terms and conditions. And with a new indirectness now introduced into relations of textual and social signification, the condition of England might be and often was thought of as primarily a crisis of representation (both political and textual), a crisis that, for Carlyle in particular, threatens to send the terms of social discourse and the conditions of everyday life into disarray.

In an attempt to account for and redress this condition of representational crisis from the 1820s through the 1840s, three writers in particular—William Cobbett in *A History of the Protestant "Reformation"* (1824–26) and *Rural Rides* (1830), Carlyle in *Past and Present* (1843), and Benjamin Disraeli in *Sybil* (1845)—argue that the signs of the times testify to a historical disruption explicitly marked by the degradation of labor and the body, the latter both material (the emaciated, unhealthy bodies of individual laborers) and metaphoric (the deteriorating condition of the social body). Ultimately, all three writers perceive this disruption as constituting a shift away from relatively stable social and productive relations toward a world in which truth and meaning are no longer guaranteed. The source of this shift, as each writer recognizes, is industrial capitalism, and its consequences are not only economic but cultural, pushing the nation, as Carlyle puts it in *Past and Present*, toward the very brink of a precipice, where "the next step now is lifted *not* over land, but into air, over ocean-deeps and roaring abysses."[7]

All three writers "diagnose" the condition of England, then, not only as a crisis concerning the material conditions of the rural and urban working classes, but also as a much more general crisis—with more far-reaching implications—playing out across the terrain of English social history, a crisis that threatens, in fact, to displace the historical underpinnings of social organization and meaning itself, and to erode the significance of labor into little more than an empty gesture. I have chosen to focus on Cobbett, Carlyle, and Disraeli because each reads the "signs of the times" as indicative of their society's progressive destabilization, discernable in three interrelated "conditions": the sharp disjunction between the past and the present, the rapid degradation of working and living conditions for the laboring class, and the concomitant debilitation of the laboring (and social) body. In response, each writer seeks in his own way to intervene in this process of social devolution by refashioning these terms and conditions of the times—history, labor, and the body—into mutually dependent guarantors of stability and meaning.

Of course, to seek stability and order in the midst of uncertain times is not a strategy unique to these authors; indeed, the three have often been lumped together with other nineteenth-century writers, artists, architects, and theologians under the usually pejorative category of the "medieval revival." Because such "revivalists" are often viewed as seeking little more than a nostalgic return to an imagined, idealized past when stability, hierarchy, and meaningfulness reigned (and therefore seen as failing to contend directly and pragmatically with the increasingly rapid social changes driven by industrial capitalism), Carlyle, Cobbett and Disraeli have too often been easily dismissed (then and now) as rather minor voices articulating a decidedly futile (even frivolous) response to the economic and social crises of their time.[8]

However, given the recent attention in our own time to terms such as "history" and "the body" in the field of literary and cultural studies, and especially given the generalized "foregrounding of representation"[9] that has characterized nineteenth-century studies over the last two decades, the Romantic and Victorian literary landscape appears increasingly complex and textured, a landscape shaped and reshaped not only by the profound changes in the modes and relations of production, but also by the interplay of various competing but interdependent discourses attempting to order and make sense of this "perplexed scene." Various critical works published in the 1980s and 1990s, from Gareth Stedman Jones's essay collection *The Languages of Class* (1983) and Catherine Gallagher's *The Industrial Reformation of English Fiction* (1985), to Mary Poovey's *Making a Social Body* (1995) and Kevin Gilmartin's *Print Politics* (1997), have carefully and closely examined the "terms and conditions" of such discourses in order to better account for their relative successes and failures.[10] Other works, particularly those by writers whose critical practice is informed by feminist and gender theory—Christina Crosby's *The Ends of History: Victorians and "the Woman Question"* (1991); the essay collection *Rewriting the Victorians: Theory, History, and the Politics of Gender* (1992), edited by Linda Shires; and Joan Wallach Scott's recently updated *Gender and the Politics of History* (1999), to name only a few—have drawn much-needed attention to the way history, class, and gender are inextricably bound together in various discursive formations throughout the nineteenth century.[11]

While this trend in literary studies toward the "foregrounding of representation" and textuality has sometimes been lamented, in the case of nineteenth-century studies the end result has meant not so much the "foregrounding of representation" (i.e., the heavy-handed application of "theory") as the recognition that the various competing threads of Victorian and pre-Victorian social discourse *had already foregrounded* the question of representation, both textual and political. Indeed, this "foregrounding" is one of the primary characteristics not only of the Romantic and Victorian periods, but also, and most especially, of the Romantic/Victorian borderland, precisely when settling the question of representation was seen as crucial to resolving the series of social, economic, and political crises that characterized the increasingly turbulent decades from the 1820s to the 1840s.[12]

In seeking to "foreground" a particular convergence of attention to history, labor, and the body among three writers of the decades before and after the first Reform Bill, I have chosen four generically disparate texts: Cobbett's *History of the Protestant "Reformation"* and *Rural Rides* are quintessential examples of polemical historiography and political travelogue, respectively; Carlyle's *Past and Present* is direct social criticism of the sort that can perhaps only be described as Carlylean; and Disraeli's *Sybil; or, The Two Nations* belongs to the subgenre of the Victorian industrial novel. Situating Disraeli's novel in the context of nonfictional prose, rather than within its established subgenre, would seem to accord *Sybil* a certain singularity with respect to its industrial-novel peers. And, indeed, my argument will suggest that Disraeli's *Sybil* has more in common with Carlyle's *Past and Present* and Cobbett's *Rural Rides* and *A History of the Protestant "Reformation"* than with *Alton Locke*, *Mary Barton*, *North and South*, *Hard Times*, or *Felix Holt*.[13]

While the industrial novels of Kingsley, Gaskell, Dickens, and Eliot also attend, of course, to industrialism's degradation of the working class, and thus to the condition of labor and the laboring body, Disraeli's particular emphasis on the historical context of that degradation, coupled with the sense in which *Sybil* functions (in Disraeli's view) as a counternarrative to the accepted view of historical progress in his time, places him more firmly in line, I believe, with his nonfictional prose antecedents, who are also seeking to establish a stable, meaningful relationship between the past and the present in an effort to strengthen the seemingly moribund social body.

As Linda Shires argues in her afterword to *Rewriting the Victorians*, "[c]ultural change always comes about by at least a three-pronged process of readjustment: a reorganization of the material conditions of production, a reorganization of cultural symbols, and a rearticulation of current vocabulary in new ways. Such alterations are not imposed from without, but occur from within the cultural formation by agents and collectives of agents."[14] It is precisely as such agents of "readjustment" that I have sought to represent Carlyle, Disraeli, and Cobbett in these pages. Whereas in 1829 Carlyle advocated the "true discernment" of the "signs of the times" in order to "wisely adjust our own position in it," for Carlyle in 1843, and for Cobbett before him and Disraeli shortly after, the question became not so much one of *self*-adjustment, as it did one of *cultural readjustment*, a process that necessitated for each a recentering or realigning of social signification, which each sees as a necessary prelude to the resolution of the condition-of-England crisis. As I intend to show in the following chapters, these three writers are not merely wallowing in a wistful nostalgia for the past; instead, each writer's intense level of engagement with his *present times* is founded on two mutually important characteristics: a passionate belief in the power of writing to shape the way people understand their position relative to the past, present, and future; and a relentlessly self-conscious approach to discerning the texture of those times—to the complex, "perplexing" interrelation between the materiality and the textuality of history, labor, and the body.

Though Cobbett's *A History of the Protestant "Reformation"* is usually dismissed as little more than a typical example of the medieval revivalist tendency to idealize the past, in chapter 1 I argue that Cobbett's book foregrounds the textuality of history in order to assert that the historical truth actually lies elsewhere—inscribed on the *present* material bodies of ordinary laborers. According to Cobbett, it is on the very bodies of the people that the violent effects of history, including poverty, hunger, and dispossession, have been inscribed; in this way, the bodies of the people become not only signs of the present condition of England and Ireland, but also signs of its history, signs that offer, for Cobbett, a "true description" of England, past and present.

Because Cobbett ultimately intends, through his writing, to improve the material lives of those laborers, his writing thus seeks the alteration of those bodies—their "reformation," if you will, a "reformation" that will erase the signs of the violent separation of the laboring bodies from the wealth resulting from their labor. Cobbett's *A History of the Protestant "Reformation"* may thus be seen as an attempt at the reformation of historical representation, a rewriting that seeks simultaneously to establish a sign relation between the material bodies of the present and the historical events of the past, and to erase that relation through a re-formation, or alteration, of the bodies of present workers. In Cobbett's ideal, reformed world, then, the bodies of laborers would no longer be marked by the signs of the historical "reformation"; as reformed bodies, their signification would thus break with the past and return to the body itself, empowering that body with the ability to inscribe its own history.

For Cobbett, the matter of attending to the material and metaphoric body thus lies at the very heart of what Carlyle later would call the "Condition-of-England question." The site of Cobbett's textual and political struggle, therefore, is always the (unhealthy) body in all of its manifestations—individual and social, material and metaphoric—and such a terrain of struggle therefore necessitates strategies that will redress the condition of the body at both the material and representational levels. Chapter 2 interrogates these sometimes paradoxical strategies, including radical husbandry and parliamentary reform, with attention to the way the rhetoric of Cobbett's "body/politics" in *Rural Rides* (his use of the term "Wen," for example) seeks to link inextricably the symbolic with the material, the political with the everyday, in an attempt to restore the health of the people, and of the national body as a whole.

Chapter 2 concludes with an examination of the way these strategies find their combined symbolic embodiment in the romanticized body-image of William Cobbett himself. As I argue, the irony of his failure and demise—that his labor to restore the health of both the body of Parliament and the nation through his physical presence in the House of Commons ultimately destroyed his own health—is further deepened by Cobbett's attempt throughout his writings to project a healthy and robust self-image, an image perpetuated by Cobbett's commentators (including Carlyle), and one that tends to obscure his practical efforts to alter—materially and metaphorically—the body of the people.

In contrast to Cobbett's view of history as "textual" in the sense that it is subject to erasure and rewriting, Carlyle's *Past and Present* problematizes the enterprise of historiography itself, foregrounding the textuality of history as a way of establishing its relative inaccessibility and thus its status as a representation or trace of an unrecoverable object, itself always already a (dead) text—a corpse/corpus. As I argue in chapter 3, for Carlyle the past is utterly dead and other; to touch it or "resurrect" it would transgress that difference on which the very practice of historiography itself is predicated, a paradoxical practice of tracing of the other, of what Michel de Certeau terms a "labor of death and a labor against death."[15]

This paradoxical historiographic practice is "embodied" in Carlyle's translation of the twelfth-century *Chronica Jocelini de Brakelonda*, a translation Carlyle metaphorically links to the unwrapping of a corpse's cerements. Two subsequent metaphors—the magical speculum and the camera lucida—structure Carlyle's approach to Jocelin's corpse/corpus, each offering us, seemingly, the means to apprehend directly what is utterly dead and other, but simultaneously denying us those means, substituting instead a mediated translation based on a logic of displacement and virtual representation.

At the center of Jocelin's text, too, lies another corpse, the body of St. Edmund—and it is Jocelin's account of the "translation" or movement of the saint's body that provides Carlyle with his most vivid (and most often misread) metaphor for the relationship between the past and the present. As we shall see, Carlyle's "translation" of Jocelin's corpus also functions as the theoretical ground for the later sections of *Past and Present,* where a further "translation"—the symbolic movement or reinscription of "Labor" into the center of all social and productive relations—will serve as an anchor or fulcrum around which (and in relation to which) social meaning will circulate.

Chapter 4 interrogates the theory and practice of this symbolic reinscription. In the process, we find that Carlyle's social criticism envisions the devolution of social order into an abyss of simulation, resulting in a society adrift from its anchors of meaning. The question of the condition of England becomes, for Carlyle, not one of masking the truth, but, to paraphrase Jean Baudrillard, a question of substituting signs of the real for the real itself, a substitution that precipitates the dissolution of the real into the nothingness of simulation.[16] In order to address (and redress) this situation, Carlyle attempts a reanchoring of social discourse (and the social body) through the construction of a central, transcendental signifier: namely, *Labor.* By representing labor as "sacred," Carlyle underwrites its transcendent status, a status mirrored in a particular code of labor relations—the Chivalry of Work—that Carlyle offers as an ideological justification for a recentering of the workplace around the all-penetrating gaze of the Captains of Industry.

Although Carlyle and Benjamin Disraeli both pursue the condition-of-England question in terms of the interrelation between history, labor, and the body, Disraeli does not share Carlyle's self-consciously provisional approach to historical truth. For Disraeli, like Cobbett, the whole of written history is little more than a misrepresentation. According to Disraeli, the "textuality" of history is precisely what permits such distortions to occur; at the same time, however, that textuality also allows those "with the knowledge and the courage" to realign historical representation with historical truth. In chapter 5, I examine Disraeli's *Sybil* as a text that intends just such a realignment, through the emplotment of a narrative that offers a "recovery" of the dispossessed, marginalized truth of English history.

Significantly, at the time of *Sybil*'s composition, Disraeli himself was keenly aware of his own historical position with the Tory party, a position he began to view as increasingly marginalized and disaffected. Ironically, Disraeli locates the source of his marginalization in his own nontraditional view of history. With respect to its representation of history, then, Disraeli's *Sybil* might be described as encompassing a twofold project of recovery—a self-recovery (a refashioning of his own image) and a social recovery—a narrative that purports to recover or rescue the historically marginalized and dispossessed. This latter recovery, as we shall see, is really little more than a "covering-over" whereby Disraeli "re-covers" his own ideological agenda. The burden of this theme in *Sybil* is carried by the title character herself, whose "conversion" to Egremont's (and Disraeli's) position embodies the social and political trajectory Disraeli wishes to define for the working class.

Similarly, with respect to the representation of the laboring classes themselves, Disraeli's *Sybil* envisions a full "recovery" for the condition of England in the form of a disempowering redemption-from-above, a redemption that would proceed according to a recoding of the relation between the new generation of aristocracy and the working class—a realignment, if you will, of the "two nations" into one body. Chapter 6 closely examines the paradoxical implications of the fictional representation of labor in *Sybil*. Disraeli must depict the degradation of the masses in full and graphic detail in order to support his position that their redemption must come from above. He thus gives that marginalized class a voice in the novel, but a voice that the narrative itself ultimately seeks to silence, and, in certain extreme cases, to destroy. The "end" of *Sybil* thus means the "end" of the working class altogether, signified by Sybil's own conversion and transformation, and the narrative's purging of "unredeemable" elements among the working class.

Together, Cobbett, Carlyle, and Disraeli share the desire to intervene in the changing times, and to establish the terms and conditions of that change. In an effort to stabilize the times through the textual process of inscription and interpretation, the texts of Cobbett, Carlyle, and Disraeli become, ironically, signs of their own time, subject to the very practice of reading each foregrounds as necessary to both the "accurate" representation of the condition of England and to the reformation of that condition. In this way, we might assert with Linda Shires that the textual interventions of Carlyle, Disraeli, and Cobbett "foreground instability"—in other words, that they inevitably represent contradictory, dissenting, or paradoxical viewpoints even as they appear to be constructing a unified and consistent rhetorical position.[17] In the particular cases of these three writers, though, that "instability" is foregrounded precisely in an effort to dispense with it; their texts are, in this way, engaged in a struggle to instantiate stability textually, in and against a decidedly unstable context—the present "times." Thus their labor, like Michel de Certeau's historiographic enterprise, remains inherently paradoxical, desiring a clear articulation of the relationship between past and present, between the textual and the material, and at the same time demonstrating that such borders are always provisional and negotiable, capable of being rethought and redrawn. By engaging the condition-of-England question, then, the "labor" of these three writers is itself, in a sense, "conditional," subject to the same shifting historical context that their texts struggle within and against.

I

The Reformation of History and William Cobbett's *A History of the Protestant "Reformation"*

IN AN EFFORT TO ILLUSTRATE THE DEGREE to which various plots and conspiracies during the reign of Charles II were imputed to Catholics, William Cobbett directs our attention in his *A History of the Protestant "Reformation"* (1824–26) to the memorial marking the occasion of the Great Fire of London. Specifically, he points to the monument's inscription, which reads: "This monument is erected in memory of the burning of this Protestant city by the *Popish* faction, in September, A.D. 1666, for the destruction of the Protestant religion and of *old English liberty*, and for the introduction of *Popery and slavery*. But the fury of the Papists is not yet satisfied."[1] Cobbett calls this inscription a monstrous lie (XII:369), and indeed, the groundlessness of the monument's inscription attests well to the conspiratorial climate Cobbett wishes to depict.[2] However, it is not only the inscription itself that interests Cobbett, but also the inscription's *history*. Cobbett tells us that although Charles II allowed "this lying inscription to stand," the text "was effaced by his brother and successor, but when the Dutchman and the '*glorious* revolution' came, it was restored; and there it now stands, all the world, except the mere mob knowing it to contain a most malignant lie" (XII:369).[3]

For Cobbett, this process of inscription, erasure, and reinscription captures precisely the problematic relation between historical representation and "truth," especially when the "truth" of history is subject to political forces that seek the displacement, dissimulation, or misrepresentation of historical events. If this representation of the historiographic enterprise appears rather conspiratorial, that is quite clearly Cobbett's intent; in his opinion, the received versions of English history have always been a product of ulterior motive and political expediency.[4] Recent historians are little more than "modern romancers," writes Cobbett, "every one of whom has written for place, or pension" (XVI:451). The example of the inscription embodies this state of affairs; the written word is a lie, and justice demands its erasure.

After reminding his audience that all the available evidence (including a report by the House of Commons) attests to the falsity of the inscription's assertion (XV:430), Cobbett exclaims: "What infamy then to charge the Catholics with it; what an infamy to put the lying inscription on the pillar; what an act of justice, in James II., to efface it; what a shame to William to suffer it to be restored; and what is it *to us*, then, who now suffer it to remain *without petitioning for its erasure!*" (XV:430). What is it to us? Limited to its rhetorical context, the answer to that question is meant to be an indictment of sorts, suggesting that the lack of a public outcry in the face of such a lie exceeds even the shame due those who inscribed the monument in the first place. In its broader context, though—in the context of a "history" that sets itself over and against other historical accounts of the Reformation—Cobbett's question raises what is for him one of the most fundamental of historical queries: What is the relation between an understanding of history and the current circumstances of everyday life? In short, what is the relationship between past and present, and of what use is that relation to us?

Cobbett answers this question by asserting the following: "The great use of history, is, to teach us how laws, usages and institutions arose, what were their *effects on the people*, how they promoted *public happiness*, or otherwise; and these things are precisely what the greater part of historians, as they call themselves, seem to think of no consequence" (II:38). For Cobbett, then, an assessment of the material condition of the people—and especially the relation between that condition and the policies and laws of government—is the proper function of the historical record. This position is consistent with his foregrounding of the condition of the material bodies of laborers in his theory and practice of radical husbandry and the cottage economy, and in his call for parliamentary reform (see chapter 2). Even his phrase "the use of history" familiarly privileges the notions of productivity and functionality. By contrast, a "history" that attends only to the life and times of a monarch, for example, would be, as Cobbett states elsewhere, decidedly unproductive and useless. In his *Advice to Young Men* (1830), Cobbett explains that

> [y]ou hear enough, and you read enough, about the *glorious wars* in the reign of KING EDWARD the THIRD; and it is very proper that those glories should be recorded and remembered; but you never read, in the works of the historians, that, in that reign, a common labourer earned threepence-halfpenny a day; and that a *fat sheep* was sold, at the same time for one shilling and twopence. . . . These are matters which historians have deemed beneath their notice; but they are matters of real importance: they are matters which ought to have practical effect at this time; for these furnish the criterion whereby we are to judge of our condition compared with that of our forefathers.[5]

Before historical knowledge can be put to a practical, material use, however, we first need a firm grasp of history itself. And while Cobbett has already expressed dismay about the misrepresentation of history through reinscriptions like the one on the monument to the Great Fire of London, he nonetheless maintains a steadfast faith in the ability of language to convey the essence or truth of its referent: "We never understand the nature and constituent parts of a thing so well as when we ourselves have made the thing: next to making it is the seeing of it made; but, if we have neither of these advantages, we ought, at least, if possible, to get a true description of the *origin* of the thing and of the manner in which it was put together" (II:39). As this passage makes clear, though, Cobbett's faith in the descriptive power of language is nevertheless heavily qualified. He clearly positions language as thrice removed from the object of its description, while "making" and "seeing" enjoy a closer proximity to knowledge and understanding. If we apply this statement to historical knowledge (and this is indeed the contextual import of the passage), we can see that, though thrice removed, a "true description" of history may in fact be the only route to the history of the remote past, inasmuch as we have not produced or witnessed such history ourselves. And it is as just such a "true description," I would argue, that Cobbett offers his *History of the Protestant "Reformation"*—that is, as a representation that embodies the suppressed historical truth in opposition to "those books which are called '*Histories of England*' [and] are little better than romances" (II:38). Significant here is the apparent lack of mediation between this hypothetical "true description" and the actual events that such a description purports to represent. Though he recognizes that our access to the past must be mediated by language, for Cobbett historical representation seems to be simply either accurate or inaccurate, either a true account of a historical event or a deliberate distortion. Though his qualification —"if possible"—suggests that such true descriptions may lie beyond the scope of present historical knowledge, one gets the sense that if such a representation were not possible, history would remain completely inaccessible. Cobbett's vision of historical representation thus allows him to adopt a confrontational, polemic stance in which a "true description" of history, seemingly unmediated by language, faces off against historical misrepresentation and displacement, the latter figuring, in his sense, as *nothing but* language. Ultimately, as we shall see, Cobbett foregrounds the textuality of history in order to assert that the "truth" of history lies in the material—specifically, in the condition of laboring bodies, where he finds inscribed an all-too-legible account of degradation, poverty, and hunger.

In addition to the textual "reformation" of the relationship between historical representation and truth, Cobbett asserts that the same condition of displacement that characterizes contemporary historical accounts of the period of English history from the reign of Henry VIII to the present also characterizes the historical truth of that period. In other words, from Cobbett's perspective nearly all contemporary accounts of English history relating to the Reformation and its legacy willfully displace the idea of displacement itself, re-presenting that period of history in terms of an ideologically and historically necessary "reform" of the relationship between politics, religion, and society. For Cobbett, such a narrative misrepresents the way in which "authentic" social and economic relations (especially those grounded in the monastic-centered community) were summarily eradicated, an erasure, he asserts again and again, that "has impoverished and degraded the main body of the People" in England and Ireland.[6]

In this way, the history of the Protestant Reformation, for Cobbett, becomes a generalized history of the displacement of the authentic by the false, a displacement whose effects persist in the present not only historiographically, but also linguistically, in the erosion of substance from words like *charity*, *hospitality*, and especially *reformation* itself. More importantly, with respect to the relationship between the past and the present, Cobbett asserts that this effect can be detected in the altered material lives of the "main body of the People." Responding to Archdall's assertion in the preface to his *History of the Irish Monasteries* that any comparison between the society of the medieval past and that of the present would conclude "decidedly in favour of modern times," Cobbett declares:

> Are modern times proved to be "*decidedly superior*" to former times by the law that shuts Irishmen up in their houses from sunset to sunrise? Are the people's living upon pig-diet, their nakedness, their hunger, their dying by hundreds from starvation, while their ports were crowded with ships carrying provisions from their shores, and while *an army was fed in the country*, the business of which army was to *keep the starving people quiet*: are these amongst the facts on which you found your "comparison so *decidedly in favour of modern times*"? (V:148)

It is on the very bodies of the people, then, that the violent effects of history have been inscribed in terms of poverty, hunger, and dispossession; in this way, the bodies of the people become not only signs of the present condition of England and Ireland (as is the case throughout *Rural Rides*), but also signs of its history, signs that offer, for Cobbett, a "true description" of England, past and present.

Central to Cobbett's assertion that the displacement of the wealth and property of the Catholic Church in the sixteenth century contributed to a deterioration of the material living conditions of the majority of the common people is the explicit assumption that, contrary to Archdall and others, the conditions of everyday life prior to the "Reformation" were substantially better than they were afterward. "If I do not *prove*," writes Cobbett, "that before the 'Reformation,' England was *greater, more wealthy, more moral*, and *more happy*, than she has ever been since; . . . I will be content to pass, for the rest of my life, for a vain pretender" (VI:182). It is on this point, perhaps more than any other, that Cobbett has been accused of idealizing the medieval period.[7] The accusation is not unjust, but it is often inextricably (and unnecessarily) bound to the further accusation that Cobbett proposes a return to the past as a method of reforming the present.[8] For Cobbett, though, there can be no "return" to the past other than through direct historical representation—through his "true description." And if we understand that true description to be embodied, at least in part, by the physical condition of laborers *in the present*, and further understand that Cobbett ultimately intends, through his writing, to improve the material lives of those laborers, his writing thus seeks the alteration of those bodies—their "reformation" if you will, a "reformation" that will erase the signs of the violent separation of the laboring bodies from the wealth produced by their labor. After all, the word *reformation*, Cobbett writes, "means, an alteration *for the better*" (I:3). In this way, Cobbett's *History of the "Reformation"* might be seen as an attempt at the re-formation of historical representation, a rewriting or reinscription that seeks simultaneously to establish a sign relation between the material bodies of the present and the historical events of the past, and to petition for the erasure of that relation through a re-formation, or alteration, of the bodies of present workers. In Cobbett's "ideal" world, then, the bodies of laborers would no longer be marked by the signs of historical "reformation"; as "re-formed" bodies, their signification would thus break with the past and "return" to the body itself, to the material welfare of the individual laborer and his or her community.

In his examination of the material welfare of medieval laborers, Cobbett turns to the monastic-centered community as an example of a small-scale society in which the material conditions of its inhabitants are the focus of monastic economic and social practice.[9] Cobbett's interest lies in the way the monasteries in particular function as guarantors of economic prosperity and social stability, and Cobbett sees both functions as predicated on the relation between the monasteries and the land. In economic terms, according to Cobbett, the monasteries functioned as a kind of fulcrum of exchange, a centering force whose power and effectiveness derived from their attachment to the land and the community. In contrast to the profit-oriented absentee landowners of his own time,

> [m]onastics could possess no private property, they could save no money, they could bequeath nothing. They had a life interest in their estate, and no more. They lived, received, and expended *in common*. Historians need not have told us they were "easy landlords." They *must* have been such, unless human nature had taken a retrograde march expressly for their accommodation. (V:151)[10]

As is clear from Cobbett's original emphasis in this passage (a portion of which appears verbatim in Disraeli's *Sybil*),[11] Cobbett wishes to highlight the monasteries' communal function, especially the way in which they ensured that the wealth derived from the land would be directed back to the community whose labor created the wealth in the first place. "From the land all good things come," writes Cobbett, and "one of the great advantages attending the Monasteries, was, that they, of necessity, caused the revenues of a large part of the lands of the country to be spent on the spot whence those revenues arose" (V:150). Cobbett thus attributes to the monasteries the crucial function of restricting the production, consumption, and reproduction of wealth to the confines of the community itself, a task that is at once a kind of *centering* function (in the sense that the activity revolves around the monastery and thereby remains locally grounded) and a *distributive* function, whereby wealth does not become concentrated in the monastic center of the community, but is instead redistributed—centrifugally, as it were—around that center. It is in this latter sense that Cobbett refers to the monasteries as "great diffusers of general prosperity" (V:149); they thus operate as a communal point of exchange and distribution, rather than as a parasitic point of unilateral profit and accumulation.

To a certain extent, this "diffusion" of wealth throughout the community also accounts for the monasteries' ability to maintain social order within the community. Cobbett, however, ascribes a large portion of that ability to their geographic centrality—specifically, to the permanence of that centrality:

> The Monastery was a proprietor that *never died;* its tenantry had to do with a deathless landlord; its lands and houses never changed owners; its tenants were liable to none of many of the uncertainties that other tenants were; . . . its villagers had all been born and bred up under its eye and care; their character was of necessity a thing of great value, and, as such, would naturally be an object of great attention. A monastery was the centre of a circle in the country, naturally drawing to it, all that were in need of relief, advice, and protection, and containing a body of men, or of women, having no cares of their own, and having wisdom to guide the inexperienced, and wealth to relieve the distressed. (V:152)

It is this permanence or "fixedness" (V:152) of the monasteries that at once allows the monastic institution to transcend the primary limitation of the material body and to underwrite the material well-being of the individuals in the community. In addition, it is this centralized "fixedness" that enables the monasteries to guarantee social stability; in this latter function we will find a similar geographic/social plan taken up by Carlyle in his panoptic reorganization of the workplace, and by Disraeli in his similarly panoptic model of Trafford's factory and village.[12] In each case, we are presented with a social body organized and ordered according to the logic of a centralized, paternal scrutiny ("under the eye and care"); moreover, in the case of the monasteries, as

Cobbett describes it, this centralized power of social ordering also operates centripetally, "drawing to it all those in need of relief."

In Cobbett's view, then, the monastery functions simultaneously as a centrifugal economic force and a centripetal social force. As the center of social union and economic diffusion, however, the monastery's effectiveness, as is clear from the above passage, depends entirely on its "fixedness" or permanence. It is this unchanging character of the monastic presence, of course, that was forever altered by the Reformation. With that presence erased, the dual centrifugal/centripetal force of the monasteries lost its stabilizing origin, and that displaced origin was supplanted not by a new center, but by an *absence*—"by those who . . . live at a great distance from their lands, and draw away the revenues of them to be spent elsewhere" (V:151).[13]

The post-Reformation societies of England and Ireland might thus be described as "decentered," with an impoverishing system of transference displacing the even, centrifugal diffusion of wealth, and a divisive system of class difference displacing the centripetal cohesion guaranteed by a unifying social center. In raising the matter of this relation between the past and the present, Cobbett casts the historical moment of alteration, of "reform," in terms of an exchange: "Go into any county, and survey, even at this day, the ruins of its, perhaps, twenty Abbeys and Priories; and, then, ask yourself, 'what have we *in exchange for these*'?" (V:155). Cobbett leaves the answer rhetorically implied here, but later states the matter directly: "Nothing has ever yet come to supply the place of what was then destroyed" (VI:182).

The unilateral character of this "exchange"—the "substance" of the monastic presence exchanged for the "nothingness" of absenteeship, social separation, and economic exploitation—neatly inverts the typical association of the past with "absence," and the present with "presence." Here, the past is re-presented as substantive, characterized by the presence of centers and origins, while the present remains marked by the absence of that substance. Decentered, with its social, economic, and political "origin" founded on a moment of displacement, the present, for Cobbett, lacks material significance, a condition he finds reflected in the physical inanition of the laborers, in the proliferation of ready-made products, in the correspondingly hegemonic pursuit of immaterial signs of class status, and in a financial system based on mere paper and burdened by a national debt. In short, the immaterial present has turned away from the material concern with the welfare of the individual and the social body that Cobbett says epitomizes the function of the Catholic Church:

> [T]he Catholic Church was not, and is not, an affair of mere *abstract faith*; . . . it was not so *very spiritual* a concern as to scorn all cares relative to the *bodies* of the people; . . . the *tithes* and *offerings* and *income from real property*, of the Catholic Church, went, in a great part, to feed the hungry, to clothe the naked, to lodge and feed the stranger, to sustain the widow and the orphan, and to heal the wounded and the sick. (XI:327)[14]

Significantly, Cobbett ties the disappearance of this attention to the material body to a corresponding disappearance of the substantive meanings of words, including the word "charity" itself. Cobbett asserts that in its deemphasizing of good works, the "reformation" caused charity, that "well-known *Catholic* commodity," to be "set wholly at nought" (XI:328). Thus, although "the *name* of charity is retained by some of these [Protestant] establishments . . . the substance no where exists" (XI:329). Cobbett cites a similar instance of this erosion of meaning in an earlier part of his *History*, with respect to the word "hospitality." Due to the disappearance of the monastic institution, writes Cobbett, "[t]here is now no *hospitality* in England. Words have changed their meaning. We now give entertainment to those who entertain us in return. We entertain people because we *like them personally*; and, very seldom, because they stand in need of entertainment" (VI:183).[15] This passage elaborates the point he makes at the conclusion of his first letter—that the "reformation" has displaced the practice of "Old English hospitality," and "we have since known nothing but the name" (I:36).[16]

Given his diagnosis of the impoverished and degraded present, coupled with his lament about the use of terms like *charity* and *hospitality* "in name only," Cobbett's view of language lies open to the charge of a nostalgic longing for authenticity, a desire that would resist change in favor of a return to a linguistically idyllic past. As Derek Attridge observes, any approach to language that values the "authentic meanings" of words (usually arrived at etymologically) and resists historical changes to those meanings "must depend on a diagnosis of cultural decline . . . or a faith in a lost Golden Age of lexical purity and precision."[17] Ultimately, according to Attridge, the problem with this view of language is really a historical problem: "Although [this view] flirts with history, it's a deeply anti-historical attitude, replacing the social and historical determination of meaning . . . by a transcendent 'true' meaning."[18] Such a view of language is antihistorical, in other words, because it equates a historical change in meaning with a false, unreal, inauthentic (even arbitrary) instance of signification, an instance that breaks with the natural "original" relationship between signifier and signified. The past thus becomes the privileged realm of authentic signification, while the present remains a degraded, inauthentic realm of simulation and self-referentiality.

Perhaps the most damning example of Cobbett's privileging of an "authentic" or "original" meaning may be found in his reaction to the post-Reformation proliferation of Protestant sects, each claiming to have sole access to religious truth. Grounding his argument in the "one true religion" premise, Cobbett raises the issue of the effect on the public of the legal tolerance of such dissent, given that each sect now routinely charges the others with practicing a false religion. "The natural, the necessary effect is," claims Cobbett, "that many men will believe that *none of them have truth on their side*, and of course that the thing is false altogether" (VII:203). Such a claim puts Cobbett in a peculiar bind. On the one hand, such a crisis of belief—of signification really—strikes him as extremely dangerous; the absence of an acknowledged "one true religion" (like the absence of authentic, meaningful words) can only push society farther in the direction of chaotic self-referentiality. On the other hand, "the effect" Cobbett warns against is precisely the conclusion he wishes his audience to embrace—namely, that authentic "truth" cannot be established in the context of a wide variety of legally sanctioned but mutually contradictory claims. The "truth," in this case, then, appears forever undecidable. In this way, Cobbett's own argument would seem to hasten the inevitable conclusion that "the thing is false altogether." A related and perhaps even more chaotic situation, according to Cobbett, occurred during the Puritan revolution. With nearly everyone claiming a right to preach, "[e]very one interpreted the Bible in his own way," resulting in the proliferation "of all sorts of blasphemies and . . . horrors" (XII:366). After all, writes Cobbett, "if every man be his own interpreter of that book, who is to say that he acts contrary to his own interpretation? Why not all these new monstrous sects? If there could be one new religion, one new creed made, why not a thousand?" (XII:366).

In attempting to resolve this issue, Cobbett offers his own mutually contradictory choice: "The law should acknowledge and tolerate but one religion," he concludes, "or it should *know nothing at all about the matter*" (VII:204). With its peculiar Cobbettian mix of intolerance and ambivalence, this statement's either/or proposition enables Cobbett to press for the legal authorization, as it were, of truth, or, failing that, to assert the necessity of erasing such authorization altogether. Presumably, such an erasure would at least, in Cobbett's view, render the question of the law's endorsement of "falsehood" more problematic; one could not as easily conclude (as Cobbett and his audience apparently have) that because the law authorizes almost all claims to (religious) truth, then no signified truth exists. As to the first part of the proposition, the intolerance of his endorsement of one religion recognized by law overshadows his more general (and paradoxical) premise that the legitimacy of such a religion's claim to "truth" remains irrelevant. In holding up the pre-Reformation Catholic Church as an example of a religious institution that claimed to be the "one true religion" and exercised its power to enforce that claim, Cobbett writes: "Whether that were the true religion or not, we have not now to inquire . . . but . . . its long continuance, and in so many nations too, was a strong presumptive proof of its good moral effects upon the people" (VII:204). In this latter statement, Cobbett subordinates the question of the Catholic Church's claim to truth in favor of what are for him more discernable and pertinent facts—namely the relation between the establishment of that church in all of its monolithic grandeur, and the social welfare of the people. For Cobbett, evidence that the people benefited, morally or physically, is enough to warrant having one "true" religion legally recognized, regardless of its theological accuracy. "Truth," in this case, is measured in terms of its ideological and economic "effect"; where Cobbett finds that effect to be wanting, the "truth" too must be lacking.

Although Cobbett's rhetoric, at the surface, *seems* to privilege an "authentic truth," Cobbett approaches language not as an essentialist etymologist (with whom he would nonetheless surely sympathize) but as a materialist. For him, language becomes "inauthentic" when it ceases to refer to the material world (especially the physical body) or otherwise fails to convey the material truth; in either case, such language is "inauthentic," in Cobbett's view, because it cannot be put to any sort of practical use.[19] With respect to the condition-of-England question, such an "inauthenticity" produces little beyond outright contradiction and hypocrisy. As Cobbett remarks, "Yea, verily, this is the picture we now exhibit to the world: the Law-Church parsons putting up all the churches thanksgiving for a plenteous harvest, and the main mass of the labouring people fed and clad worse than the felons in the gaols!" (XIV:412). This picture, which Cobbett terms "starvation in the midst of abundance!" (XIV:412), illustrates the degree to which the material lives of ordinary laborers have been de-signified, rendered absent (or more precisely, rendered as becoming absent, through the debilitating, withering effects of inanition) in the midst, ironically, of an "abundant" presence—represented by the self-referential discourse of thanksgiving, wherein "productivity" and "abundance" become ends in themselves, not a means to consumption and sustenance. As Elaine Scarry writes in her introduction to the volume *Literature and the Body*, "When language and the body are placed side by side, the weightlessness of any language that has lost its referential aspirations becomes especially noticeable. But what becomes noticeable in addition to this problematic deficit of linguistic consequence is the problematic surfeit of consequence, the danger that results from excluding the material world."[20] This danger, for Scarry, derives from a de-signification of the material world, a world in which matter, following Scarry's earlier pun, no longer matters.[21] For Cobbett, the danger extends even further; the exclusion of the material body from signification renders that body vulnerable to inanition and neglect, to a withering that mirrors the decay of the signified in language itself. The body thus experiences an alteration in its referential function, a shift from its role as the material signified of "healthy" social discourse and activity to a (disappearing) role as the withering sign of social degradation.

Cobbett's *A History of the Protestant "Reformation,"* as I have suggested, is an attempt to redress the consequences of this shift by turning our attention to its historical "origin" and tracing the progress of its effects on "the main body of the people" from the Reformation to the present. As a historiographer whose subject is thus "the material" itself, Cobbett recognizes that the representation of that material poses an immediate problem. How does one narrate the material conditions of everyday life, past and present, with a language that itself has, in certain instances, seen its substantive meaning eroded to the point that words have not only exchanged one meaning for another, but become weightless (in Scarry's sense), having lost their referentiality altogether? For Cobbett, the answer lies in his attempt simultaneously to foreground the self-referentiality of such language and to reclaim that language for his own purposes, toward the construction of a "true description" that would accurately represent the condition of the working poor in England and Ireland and diagnose its causal "origin" as well.[22] Nowhere is this strategy more evident than in Cobbett's treatment of the word *reformation* itself. Cobbett always places quotation marks around the word to foreground its status as an ironic signifier.[23] Although "the word REFORMATION . . . means, an alteration *for the better*," writes Cobbett, "this was an alteration greatly for *the worse*" (I:3–4). It is hardly surprising, then, that "the makers of this great alteration . . . have contrived to give it a *good name*" (I:3). Cobbett's quotation marks give the word "reformation" a qualified, provisional status, displacing it out of its inauthentic narrative context (that of the received history of the Reformation) in order to allow the reinscription of the word in a text in which "Reformation" (in quotation marks) becomes a privileged sign of that counter-narrative itself. Far from nostalgizing the "authentic" meaning of the word *reformation*, Cobbett instead rewrites the terms of its signification—that is, he changes its meaning—in an effort to once again align signifier and signified in a relation of "true description." The seemingly simple gesture of placing quotation marks around the word thus performs a rather complex treatment of the term, subverting its use in other historical narratives by calling attention to its disconnectedness from the material truth, while at the same time appropriating it for his own use, as a privileged sign of counter-historical truth.

The antihistorical view of language that privileges authentic meanings, as we have seen, depends upon a resistance to change. Cobbett would gladly join in such resistance, but only if it means resistance to an alteration, like the "reformation," that is "greatly for the worse." In his *History of the Protestant "Reformation"* and throughout his writings, Cobbett insists that any assessment of such change must be measured strictly in terms of the material lives of the people in general. In the face of an "alteration greatly for the worse," Cobbett advocates not a return to the past but a reform of the present, a reform that would produce a tangible change in the material conditions of everyday life. As Raymond Williams asserts, "Cobbett's real drive in the case of history as in everything else, was to change conditions in his own place and time."[24] It is his historicization of that condition that necessarily turns Cobbett in the direction of the past (both the eighteenth century of his boyhood and the pre-Reformation medieval period); in the process, his representation of the past itself provides the historical referent of "truth" for his project of reform.[25] In seeking to relate the history of the "reformation" indexically with the material conditions of the people, the "change" signified by the word *reformation* is thus itself changed—re-formed—into the weighty matter of material life. The historicized body for Cobbett is a changed and changing body, caught in the context of a larger shift away from a material social order centered on the welfare of the body politic, to a nation in which the body politic has become increasingly marginalized and decentered, a situation that has "degraded and impoverished the main body of the people" (II:37).

In tracing the history of the "reformation" in terms of its effect on the material body of common laborers, then, Cobbett's text functions in concert with his other principal writings of the time, like *Cottage Economy* (1822), and especially with those published in his *Political Register* and later collected under the title *Rural Rides* (1830).[26] As a text that in a sense represents the past in terms of the present (i.e., through the repeated comparison of pre-and post-Reformation life with the current condition of the "main body" of the people as a whole), Cobbett's *History of the Protestant "Reformation"* might be said to have a practical "use" with regard to its audience, as a kind of handbook of historical displacement and dispossession that not only documents that particular aspect of the "Reformation" but petitions for the erasure of its lingering effects.[27]

In representing Cobbett's text in this way, though, I have so far evaded the question of the *accuracy* of his historical investigation—specifically, the fact that nearly all his commentators agree that the text falls well short of his claim to have produced an authentic "true description" of historical events. What to do, then, about Cobbett's assertion of a meaningful, accurate historical truth for a narrative that, everyone agrees, is extremely polemical and rife with exaggeration and error? Precisely because of its historical inaccuracies and inflammatory rhetoric, some critics have tended to treat the text as a sort of aberration, an ultimately insignificant departure from his other writings of the time and especially from *Rural Rides*, which stands alone as "a far different and far better work."[28] Raymond Williams shares this perspective to a certain extent, asserting that "Cobbett's *History of the Protestant Reformation* . . . belongs to this decade [the 1820s] but for all its polemical vigour is without its central qualities."[29] By "central qualities" Williams means those most evident in *Cottage Economy* and *Rural Rides;* namely, a rhetorical effect of "writing and talking *with* people and current events," as opposed to the "much lower dimension of 'popular' writing" that *A History of the Protestant "Reformation"* leans toward, with its concomitant rhetorical effect "of writing *to* or *at* 'the people.'"[30]

Despite such an assessment of the place of Cobbett's *History* with respect to his other works of the time, when it comes to the question of Cobbett's rhetorical stance vis-à-vis history itself, Williams defends Cobbett to the last, in a tone barely separable from the "vigorous polemic" of his subject:

> If he is the voice of anything that can be called, for rhetorical purposes, Old England, he is also in that act the voice of protest

> against finance capital, imperialism and the aristocratic State, and the voice of encouragement of working-class organization, democratic protest and popular defiance. It is only by falsifying selection that he can be enrolled for that now common nostalgia, in which an image of old rural England is emblazoned against the actual people of England, often by the literal descendents of the nabobs, negro-drivers, generals, admirals, governors, commissioners, bankers, stock-jobbers and lawyers.[31]

If we apply this line of general defense to the specific work of *A History of the Protestant "Reformation,"* clearly the question of its truthfulness, of its accuracy, matters a good deal less in the context of its significance as a text that participates in just such a "protest" against the current prevailing conditions of everyday life. Cole, for example, cites Cobbett's *History* as providing "just that basis of popular support" for Catholic Emancipation that the movement needed, ultimately, to enable its legislative realization.[32] For Cole, then, specifically, and for Williams more generally, the *practical effect* of Cobbett's texts becomes the standard by which to judge the merits of his writing, a standard that is itself "Cobbettian" in its attention to the *usefulness* of textual representation, and one that, as I have mentioned, renders the question of the relationship of that representation to historical "truth" a moot one.

Among more recent critics, only Ian Dyck has attempted to engage the question of Cobbett's claim to a direct, unmediated representation of the truth head-on, with a thesis that underscores the radicality of Cobbett's position by asserting that *A History of the Protestant "Reformation,"* in addition to his other texts that treat both the recent and remote past, really does *directly represent the truth*.[33] For Dyck, Cobbett's historical narratives constitute a kind of "people's history" (127), drawing on and reinforcing representations of the past that were already present among agrarian laborers (as evidenced, for example, in popular songs and ballads of the time); as such, writes Dyck, "Cobbett's histories were composed in conscious opposition to the dominant historiography of his day" (126), and thus "were intended to preserve and fortify the independence of the people's historical consciousness" (127). As Dyck explains:

> True and relevant history, Cobbett believed, could not be assembled within the halls of the social, economic and political establishment. Meaningful and democratic history dwelt in the folk mind, where it was orally conveyed from generation to generation with minimal interference from either the dominant culture or the 'novelty of experience'. (132)

While Dyck asserts later in his chapter that the concept of "Old England," for Cobbett and his agrarian audience alike, "was a construction of class experience and of their perception of relative economic prosperity in the past" (138), we see in the above quotation how that very "construction," a term that one might expect would have a mitigating effect on the claim to an authentic "truth," actually functions as an indisputable instance of that truth, and does so in a way that claims that truth to be (paradoxically) unchanging. Interestingly, this truth, conveyed (according to Dyck) as part of an oral tradition, remains necessarily unembodied by the written word; indeed, the very fact of its orality attests to its independence from the politically motivated historical representations that, in Dyck's words, "seek to secure control of popular memory" (127). Implicit in Dyck's formulation of the oral truth "dwelling in the folk mind" is the idea that Cobbett's historical writing provides this "meaningful and democratic history" with its *legitimate* textual embodiment, an embodiment that both "fortifies" the independence of that history and enables it to engage textually, as a counter-narrative, with the historical accounts produced by "the dominant historiography."

When Dyck's analysis of the relationship between Cobbett's historical writing and the "truth" of the oral tradition is applied specifically to *A History of the Protestant "Reformation,"* the problem of Cobbett's claim of offering "true description" is thus neatly resolved; once we position the "oral truth" of the folk mind as the narrative's referent, the claim to an objective historical truth is thereby bracketed and displaced. Such a strategy is certainly attractive, taking advantage as it does of contemporary notions of the inseparability of any "truth" from its representation, a relation that necessarily foregrounds the mediation inherent in any attempt at "accurate" or "true" historical narration. I am fully at ease with that position, probably more than is Ian Dyck; Cobbett, however, would not have been. His claim of embodying a "true description" of historical events remains simply what it claims to be—an assertion of privileged access to a suppressed and displaced historical truth.

A question still needs to be asked, then, in order to come to some assessment of the relation between Cobbett's understanding of historical truth and its textual representation in *A History of the Protestant "Reformation"*; namely: When Cobbett seeks the truth in other written historical accounts, where does he find it? The answer proves rather surprising. In the final section of his *History* (i.e., in Letter XVI), Cobbett repeatedly asserts that truth (historical truth in particular) can only ever be *incidental*. In citing Fortescue's *De Laudibus Legum Angliae*, Cobbett claims: "The passage I am about to quote, relating to the state of the English, was *purely incidental;* it was not intended to answer any temporary purpose. It *must have been a true account*" (XVI:458). Similarly, in referring to the punishment for disorderly conduct under Richard II, Cobbett cites information from a transcription of a historical document in White's history of Hampshire, and claims: "This fact *must be true*. White had no purpose to answer. His mention of the fact, or rather his transcript from the record, is purely *incidental*" (XVI:462). And once more, in reference to an Act of Parliament that describes beef, pork, mutton, and veal as "food of the poorer sort," Cobbett states: "It is an incidental mention of a fact. It is an Act of Parliament. It *must have been true*" (XVI:463).

This quality that Cobbett assigns to the truth—the incidental—suggests that in written historical accounts, the truth is, for Cobbett, (always) already marginalized and displaced, subordinate to, even an accidental product of, a motivation that lies elsewhere, in some purpose other than representing the "truth."[34] Given this "incidental" nature of the truth, to what extent, we might ask, is Cobbett's own text "incidental"? In other words, does *A History of the Protestant "Reformation"* embody the truth incidentally, in the manner that Cobbett himself asserts makes a text's authenticity not only discernible, but imperative, in the sense that the "incidental" text "*must be true*"?

I think the answer is yes—Cobbett clearly locates the "truth" of his historical narrative in the incidental; that is, in the material bodies of working people. For Cobbett, the physical bodies of the people function as the incidental truth of the "reformation," because the plight of the people—the history of their bodies—remains incidental to the self-interested motivations of the major players of his historical account. Cobbett thus seeks to bring this embodied but marginalized truth front and center in an attempt to accord it the status of a central and material truth about both English history and contemporary English culture. This project is not in the service of a nostalgic wish for a return to an ideal past, but a declaration of the necessity for a radical break with the past itself—that is, a break with the historical legacy of the "reformation." The body serves as text on which is inscribed the history of the "reformation," but like the words on the monument to the Great Fire of London, that inscription is itself subject to erasure. The aim of Cobbett's *History*, then, is twofold: Cobbett first establishes the material body of the people as a text to be read, then seeks a "re-formation" of that body that would, in a sense, detextualize that body, and return it to the material. The significance of this "re-formed" body would thus be self-referential, offering a "true description" of itself, rather than signifying the history of its subjection to degradation and impoverishment. In this way, history too would be "re-formed," made anew, with the material body as its subject. As Kevin Gilmartin has stated, "Far from abandoning the highest powers of language to transform the world, Cobbett's radical prose operated as if those powers inhered reciprocally in language and in the conditions to be transformed."[35]

The relation between Cobbett's claim to truth and its historical representation is thus a rather complex one; instead of reflecting an objective truth already apparent in the folk mind, Cobbett's project "constructs" that truth out of the folk body, out of the incidental significance of the material bodies of the people themselves. In the process, his *History of the Protestant "Reformation"* seeks the re-formation of that significance, a remaking of history in the image of the material body of the laborer. The matter of just how to "re-form" these material bodies Cobbett takes up elsewhere, particularly in the selections from his *Political Register* published as *Rural Rides*. The practical matter of "reform" is addressed in chapter 2, which also examines how Cobbett's foregrounding of the textual and material body, when addressing what Carlyle would later term the "Condition-of-England question," is inextricably (and ironically) bound up with the status of his own body—the "great Cobbett" as a representation, an embodiment, of the people.

2

William Cobbett and the (Un)Healthy Body

Matter, Metaphor, and the Man

IN HIS ESSAY ON SIR WALTER SCOTT (1838), Thomas Carlyle asserts that "our best definition of Scott were perhaps even this, that he was, if no great man, then something much pleasanter to be, a robust, thoroughly healthy and withal very prosperous and victorious man. An eminently well-conditioned man, healthy in body, healthy in soul; we will call him one of the *healthiest* of men."[1] As Carlyle explains, this healthful state signifies a kind of holistic balance between body and environment, centered in the soul:

> For does not health mean harmony, the synonym of all that is true, justly-ordered, good; is it not, in some sense, the net-total, as shown by experiment, of whatever worth is in us? The healthy man is the most meritorious product of Nature so far as he goes. A healthy body is good; but a soul in right health,—it is the thing beyond all others to be prayed for; the blessedest thing this earth receives of Heaven. Without artificial medicament of philosophy, or tight-lacing of creeds (always very questionable), the healthy soul discerns what is good, and adheres to it, and retains it; discerns what is bad, and spontaneously casts it off. (SWS, 38–39)

At the root of the healthiest of men, then, lies an inherent gift of moral discernment that enables the liberation of the metaphoric body, freeing it from ideologies that, like medicaments, are needed by those who suffer from bodily disorders, or from ideologies that, like certain kinds of clothing, restrict the body, distorting it into a more fashionable appearance. Indeed, this healthful harmony itself functions, asserts Carlyle, as an *ordering* phenomenon, as a force for improvement and balance: "In the harmonious adjustment and play of all the faculties, the just balance of oneself gives a just feeling towards all men and all things. Glad light from within radiates outwards, and enlightens and embellishes" (39).

According to Carlyle, only one other writer in recent memory can equal Walter Scott in terms of this particular conception of health, one who, Carlyle admits, is "perhaps . . . the most opposite imaginable to Scott"—namely, William Cobbett (39).[2] In keeping with his notion of health as radiating outward from the soul, Carlyle calls him "the pattern John Bull of his century, strong as the rhinoceros, and with singular humanities and genialities shining through his thick skin" (39).[3] In the midst of "the sickliest of recorded ages," writes Carlyle, "when British Literature lay all puking and sprawling. . . . Nature was kind enough to send us two healthy Men, of whom she might still say, not without pride, 'These also were made in England; such limbs do I still make there!'" (39–40). This latter statement casts Cobbett and Scott as products not just of "Nature" but of the Nation itself; in this way, the body metaphor Carlyle employs throughout becomes intertwined with the metaphorics of labor, gender, and nationalism. The healthy, *masculine* natures of Cobbett and Scott thus function as ironic, *inverse* signs of the health of the national body, representing, in the context of national literature (i.e., the Romanticism of Byron and Shelley), the only exceptions to an otherwise violently ill condition. As the "pattern John Bull," then, Cobbett embodies for Carlyle the very strength and masculine "health" that the nation desperately lacks.

Carlyle's representation of Cobbett as one of the "healthiest of men" perpetuates an image Cobbett himself cultivated by proudly espousing the virtues of "early rising, sobriety, abstinence and a resolution to be active," and by consciously projecting a self-image of unassailable health and vigor in his writings.[4] Even so, Carlyle's designation is nevertheless an unintentionally ironic one: whereas Carlyle uses the word "health" as a metaphor for the state of one's soul as manifested in an innate capacity for sound moral judgment, Cobbett understands "health" as primarily a material condition, to be ascertained with reference to the physical body. Indeed, when it comes to assessing the health of the nation, the contrast between Carlyle and Cobbett proves similarly pronounced. Although each discusses the health of the nation with reference to the health of the people themselves, Carlyle subsumes the material inanition of the laboring masses under the larger problem of English spiritual inanition, rendering the emaciated bodies of laborers merely an outward manifestation of the nation's inner lack of moral, meaning, and spirit.[5]

In contrast, Cobbett's investigation of the health of the nation over the course of more than ten years (from 1821 to 1832, as first reported in his *Political Register,* and collected in the first edition of *Rural Rides* [1830] and later expanded editions) begins and ends with the material condition of the people themselves, especially agrarian laborers. Though Carlyle locates in Cobbett's "healthy soul" the ability to discern and adhere to "what is good," Cobbett's definition of "good" is strictly material: "I will allow nothing to be good with regard to the labouring classes," writes Cobbett, "unless it make an addition to their victuals, drink or clothing" (*RR,* 1:176). Although commentators have often remarked on the materiality of his rhetoric, Cobbett by no means resists engaging in the play of body metaphors already a part of what Carlyle would later term the "Condition-of-England question."[6] Indeed, as his frequent use of the term "Wen" indicates, Cobbett often represents the nation according to a self-conscious metaphorics of the body, maintaining a steadfast belief in the status of the healthy laboring body as a transparent sign of the nation's health.[7] Thus, his "body politics" may be seen as advocating a materialist version of the social body metaphor, one that recenters the national body around individual rural laborers and the satisfaction of their material needs.[8] Cobbett's materialist social body thus contrasts sharply with the bourgeois version of the metaphor being shaped, in various conflicting ways, by economists, social reformers, politicians, and cultural critics in the first half of the nineteenth century. This bourgeois vision of the social body as an organic whole sought the incorporation of the working class into the larger aggregate, bringing a heterogeneous portion of the social body (the laboring masses) into harmony with the larger homogeneous society.[9] Cobbett's project takes the opposite view, assimilating the larger whole to the material bodies of rural laborers, a process that Cobbett thought would necessitate the dismantling (or at least the attenuation) of capitalist encroachment into the countryside.

Although part of his own critique (and indeed, part of his very solution to the national crisis) rests on a reconfiguration of the current system of political representation, as we will see, Cobbett does not settle for a merely symbolic remedy for the nation's ills. Instead, Cobbett's rhetoric seeks to link inextricably the symbolic with the material, the political with the everyday, in order to restore the health of the people, and thus the national body as a whole. Toward this end, Cobbett advocates not only a re-formation of the body of Parliament, but also a localized recentering of the cycle of production and consumption within the individual home and community through the practice of "radical husbandry." This practice intends to address the material needs of rural laborers, while also invoking, symbolically, the larger system of political reform Cobbett insists would disperse the wealth now concentrated in England's "Wen" (London) and bring down the "Thing" itself—the system of finance, industry, and agriculture that determines (and undermines) the health of the nation.

As Kevin Gilmartin argues, "the *Rural Rides* mapped a corrupt system onto the English countryside. . . . [T]hey struggled to *realize* the figure of corruption in order to manifest its effects and accelerate its downfall."[10] One way that Cobbett attempts to achieve just such a realization is through his consistent identification of London as the "great Wen," the primary symptom of the Thing's unhealthy effect upon the social body. Cobbett's metaphorical substitution of "Wen" for "London" is almost always matter-of-fact, and not overtly pejorative; as Chesterton puts it, Cobbett "is careful to say quite carelessly, 'I was coming from the Wen,' as if he were saying, 'I was coming from the Wood.'"[11] As a result, the ubiquity of the term "the Wen" strengthens its metaphorical identification with London, until "London" itself disappears into the metaphor. Although others before and after Cobbett have employed a similar metaphor for this city, for Cobbett "the Wen" not only captures the sense in which London figures as a locus of ugliness and disease on the national body, but also emphasizes the city's role as an accumulation point for all those individuals whose contributions to society are decidedly unproductive, if not downright counterproductive.[12] By labeling such a collection point "the Wen," Cobbett decenters London's significance as a financial and political hub, ironically displacing that center to a point of concentrated but extraneous excess.

Two related body metaphors reinforce this sense of eccentricity and excess: the term "tax-eaters," and a subset of the tax-eating class Cobbett derisively refers to as "dead weight." In using the term "tax-eater" to designate those whose material wealth derives, through taxation, from the labor of others (Cobbett's list of tax-eaters includes pensioners, sinecurists, members of the "standing army," the established clergy, and Jews),[13] he consciously foregrounds their *consumptive* character, a consumption that comes at the expense (literally and metaphorically) of the laboring body; as Cobbett asserts, it is "unsparing taxation" that results in the laborer "famishing in the midst of abundance" (*RR*, 1:59). Feeding on the productivity of others, the tax-eaters are themselves "over-fed" (*RR*, 1:94); gluttonous and swollen, they congregate in London and thus form that larger sebaceous mass of excessive swelling, the "Great Wen." As a subset of the tax-eaters, "dead weight" refers specifically to those receiving pensions and half-pay in reward for their service in the Napoleonic Wars. As a metaphor, "dead weight" foregrounds not the parasitic consumption conveyed by "tax-eaters," but the excessive burden such consumption places on the economy.[14] By representing this class of tax-eaters as metaphorically "dead," Cobbett turns the body metaphor in an ironic, contradictory, even vampiric direction, one that casts the sheer wastefulness of such expenditure in seemingly absurd terms—as the feeding of dead bodies.

In a similar vein, Cobbett metaphorizes his rather vague and abstract term "the Thing" as a dead body, with the emphasis on decay and putridity.[15] For example, when venturing into one of the lesser Wens (Cheltenham, in this case), and finding it to be a rather deserted, depressed town with falling housing prices, Cobbett cannot contain his glee: "'Oh!' I said to myself, 'the accursed THING has certainly got a *blow*, then, in every part of its corrupt and corrupting carcass'" (*RR*, 2:446–47). Here, Cobbett symbolizes the "THING" as a decaying mass of flesh, whose advance into the countryside and throughout the nation is thus not so much the product of a willful movement forward, but rather the slow spreading of its rottenness and decay. "Rottenness, putridity is excellent for land," Cobbett writes, "but bad for Boroughs" (*RR*, 1:231). Though intended as a pun on the idea of "rotten boroughs," Cobbett's observation may be applied to the THING as well, of which rotten boroughs are a component. Indeed, the "corruption" of the THING will ultimately be good for the land, in Cobbett's view, because such decay signals the weakness and inevitable end of the THING, already artificially propped up by the manipulation of paper money. In a sense, then, its decay will nourish and revitalize the agrarian interest, allowing it to "grow." In this way the "dead weight" metaphor is taken a step further and given yet another layer of irony, playing on the beneficial aspects of waste and decay.

As Kevin Gilmartin notes, this metaphorization of corruption as a rotting carcass leads Cobbett, on at least one occasion, to "collapse the boundary between the figural and the real."[16] Even so, this collapse between the figural and the real does not seem to extend to the specific matter of what to do about the Great Wen itself. In contrast to Southey's description of the manufacturing system as a "fungous excrescence" that has become so inextricable from the vital circulatory system of the body politic "that to remove it by absorption is impossible, and excision would be fatal,"[17] Cobbett's "Wen" instead appears to be decidedly extricable, as an excessive, extraneous growth on the national body. The question, though, in keeping with the metaphor, remains: How might the Wen be removed? The answer, for Cobbett, is not so easily articulated. "The dispersion of the wen," writes Cobbett, "is the only real difficulty that I see in settling the affairs of the nation and restoring it to a happy state" (*RR*, 1:39). A little later he asks, rhetorically, "But how is this Wen to be *dispersed?* I know not whether it be to be done by knife or by caustic; but dispersed it must be!" (*RR*, 1:60).

Cobbett's use of the term "dispersion" here is significant, for it at once asserts that "the Wen" must be removed and suggests the method

—through a dispersal or redistribution of the population. Though his metaphors for the process of the removal of the wen—excision ("by knife") and corrosion ("by caustic")—are in keeping with the medical technology of the time, neither could be said to effect a "dispersal" in the sense of a breaking up, or scattering, of elements congregated closely in one place. At the root of this contradictory use of the body metaphor is Cobbett's persistent concern with the material, physical body. No matter how often Cobbett equates London (and other urbanized locales) with a bodily excrescence like a wen, he finds that he cannot resolve the question of London's political and economic effect on the rest of the national body *as if it really were* a wen.[18] He recognizes that the "Great Wen" is actually a dense mass of individual bodies (many of whom he considers to be parasitic "tax-eaters," feasting on the national body from within), and it is this perception that necessitates his use of the word "dispersion"—a dispersion of people and of wealth.

In this way, Cobbett's foray into the metaphorics of the unhealthy social body immediately problematizes his ability to represent a "cure" for the nation's ills in those metaphorical terms. Cobbett seeks to resolve this metaphorical paradox by representing the condition of England in terms of another organic metaphor, this one much closer to Cobbett's own area of expertise, and one that enables him to foreground the material needs of agrarian laborers—namely, the metaphorics of a "radical system of husbandry":

> *Radical* means, *belonging to the root; going to the root*. And the main principle of this system [of radical husbandry] . . . is, that the root of the plant is to be fed by *deep tillage*, while it is growing; and to do this we must have our *wide distances*. Our system of husbandry is happily illustrative of our system of politics. Our lines of movement are fair and straightforward. We destroy all weeds, which, like tax-eaters, do nothing but devour the sustenance that ought to feed the valuable plants. Our plants are all *well fed*; and our nations of Swedes and of cabbages present a happy uniformity of enjoyments and of bulk, and not, as in the broad-cast system of Corruption, here and there one of enor-

> mous size, surrounded by thousands of poor little starveling things, scarcely distinguishable by the keenest eye, or, if seen, seen only to inspire a contempt of the husbandman. The Norfolk boys are, therefore, right in calling their Swedes *Radical Swedes*. (*RR*, 1:24)

Here, the themes encapsulated in the "Wen" metaphor—the interrelated matters of health and space in particular—are recast in agricultural terms. The "radical" system of husbandry at once refers to a real method of raising animals and produce (popularized by Cobbett in *A Year's Residence in America* [1818–19] and *Cottage Economy*, among other texts) and to a "radical" understanding of social organization that articulates (metaphorically) a method for the cultivation of value. Such a cultivation of value depends, ultimately, upon space—upon the even dispersion of labor, as it were, across the national landscape. When applied in agriculture, this method requires the planned and orderly distribution of individual plants in rows, separated by the wide spaces necessary for the deep tillage that ensures that the roots will have adequate access to air, moisture, and nutrients. In contrast to this system of "radical" husbandry, "the broad-cast system of Corruption" distributes value randomly and haphazardly—just as seeds are often cast randomly and haphazardly—inevitably concentrating that value in only a few individuals at the expense of the many, and decreasing the overall return.

This metaphor of radical husbandry, of course, conveys some of the same ideas that Cobbett's use of the term "Wen" does; in both instances the concentration of wealth or value, its uneven distribution, is cast as a threat to the health of the nation. The difference lies in the way "radical husbandry" not only addresses the condition of England metaphorically, but seeks to redress that condition *literally*. Through the theory and practice of radical husbandry (along with methods for household management collected under the title *Cottage Economy*), Cobbett intends to improve the condition of small farmers, agricultural laborers, and their families, by giving them the means to better manage their own labor. "Economy means management," writes Cobbett, "and nothing more; and it is generally applied to the affairs of a house and family, which affairs are an object of the greatest importance, whether as relating to individuals or to a nation."[19] This strategy for the management of cottagers ultimately rests on the practice of radical husbandry itself, metaphorically and literally, providing a means for the self-production of material goods, especially food.

Cobbett thus saw the practice of his "cottage economy" as establishing an alternative strategy for everyday living both within and against the shift toward a capitalist method of farm production and Wen-centered values. In particular, Cobbett targeted the altered relation between laborers, farmers, and landowners as the source of the degradation of the laboring body, particularly its malnourishment. Cobbett best illustrates the disruption of this relation through his account of the fate of the tenant farmer Charington. Attending a sale at the farmer's home in October 1825, Cobbett notes that the house contained a wide assortment of centuries-old oak furniture, including chests, dressers, beds, and tables, "[b]ut all appeared to be in a state of decay and nearly of *disuse*" (*RR*, 1:276). Such furniture, according to Cobbett, was plainly designed to accommodate not just the farmer and his family, but also all the laborers hired to work the land; Cobbett thus designates the decay of the furniture (itself of solid and durable material) as a sign of an alteration in the productive relations between farmer and farm worker. A closer inspection of the household reveals further signs, this time of the trappings of class: fine dishes and glassware, a carpet, a bell-pull, and "worst of all," writes Cobbett, "there was a *parlour*," done up "just in the true stock-jobber style" (*RR*, 1:276–77). Though his station in life was that of a tenant farmer,

> the '*Squire* had many *wine-decanters* and *wine glasses* and "*a dinner set*," and a "*breakfast set*," and "*dessert knives*"; and these evidently imply carryings on and a consumption that must of necessity have greatly robbed the long oak table if it had remained fully tenanted. That long table could not share in the work of the decanters and the dinner set. Therefore, it became almost untenanted; the labourers retreated to hovels, called cottages; and instead of board and lodging, they got money. (*RR*, 1:277)

In this passage, Cobbett develops the long oak table into a symbol of a solid, "concrete" value through all its attendant qualities—sturdiness, durability, functionality, and especially communality (as a place where the extended family that included the laborers shared their meals). In short, the long oak table signifies the material value Cobbett identifies with the productive labor of farm workers, and with the farmhouse-centered way of life. According to the scenario in the above passage, this value, with its basis in an economy of production and mutual dependency, has been completely displaced by a new kind of value based on an economy of consumption—the consumption of signs—in which the long oak table's use-value, along with its sign-value, disappears.[20] In addition, by describing the oak table metaphorically as "untenanted," Cobbett neatly ironizes the very process of untenanting now affecting farmers who are themselves tenants, and who, like Charington, can no longer afford to pay their own rent, let alone the wages needed to hire laborers. With respect to the localized micro-economy of the small farm, it appears that Cobbett's advocation of "dispersal" (as in the case of the Wen) does not apply here; indeed, if anything, the trend is reversed. Agrarian life and labor needs to be repopulated, recentered, relocalized, in order to effect the restoration of its productive value. Until such time, the long oak table—bare and unused—represents the loss or erasure of that pure value, supplanted by the larger emptiness of objects whose only value lies in their function as signs.[21]

Cobbett identifies this erasure of mutual obligation and social stability as an effect of the "accursed system," which "has, in all likelihood, transmuted [the Charingtons] into a species of mock gentlefolks, while it has ground the labourers down into real slaves" (*RR*, 1:277). Although careful to exempt the Charingtons and others like them from any direct blame ("There was no reason to expect that farmers would not endeavour to keep pace, in point of show and luxury, with fundholders" [*RR*, 1:278]), implicit in Cobbett's tone is the sense that the Charingtons are nonetheless wrong to pursue the trappings of the landowning bourgeoisie and gentry, because to do so is to betray their "natural" class affiliation; or rather, to do so is to betray their role in a society that, prior to the ascendancy of stockjobbing and the growth of the "Wen," lacked such clearly demarcated class differences.[22] Their "transmutation" is thus more sartorial than substantive, "a *show* not warranted by the reality" (*RR*, 1:278). This assessment of the Charingtons' transmutation attests to Cobbett's "defensive" position, as Williams expresses it, with regard to the increasingly entrenched class system, and further reveals Cobbett's suspicion of class mobility, here rendered as nothing more than self-deluded play-acting, signifying (more to the point) a shift from a "real" system of social relations with stable social identities, to a spectacular system, in which commodities function as signs, and useful objects (like the oak table) fall away into decay and disuse.

As a result, Cobbett also deplores the corresponding shift away from self-reliance and self-sufficiency, and toward a dependence on commodities readily available in the market economy:

> To buy the thing, *ready made*, is the taste of the day; thousands, who *are housekeepers*, buy their dinners ready cooked: nothing is so common as to *rent breasts* for children to suck: a man *actually advertised*, in the London papers, about two months ago, to *supply childless husbands with heirs*! In this case, the articles were, of course, to be *ready made*; for to make them "*to order*" would be the devil of a business; though, in desperate cases, even this is, I believe, sometimes resorted to. (*RR*, 2:508)

In a world where "all is to be had by *trafficking*" (*RR*, 2:508), the "ready made" object reigns; commodities are purchased and consumed, and the labor of others purchased to perform what for Cobbett are some of the most basic and natural of human labors—physical reproduction and the care of children. Traditional gender roles are disrupted; (re)production is in this way effectively displaced from the individual body that would "naturally" engage in it, transformed by the marketplace of commodified bodies and body parts (the breasts of women, children available for adoption at the right price); and, as Cobbett's half-serious joke about making children "to order" implies, sexual intercourse itself takes on both physical and commercial properties. In short, the "ready made" displaces labor altogether, concealing it behind a seemingly impersonal, agentless object, one that appears always (al)ready made, and only accessible through money.

As a counter to the culture of the ready-made, Cobbett offers the localized culture of the handmade, the production of material goods within the domestic setting. The most detailed example of this particular mode of production occurs in the section of *Cottage Economy* devoted to the making of straw plat for hats, fashioned from raw material grown in England (*CE*, 153–82), and this example, among others, is taken up at various moments throughout *Rural Rides*. Cobbett thought the task most suitable for women and children, who have lost most of "their natural employment" to the wen-centered capitalist mode of production (*RR*, 1:160). Cobbett's advocacy of straw plat thus suggests a means to restore traditional gender and family roles undermined by the capitalist culture of the ready-made. Although Tim Fulford has argued eloquently in his book *Romanticism and Masculinity* that during the Caroline affair of 1820 (when Cobbett exhorted women to act collectively in protest of Caroline's trial), "the implications of [Cobbett's] rhetoric" went well beyond his traditional view of gender roles, here Cobbett's rhetoric is without the mitigating call for collective political struggle.[23] Instead, women and children are urged to return to their "natural" scene of traditional domestic labor, and thus to offer a kind of resistance to capitalism within the prescribed boundaries of gender roles.

Because the production of handmade straw plat would thus take place primarily within a domestic setting, and therefore wholly outside the factory-based economy, Cobbett takes great delight in asserting the impossibility of making straw plat with the aid of machinery: "It will be impossible for any of the '*rich ruffians;*' any of the horse-power or steam-power or air-power ruffians; any of these greedy, grinding ruffians, to draw together bands of men, women and children, and to make them slaves, in the working of *straw*. The raw material *comes of itself*, and the *hand*, and the *hand alone*, can convert it to use."[24] Cobbett reiterates this point in an 1826 visit to Worcestershire, where he attributes the relative prosperity of the laborers near Worcester to their cottage-based industry of manufacturing gloves, which, like the making of straw plat, "cannot be carried on by *fire* or by *wind* or by *water*, and which is, therefore, carried on by the *hands* of human beings" (*RR*, 2:440). Cobbett also sees the cultivation of the handmade as a hedge against the wen-like tendency of the factory "to draw English people into crowds and make them slaves, and slaves too of the lowest and degraded cast" (*RR*, 1:160). Indeed, in the section on glove manufacturing near Worcester, Cobbett offers his vision of the benefits of a rural, mixed economy, without centralized production, during times of economic crisis

> where manufacturing is *mixed with agriculture*, where the wife and daughters are at the needle, or the wheel, while the men and boys are at plough, and where the manufacturing, of which one or two towns are the centres, is spread over the whole country round about, and particularly where it is, in very great part, performed by females at their *own homes*, and where the earnings come *in aid of the man's wages;* in such case the misery cannot be so great. (*RR*, 2:440).

Cobbett offered the region near Worcester where this production of handmade gloves predominated as evidence of such an economy's strength in the face of hard times, and in the preceding quotation we encounter again Cobbett's advocacy of "dispersal," according to which production must be decentralized and relocalized within the cottage. Because the industry Cobbett advocates is always land-dependent, space becomes a necessity, and a sharp contrast to the close quarters of the factory system. By equating the laborer's status within the factory to that of a slave (a common trope within radical discourse), Cobbett also associates self-employment and hand labor with the liberating reward of productive activity, in which the worker's labor is not alienated, commodified, and subject to purchase. Even so, it is also clear from the quotation that Cobbett's ideal, decentralized rural economy is dependent upon a gendered division of labor, with women serving a subordinate, supplementary role in their "proper place" (at the needle or wheel in their own homes). The liberating reward of such productive activity, then, is a restricted one for women, occurring only within prescribed, conservative boundaries set by a traditional view of gender.[25]

Furthermore, the "great thing" about hand production, and the making of straw plat in particular, writes Cobbett, is "that, to obtain the materials for the making of this article of dress (i.e., a hat or bonnet) . . . requires not a penny of capital" (*CE*, 173). Cobbett thus advocates the production of handmade goods as a practically free investment; only one's labor is required, and that too, if willingly expended, is in a certain sense "free." By contrast, the wage relation of factory production, along with what Cobbett considered to be inhuman working conditions (he calls factories "Hell-Holes of 84 degrees of heat" [*RR*, 2:440]), reduces the laborer to a mere slave of the system, a commodity completely at the mercy of the forces of capital and the culture of the ready-made.

As we have seen in the case of the farmer Charington, Cobbett blames the "accursed system" of factory production, class relations, and the "ready made" for the introduction of the wage relation into the agricultural economy. In addition, Cobbett extends his argument against the changing relationship between employers and employed to include the hypocrisy of outdoor relief as well. In September of 1822, as Cobbett traveled near his boyhood home of Farnham, he came upon a group of laborers, one of them a former childhood friend, at "parish-work." With the harvest ended and the farmers unable to pay wages for further work, these parish-work laborers proceeded "at the expense of half-ruined farmers tradesmen and landlords, to break stones into very small pieces to make nice smooth roads lest the jolting, in going along them, should create bile in the stomach of the overfed tax-eaters" (*RR*, 1:94). While "not . . . absolutely digging holes one day and filling them up the next," Cobbett judged such labor to be decidedly unproductive, especially when tasks that might be performed—the stripping of the hop poles, the mending of fences, the further cultivation of land before the frost—were left undone (*RR*, 1:94). Productive labor, here as always throughout Cobbett's writings, serves as the anchor of meaning and value; without such an anchor, the world becomes unhinged: "It is a state of things," writes Cobbett, "where all is out of order; where self-preservation, that great law of nature, seems to be set at defiance" (*RR*, 1:94). In a world where hypocrisy, irony, and disorder carry the day, where the means to self-preservation remain thwarted by a system that renders "farmers *unable* to pay men for working for them," but legislates that they must "pay them for working in doing that which is really of no use to any human being," Cobbett as always addresses the material needs of the laborers first: "We left these poor fellows, after having given them, not '*religious Tracts*,' which would, if they could, make the labourer content with half starvation, but, something to get them some bread and cheese and beer, being firmly convinced that it is the body that wants filling and not the mind" (*RR*, 1:94).

Cobbett's gesture is telling. While almost always willing to offer money or food to those laborers he encounters in distress, at the same time Cobbett continually rails against the harmful effects of charity, particularly when that benevolence is embedded in religious ideology, especially Methodism.[26] Cobbett does not consider his vituperation toward religious charity a contradiction of his own practice of spontaneously assisting, if only in a small way (perhaps only by providing enough money for one meal), those who stand in need of such assistance, inasmuch as his own "giving" does not imply that the "receiver" is obliged to subscribe to Cobbett's politics.[27] Furthermore, and perhaps more importantly, Cobbett objects to the tendency of most religious teachings (again, Methodism is usually the primary target) to devalue labor and the material world in general. In the introduction to *Cottage Economy*, Cobbett again turns to a body metaphor to make his point: "As an ailing carcass engenders vermin, a pauperised community engenders teachers of fanaticism, the very foundation of whose doctrines is, that we are to care nothing about this world, and that all our labours and exertions are in vain" (*CE*, 9).

Cobbett argues strenuously throughout his writings against this (mis)representation of the laboring body as engaging in a kind of false exchange economy, according to which one's labor produces nothing of value or use. With equal vigor, Cobbett also attacked what he saw as the devaluation of labor—indeed, the thwarting of the need to labor—by the practice of religious beneficence. Cobbett relates just such a case of benevolent ideology shortly after his encounter with the parish-work laborers, as he passes by the estate of Sir Thomas and Lady Baring. The Barings, according to Cobbett, are known to be quite benevolent toward the poor in their vicinity, but only if those recipients of their benevolence conform to the Barings' standard of religious piety. Such a condition, in Cobbett's view, utterly undermines their good intentions: "I am very certain that, by pursuing this principle of action, where they make one good man or woman, they will make one hundred hypocrites" (*RR*, 1:96). Contrary to the Barings' practice of charity, Cobbett reaffirms that the primary target of redress is the material, rather than the spiritual, condition of the people: "Amongst the labouring people, the first thing you have to look after is, *common honesty, speaking the truth*, and *refraining from thieving;* and to secure these, the labourer must have *his belly full* and be *free from fear;* and this belly full must come to him from out of his *wages*, and not from benevolence of any description" (*RR*, 1:97). Here, Cobbett's anti-benevolence position is grounded in the basic principle of just compensation, taken up later by the Chartists as "a fair day's wages for a fair day's work." Charity, as far as Cobbett is concerned, draws humans into an unproductive exchange relation, one in which the participants in the exchange each act according to ulterior motives—the misguided religious agenda of the Barings, for example, and the willingness of the poor to pay lip service to such an agenda in order to gain access to material goods. In this way, something (food, money) is received for nothing, nothing more than an empty gesture, an "exchange" comparable in its structure to the feeding of "dead weight," and equally as unproductive, in Cobbett's view.

In addition to asserting the principle of just compensation, which pertains primarily to the wage relation between employer and employed, the above passage also articulates another kind of secondary exchange, with its basis in the payment of just wages for hard work, but exacted on the social rather than the strictly economic terrain. In return for the security of a full belly, the "you" of the above passage—presumably the payer of wages that enables the full belly—gains, in return, the benefit of three qualities in the laborer: honesty, truth, and respect for property. What motivates the employer to pay fair wages, then, is not necessarily a recognition of the principle of just compensation, but the opportunity to gain possession and control over the laboring body, "to secure" order. What passes at first glance as an assertion of social right on the part of the laboring class also ends up asserting the necessity of their passivity; the security of the laborer (belly full, free from fear) secures, in turn, the rights of property.

As we have seen, in Cobbett's consistent emphasis on "filling the belly" lies the material connection between the practice of radical husbandry and the improvement of the condition of agrarian laborers. To what extent, though, is this practice really radical, if radical husbandry serves primarily as a supplement to the wage relation, which itself secures the interests of property? In other words, does Cobbett's method of making the small farmers and laborers more self-sufficient secure them anything beyond their mere survival? Ian Dyck answers these questions by noting that Cobbett did not overtly "encourage labourers to cease waged employment, but nor did he disguise the fact that the introduction of more non-wage forms of survival would reverse proletarianization and reduce the pool of reserve labour upon which large-scale capitalist agriculture depended."[28] Raymond Williams also attests to the radicality of Cobbett's position, acknowledging that "Cobbett was all for Law and Order, and for the Traditions of his Country," but not when "he saw people starving or half-starving in the shadow of such ideas."[29] For Williams, Cobbett's material politics is the very essence of his radicalism, especially as it developed through the 1820s, when Cobbett began to "shift from an idea of constitutional reform to an idea of democracy," which included an embrace of popular struggle, whether manifested as the exercise of political pressure or open revolt.[30] As E. P. Thompson writes, Cobbett "stopped short before any radical critique of property rights," but "accepted that if existing property-relations violated . . . essential claims to human realisation, then any remedy, however drastic, was open to discussion."[31]

When Cobbett did discuss political remedies for the condition of the national body, though, he usually stuck to the issue of parliamentary reform, even alongside his claims throughout *Rural Rides* that the accursed system is "unnatural," a system "that must be destroyed, or that will destroy the country" (*RR*, 1:222). Although parliamentary reform seems an unlikely avenue for the destruction of the system, as Williams remarks, for Cobbett it was an article of faith that "a reformed parliament would end poverty."[32] As would befit someone whose material politics begin and end with attention to the condition of the laboring body, Cobbett also expressed his vision of parliamentary reform in terms of the body, again both metaphorically and literally:

> Would a dissolution of Parliament mend the matter? No: for the *same men* would be there still. They are the *same men* that have been there for these *thirty years*; and the *same men* they will be, and they *must be*, until there be *a reform*. To be sure when one dies, or cuts his throat (as in the case of *Castlereagh*), another *one* comes; but it is the *same body*. And, as long as it is that same body, things will always go on as they now go on. However, as Mr. Canning says the body "*works well*," we must not say the contrary. (*RR*, 1:132)

Cobbett's ironic appropriation of Canning's assertion that Parliament, despite its critics, "works well," foregrounds his concern not just with the body as such, but with that body's labor. Just as Cobbett establishes a link between the health of the national body and the condition of the bodies of individual agrarian workers based on his valuation of material production, so too does his use of the body metaphor to articulate his vision of parliamentary reform depend upon his privileging of productive labor. And just as the health and productivity of individual laborers determines the health and productivity of the metaphorical national body, the productivity of individual members of Parliament serves as a measure—indeed the determinant—of whether or not the larger "body" as a whole "works well."

Although Cobbett's literal and metaphorical use of the body with respect to Parliament thus appears consistent with his earlier use of body terminology, the remedy for Parliament's ailing body, as stated above, appears to differ, at least on the surface. We have seen Cobbett advocate a self-sustaining mode of production for small farmers and agrarian laborers, a management of their productivity that would directly "profit" individuals and their families by filling their bellies. With respect to Parliament, however, Cobbett seeks not the improved performance of individual laboring bodies, but the displacement of those bodies altogether. Behind Cobbett's reasoning lies a fundamental difference between the condition of rural laborers and members of

Parliament: agrarian laborers, no matter how degraded and malnourished, continue to embody at least the potential for productive labor, while "the same faces and names" that Cobbett has seen throughout his life occupying the seats of Parliament have ceased to be productive altogether (*RR*, 1:137). In this way, the body of Parliament is not so much "sick" as it is unproductive, even counterproductive.

In explaining his reasoning in a passage addressed to Canning, Cobbett shifts from a metaphorics of the body to that of the machine:

> Show us, prove to us, that the House "works well," and I, for my part, give the matter up. It is not the *construction* or the *motions* of a machine that I ever look at: all I look after is *the effect*. When, indeed, I find that the effect is deficient or evil, I look to the construction. And as I now see, and have for many years seen, *evil effect*, I seek a remedy in an *alteration in the machine*. (*RR*, 1:135).

Though this shift may at first seem contrary to his previous emphasis on the material body, in focusing on "the effect" of the machine, Cobbett once again foregrounds productivity as the standard by which he measures value.[33] Further, the significance of the House's "effect" as sign of *internal* trouble (in this case, of problems among the individual representatives who, like the components of a machine, are primarily responsible for its productivity) finds its corollary (ironically) in the very signs that determine whether or not that effect is "evil" in the first place—that is, in the bodies of individual laborers. The physical condition of the laborers' bodies thus functions as a sign of a twofold *internal* and *bodily* crisis: a crisis of material inanition (the physical body of the laborer lacks nourishment), and a crisis of political administration (the governing political body lacks productive components, and fails to "work well"). Because Cobbett seeks throughout his writings to trace the condition of the laboring body-as-sign back to its source, and inasmuch as the sign is here represented as a product of political and administrative "work," the body of Parliament might be said, in Cobbett's view, not only to *affect*, but also to *effect*—to produce—the laboring body.

At least one commentator has attempted to draw a parallel between Cobbett's call for the reform of parliament and his horticultural practice, especially with respect to trenching and crop rotation.[34] The connection between crop rotation and the displacement of the bodies of members of Parliament has particular merit, and Cobbett himself provides support for this connection by asserting that a reform of Parliament will "effect" for the agrarian laborer exactly what the practices of radical husbandry and cottage economy will. In his *Political Register* for April 2, 1831, Cobbett writes:

> Will a reform of the Parliament give the labouring man a cow or a pig; will it put bread and cheese in his satchell instead of infernal cold potatoes; will it give him a bottle of beer to carry to the field instead of making him to lie down on his belly to drink out of the brook; will it put upon his back a Sunday coat and send him to church? . . . [The] enemies of reform jeeringly ask us, whether reform would do these things for us; and I would answer distinctly that IT WOULD DO THEM ALL![35]

Cobbett's effort to improve the condition of agrarian laborers thus proceeds according to a two-pronged attack: through the material politics of radical husbandry and cottage economy on the one hand, and through the representational politics of parliamentary reform on the other. Both find their justification, says Cobbett, in their material effect; both will address the needs of the bodies (and especially the bellies) of rural workers. Admittedly, the practice of radical husbandry and cottage economy appears to address these needs much more directly than any reform of Parliament would, but for Cobbett it is imperative that the attack on the THING come from both above *and* below. The relation of "effect" between Parliament and the people, after all, has as its ground a representative relation, at least theoretically. In this sense, any alteration of the representative body that would introduce members whose interests accurately reflect those of the small farmers and rural laborers (or that would actually place small farmers and rural laborers in Parliament as members) might be said to alter the relation between the political body and the body politic, through a more direct system of representation. Toward this end, as Ian Dyck remarks, "right up until the [Reform] Bill's passage in June 1832, Cobbett pressured the ruling class to enfranchise the country workers, if not because they possessed property (the magic word for suffrage) in their labour, then because they would undo the chain of corruption and dependence that beguiled the old regime."[36] The Reform Bill of 1832, of course, did not extend that right, but Cobbett "lent it his conditional support" anyway, viewing it as "a foundation from which villagers could continue their struggle" (Dyck, 197).

If Cobbett's support for the Reform Bill would thus seem to be something of a concession, it also served a practical function as a political expedient. Dyck asserts that "not the least of his reasons for offering the [Reform] Act his provisional approval, was his quiet confidence . . . that his own presence in Parliament would enable him to achieve democracy and the cottage charter for English villagers" (197).[37] Cobbett had stood for election twice before, in 1820 for Coventry and in 1826 for Preston, but was defeated both times.[38] In the general election following the passage of the Reform Bill, though, Cobbett finally won a seat in the House of Commons, representing Oldham, near Manchester.[39] And it is at this moment—when Cobbett himself enters the House—that his body-centered social analysis comes home, as it were.[40] What better way, after all, to embody both the material politics of radical husbandry and the representative politics of parliamentary reform, than with the healthful presence (following Carlyle's designation) of his own body? As a former farmer and laborer himself, Cobbett's presence in Parliament would thus represent, both literally and metaphorically, the "presence" of what he considered to be his true constituency—the rural poor—a presence decidedly absent from a Parliament comprising the same faces and names for the last thirty years.

Not surprisingly, then, Cobbett's labor within Parliament directly reflected his longstanding concern with the physical condition of laborers. He argued strenuously for a repeal of the malt tax, which he considered to be the primary obstacle to home-brewing (one of the primary practices of his cottage economy),[41] and argued equally strenuously against the Poor Law Amendment Act of 1834, both before and after the bill became law. In both cases Cobbett's position was heard but largely ignored, as were nearly all the other positions he advocated during the ten months he served in Parliament. Such ineffectiveness must be qualified, of course, by the brevity of his tenure and the relative powerlessness of the small minority of Radical members—and indeed, most commentators make a point of acknowledging these limitations.[42]

Perhaps his greatest limitation, though, and certainly the most ironic, was ultimately the one that led to his death—his declining health. Cole writes that "from the very moment of his election, his health suffered, and his absences owing to illness became more and more frequent. Colds and coughs attacked him with increasing violence; he lost his voice on several occasions" (389). Cobbett was seventy years old when he entered Parliament, and as Macaulay reflected in 1855, "In truth his faculties were impaired by age; and the late hours of the House probably assisted to enfeeble his body & consequently his mind."[43] This assertion that Cobbett's service in the House actually contributed to his decline was generally accepted at the time of his death; Cobbett's obituary in the *Times* rather caustically stated that "The House of Commons, into which he ought never to have entered, and where he never made any figure, has, perhaps, hastened his death."[44]

The irony of his demise—that his labor to reform both the body of Parliament and the nation through his physical presence in the House ultimately destroyed his own health, leaving him physically and mentally "enfeebled"—is further deepened by Cobbett's attempt throughout his writings (and in *Rural Rides* in particular) to project a healthy and robust self-image,[45] an image commentators from William Hazlitt to Raymond Williams have willingly reproduced. For Williams, Cobbett stands—literally—for the challenge to authority and received opinion now too readily consigned to the ash heap of irrelevance and "lost causes."[46] In his brief book *Cobbett*, Williams begins and ends with the image of Cobbett as a healthy, imposing and manly figure, rising in a hostile crowd that threatened to remove him from the premises "that they might see the man that they had to put out."[47] In the end, for Williams, Cobbett remains a "disturbing presence": "In fact he keeps getting up: 'that they might see the man'. He does not ask permission or approval, least of all from the privileged or the worldly-wise. There is a challenge, and it has to be made. There is an argument, and it has to be carried on" (81). The "he" in this passage is a generalized "he," signifying not just Cobbett, but also "his kind"; Williams intends in this closing passage to recover Cobbett and his "succession," to stake a claim that material politics *matters*. To do so requires a kind of faith in the value of the material, in the need for a *physical* presence as a point from which a material challenge might be articulated; this faith is, for Williams, fundamental to the advancement of a radical, materialist politics, and it is this faith that he finds fundamentally valuable (and valued) in Cobbett. That this physical presence is an exclusively *masculine* one does not seem to occur to Williams. Instead, for Williams, matter, metaphor, and the man converge in Cobbett's bodily presence; as the embodiment of the radical tradition, Cobbett's masculinity figures as the last stand against "the privileged" and "the worldly-wise."

For Williams and others, then, this representation of Cobbett proceeds according to the logic of romanticized, manly signs—Cobbett as the man continually rising to the challenge, stout and ruddy-complected ("just the weight of a four-bushel sack of good wheat," Cobbett himself wrote in 1821 [*RR*, 1:28]), rendering that challenge formidably visible. This romanticized, manly Cobbett offered his presence, both among agrarian workers (as recorded in the *Rural Rides* and elsewhere) and in Parliament, as a challenge to the corruption of the national body, a presence both literal and literary, material and metaphoric. This romanticization, characterized by the foregrounding of the masculine presence, is hardly surprising; in fact, it is perfectly in keeping with Cobbett's representation of himself throughout his writings.[48] On the subject of Cobbett's self-representation, Hazlitt asserts that Cobbett's writing bodied forth the man himself: "He writes himself plain William Cobbett, strips himself quite as naked as anybody could wish."[49] Cobbett's bodily presence, then, is ironically also a textual presence, a representation that Cobbett himself hoped would remain even after death, as a textual legacy—the body of his written work as a transparent sign of the man.

But as Kevin Gilmartin observes, although it was Cobbett's intention to represent "his own vigorous body as the medium through which a people would again become 'one firm and united body' . . . the central standard-bearer of reform was himself radically decentered and displaced, an itinerant sign of the system's ravaging effects on its victims."[50] By "decentered and displaced," Gilmartin has in mind both Cobbett's political marginality and his displacement from his home in Botley, a displacement geographically articulated, according to Gilmartin, by Cobbett's wanderings described in *Rural Rides*.[51] And when this displaced and decentered body loses its vigor just at the moment Cobbett assumes the mantle of political "representative," this loss of vigor ironically undermines his body/politics, his efforts to secure a "re-formation" of the body of the people by merging the symbolic (the representative body) with the material (his own body). The notion of failure implicit here is also present in Carlyle's representation of Cobbett; Scott and Cobbett, after all, are not "great men," but "healthy men," something "pleasanter to be," but whose material impact on and legacy to their world remains negligible.

To romanticize Cobbett's body, then, threatens to oversimplify and overshadow his complex, contradictory efforts, both textual and material, to alter the condition of the decidedly unromanticized bodies of agrarian laborers. It also tends to obscure Cobbett's many weaknesses, failures, and prejudices, including his anti-Semitism. Many commentators, despite their attention to Cobbett's materialist politics, have given us an unblemished Cobbett, rather than a portrait of the man "wens and all," as it were. A materialist reading of Cobbett, though it must surely take up his emphasis, both literal and metaphoric, on the bodies of the people and the body of the nation, cannot, at the same time, generate an uncritical representation of "the man," especially when it merely reproduces Cobbett's self-projected image of unassailable health and vigor. To do so renders Cobbett ironically *immaterial*, unhinged from the material product of his body's labor—the body of his written work.

3

"A labor of death and a labor against death"

The Writing of History in Thomas Carlyle's *Past and Present*

THOMAS CARLYLE FIRST VISITED LONDON in June 1824, at the age of 28. After several months in "this enormous Babel of a place," he declared to his brother Alexander: "No wonder Cobbett calls this place a Wen! It is a monstrous Wen! The thick smoke of it beclouds a space of thirty square miles; and a million of vehicles, from dog- or cuddy-barrow to the giant waggon, grind its streets forever."[1] Like Cobbett, Carlyle finds most distasteful the density of London's population and its intense, commercial, money-grubbing atmosphere:

> You are packed into paltry shells of brick-houses (calculated to endure for forty years, then fall); every door that slams to in the street is audible in your most secret chamber; the necessaries of life are hawked about thro' multitudes of hands, and reach you, frequently adulterated, always at rather more than *twice* their cost elsewhere; people's friends must visit them by rule and measure; and when you issue from your door, you are assailed by vast shoals of quacks, and showmen, and street-sweepers, and pickpockets, and mendicants of every degree and shape, all ply-

ing in noise or silent craft their several vocations, all in their hearts like 'lions ravening for their prey.' (*CL*, 3:219)

Despite this litany of urban irritants, Carlyle's attitude toward London is ultimately more ambivalent than Cobbett's. Though he professes repulsion at the "false and tumultuous manner of existence" (*CL*, 3:219) that appears to abound in the city, he nevertheless writes to Jane Welsh that "it has much in it, this monster of a city, that will amuse you and awaken you to new thoughts; and with all its imperfection it is London, the London everyone delights to see or to have seen" (*CL*, 3:216). In fact, ten years after his initial visit, in June 1834, the Carlyles moved to Cobbett's Wen permanently, settling into an old brick house on Cheyne Row, in a neighborhood that afforded something of a respite from the tumultuousness Carlyle loathed. As Fred Kaplan notes, "Among its advantages were village-like quietness within a half-hour walk or ten-minute ride of the center of London and a prevailing west wind that blew the urban pollution away from them."[2] It is from this vantage point, then, seemingly "at the heart of all the universe" (*CL*, 3:218) (though in reality somewhat on the fringes of the very center of that heart), that Carlyle began to turn his attention most directly upon the volatile social conditions of the late 1830s and early 1840s, especially in his long essay *Chartism* (1839) and his book *Past and Present* (1843).

Like Cobbett, Carlyle's social analysis in these works is permeated with repeated references to the body, both literal and metaphoric. Indeed, the very phrase the "Condition-of-England question," coined by Carlyle in *Chartism* to designate the various discourses addressing the series of social and economic crises facing English society, itself denotes the matter of the nation's health, and thus implicitly metaphorizes the nation as a body subject to analogous afflictions and maladies. Also like Cobbett, when Carlyle addresses the condition-of-England question, he looks to the remote past for comparison and context. Both writers self-consciously call attention to the "textuality" of history, but for Carlyle this textuality also calls into question the very accessibility of the past itself, and thus problematizes the authorial power of historiography.

This paradoxical view of history, evident in Carlyle's early essays "On History" and "On History Again," reaches its culmination, and finds its ultimate relationship with the present times, in his *Past and Present*, a text that endeavors to generate a "mutual elucidation"[3] between the remote past and the volatile, rapidly changing present.

Thomas Carlyle wrote the bulk of the manuscript for *Past and Present* between November 1842 and March 1843, when he was supposed to be writing a book on Oliver Cromwell. As nearly every Carlyle scholar agrees, the event responsible for this diversion of his creative energy was his trip through East Anglia during the first week of September 1842.[4] Ostensibly a research-gathering tour of a region Cromwell once lived in, Carlyle's journey introduced him instead to the St. Ives workhouse and the ruined abbey of Bury St. Edmunds. For Carlyle, the "half hundred or more" (*PP*, 8) able but idle men at the former embodied the ironic ineffectiveness of the Poor Law Amendment Act of 1834, while the "old grim walls" (54) of the latter stood as evidence of what had once been that area's monastic-centered community. The immediate context for Carlyle's writing of *Past and Present* would thus seem to be his eyewitness experience of what may be more generally termed "the condition of England," with the publication of the book itself (in April 1843) marking yet another entry into the genre of occasional political tracts and pamphlets.

But Carlyle's trip through East Anglia did not resolve the specific impediment to his completion (or even the commencement) of the Cromwell biography. Less than a week before his journey, in a famous letter to Emerson, Carlyle defined his main obstacle "to be that I cannot write *two Books at once*; cannot be in the seventeenth century and in the nineteenth at one and the same moment" (*CL*, 15:57). The immediate event that allowed Carlyle to write "two Books at once" was not his experience of the St. Ives workhouse or the ruined abbey at Bury St. Edmunds (as Kaplan tells us, "He wrote nothing in September"),[5] but his visit on 12 October 1842 to the London Library, from which he borrowed *Chronica Jocelini de Brakelonda*, a twelfth-century manuscript written by a monk of the St. Edmundsbury abbey, Jocelin of Brakelond, and published two years earlier by the antiquarian Camden Society.[6] Jocelin's text (a partial translation and retelling of which occupies nearly all of *Past and Present*'s Book 2) provided Carlyle with the rhetorical strategy he needed to write two books at once, to be (in this case) in the twelfth century and the nineteenth century at the same time.

This strategy, which Carlyle terms a "mutual elucidation" (45) of the medieval past and the mid-nineteenth-century present, allows Carlyle to re-present the text of Jocelin's chronicle in the context of the political and economic crises facing England in the 1840s. This rhetorical turn toward the medieval as an agent for contemporary social commentary is not an innovation peculiar to *Past and Present*, but a strategy shared by a number of other writers often associated with the revival of literary, architectural, and historiographical interest in the Middle Ages, a phenomenon which had been growing since the mid-eighteenth century. Generally referred to as the "Gothic Revival" (though even today that term still signifies primarily the theory and practice of revivalist architecture), and less often as the "medieval revival" or simply "medievalism," this rather amorphous "fashion" includes such diverse elements as the antiquarian societies of the early eighteenth century; the so-called graveyard poets (especially Thomas Gray); Richard Hurd's *Letters on Chivalry and Romance* (1762) and Thomas Percy's *Reliques of Ancient English Poetry* (1765); the gothic novels of Horace Walpole and Ann Radcliffe (and their legacy); the historical romances of Sir Walter Scott; the historiography of William Cobbett and Robert Southey; the gothic architecture of Augustus Welby Pugin; the staging of medieval spectacle (from the building of sham ruins in the mid-to-late eighteenth century onward, to the staging of the Eglinton Tournament in 1839); the paintings of Daniel Maclise and John Rogers Herbert; the Oxford Movement; the Cambridge Camden Society; and Young England.[7]

While Carlyle's *Past and Present* has been called "the most remarkable fruit in English literature of the medieval revival,"[8] very few attempts have been made, until relatively recently, to articulate the relationship of Carlyle's project to the various efforts at revivalism that we might loosely term "historiographic."[9] Most of these latter-day accounts of the medieval revival assert that its literature is unified thematically by an idyllic return to the past, and that this tendency is itself quite literally reactionary, precipitated by the social upheavals associated with industrialism and political revolution.[10] As Alice Chandler observes:

> The more the world changed, and the period of the medieval revival was an era of ever accelerating social transformation, the more the partly historical but basically mythical Middle Ages that had become a tradition in literature served to remind men of a Golden Age. The Middle Ages were idealized as a period of faith, order, joy, munificence and creativity. Feudalism was seen as fatherhood, and the medieval world—to adopt Carlyle's phrase—was thought to be "godlike and my Father's."[11]

Chandler's assertion here is by no means a unique critical assessment of the Gothic Revival's unifying theme; instead it marks a kind of return —to the very charges of "idealization" leveled at revivalists by Whig critics and historians in the mid-nineteenth century.[12] These contemporary critics, like their Whig predecessors, tend to assess the literary products of the Gothic Revival as the symptom of a conservative, nostalgic wish for a return to an idyllic past, a wish rendered impractical and ultimately impossible by the immediate context of the volatile contemporary politics of the time. Moreover, they dismiss the vast majority of these works because the object of that nostalgic wish, the past, is merely a product, at best, of bad historiography, or at worst, of an idle imagination.

Although the literature of the Gothic Revival provides *Past and Present* with its generic context, Carlyle explicitly refuses to idealize the medieval past and, indeed, problematizes the very practice of historiography. In fact, as we shall see, it is precisely the past in this work which cannot be returned to or touched; when Carlyle embodies the past, he provides us with only the lineaments of a corpse (St. Edmund's) and the translation of a corpus (Jocelin's), not the decayed flesh or the originary text itself. Carlyle's practice of historiography self-consciously recognizes the textual status of historical "truth," and thus foregrounds the paradoxical nature of the historiographic enterprise;

the task necessitates the "bodying forth" of the past—of that which defies, by its very definition, the attempt to "revive" or re-present it.

For Carlyle, then, history is always already textual, and therefore not something that may be fully interpreted, represented, or "revived." As early as 1830, in his essay "On History," Carlyle insisted that the past presents itself as a text to be read, but only partly deciphered:

> [T]hough the whole meaning lies far beyond our ken[,] yet in that complex Manuscript, covered over with formless inextricably-entangled unknown characters,—nay, which is a *Palimpsest*, and had once prophetic writing, still dimly legible there,—some letters, some words, may be deciphered; . . . well understanding, in the mean while, that it is only a little portion we have deciphered . . . that History is a real Prophetic Manuscript, and can be fully interpreted by no man.[13]

Carlyle's use of the palimpsest metaphor here allows him to conceal the nihilist undercurrent of his theory of history (if all historical truth is constructed, the only truth may well be that there is no truth), by positing an originary, prophetic, and *ultimately unrecoverable* text to serve as the truth under erasure, as the logical ground for his historiographic enterprise.[14] This palimpsest metaphor is all the more remarkable for its assertion that History, in the abstract, is always already a text, when in the preceding paragraph Carlyle purports that one of the primary limitations of representing the past is precisely that "Narrative is *linear*, Action is *solid*" (89). In other words, history "happens," if you will, all at once; it is the sum of the world's events, many of them occurring simultaneously, rather than sequentially. As Carlyle states, "every single event is the offspring of not one, but of all other events, prior or contemporaneous, and will in its turn combine with all others to give birth to new: it is an ever-living, ever-working Chaos of Being, wherein shape after shape bodies itself forth from innumerable elements" (88). The "shape" of history, then, following the body metaphor, must be solid; its textual representation through conventional written narrative, which recounts events as a linear succession, reduces the dimensions of its significance from three to one. These two metaphors for history, as a sum of activity (a solid) and as a prophetic manuscript (a text), may appear, at first, mutually exclusive. How can history (or the past), after all, be at the same time impossible to represent through writing, and always already a written text?[15] Only in this sense: that both metaphors themselves "represent" history as "unrepresentable." If the palimpsest metaphor held that the originary trace beneath those other traces was ultimately completely readable, we would face an unreconcilable pair of metaphors. Instead, because the "Prophetic Manuscript" remains unrecoverable, the historiographer's subject will always be that "web" of writings that forms the palimpsest.[16]

It is precisely this matter of the textual nature of history that helps us to define more clearly Carlyle's relationship to the medieval revival in general, and to his immediate predecessors (Scott, Cobbett, and Southey) in particular. As the most famous and prolific of the authors associated with the Gothic Revival, Walter Scott is generally hailed as the greatest popularizing force behind the revival of literary and architectural interest in the Middle Ages.[17] "If appeals to the medieval past found a prepared audience," writes R. J. Smith in *The Gothic Bequest*, "it was Scott, more than any other, who was responsible" (133). Chandler in particular believes that Carlyle "was deeply influenced by Scott," and asserts that Scott's novels "provided [Carlyle] with a persuasive description of a paternalistic age" (51, 134). But only five years before Carlyle would be charged with idealizing the past in *Past and Present*, he attributed that same nostalgic desire to Scott in an essay published in the *London and Westminster Review*. In a brief characterization of Scott's indebtedness to Goethe's drama *Götz von Berlichingen* (1773), a play Scott had translated early in his career, Carlyle equates "Götzism" with an "affectionate half-regretful looking-back into the Past," a tendency "of which Scott was representative" (SWS, 58). Thus, when assessing the relative stature of the Waverley novels, Carlyle states that "if Literature had no task but that of harmlessly amusing indolent languid men, here was the very perfection of Literature" (SWS, 73). Add to this Carlyle's indictment of Scott's obsession with Abbotsford at the expense of his own creative energy, to the extent that he "must kill himself that he may be a country gentleman, the founder of a race of

Scottish lairds" (SWS, 72), and the distance Carlyle wished to place between Scott's work and his own, at least in terms of the function of literature, could not be more clear.[18]

There remains, though, a significant exception to Carlyle's distaste for the effect Scott's art had on its audience, an exception that bears directly on Carlyle's understanding of what constitutes a valid approach to historiography. Scott's novels, writes Carlyle,

> taught all men this truth, which looks like a truism, and yet was as good as unknown to writers of history and others, till so taught: that the bygone ages of the world were actually filled by living men, not by protocols, state-papers, controversies and abstractions of men. . . . History will henceforth have to take thought of it. Her faint hearsays of "philosophy teaching by experience" will have to exchange themselves everywhere for direct inspection and embodiment. (SWS, 77–78)

This statement advocates a historiography that seems to be quite literally revivalist in its call for a reanimation of the historical, a re-presentation of history that renders the past present. It is on this basis that Hayden White, in his *Metahistory*, aligns Carlyle with what he calls the "Formist" manner of historical explanation, a method whose practitioners are readily identified by the "vividness of their reconstructions."[19] At first, though, such a call for "direct inspection and embodiment" might seem to contradict Carlyle's palimpsest metaphor and the notion of an ultimately unrecoverable text. But for Carlyle it is precisely the act of recovery, of revival and interpretation, that marks the past as utterly dead and other. If we are to understand Carlyle as participating in a tradition of medieval revivalism, then, it must be with this difference: that "returning to the past" for Carlyle is always a matter of representation, rather than an appeal for restoration.[20] What Carlyle values in Scott's art is not his nostalgic, "half-regretful looking-back into the Past," but his ability to body forth that past. While the novels of Sir Walter Scott, like those of Radcliffe, belong to this revivalist trend, in Carlyle's view they fail to function as anything other than idle amusement: the Waverley novels in particular are "Not profitable," writes Carlyle, "for doctrine, for reproof, for edification, for building up or elevating, in any shape!" (SWS, 76). While later critics would argue that Scott's novels function more explicitly in the service of a hegemony that seeks to assuage historical crisis by replotting its course through a narrative like *Ivanhoe*,[21] Carlyle remains content (as we have seen) to affirm Scott's status, if not as a great writer, then at least as "one of the *healthiest* of men" (SWS, 10).

Despite the perhaps inevitable backhandedness of such a compliment, health is a matter not to be taken lightly when coming from Carlyle, whose own crisis of faith appears inextricably bound up with his persistent bouts of ill health.[22] Indeed, the well-being of the body, mainly expressed in the physical terms of its ability to labor (but linked also to a spiritual wellness that springs from the fulfillment of what Carlyle sees as a human duty—the obligation to work), becomes for Carlyle a kind of litmus test of how well England's political and economic organization itself "works." And while Carlyle's link between the healthy body and the healthy nation is by no means unique, his particular description in *Past and Present* of the unhealthy body as marked by paralysis and petrifaction is often taken as such. However, as we shall see, the initial deployment of this body-metaphor appears in another text usually included in the literature of the medieval revival: Robert Southey's *Sir Thomas More: or, Colloquies on the Progress and Prospects of Society* (1829), a work whose influence on Carlyle has been surprisingly underrated. While Alice Chandler ventures that "it is Cobbett, whom Carlyle praised for his humaneness and great love for the poor, who seems the most immediate English influence on *Past and Present*" (134), Southey also plays a significant, and perhaps a more direct role, in influencing Carlyle's representation of the condition of England. Carlyle and Southey were of like minds concerning the deterioration of English society; indeed, Carlyle records the topic of his last conversation with Southey as "the usual one . . . steady decay of all morality, political, social, individual; this once noble England getting more and more ignoble and untrue in every fibre of it, till the gold . . . would all be eaten out, and noble England would have to collapse in shapeless ruin, whether forever or not none of us could know," and describes their agreement about these issues as one of "perfect consent."[23]

In fact, it is precisely Southey's method of representing the past that links him more closely than Cobbett to Carlyle's *Past and Present*. Although thematically Southey's *Colloquies* are very similar to Cobbett's *A History of the Protestant "Reformation"* (indeed, R. J. Smith remarks that they "express almost identical opinions" [157]), in terms of tone and rhetorical structure, the works differ dramatically. Southey offers as his rhetorical device in *Colloquies* a conversation between the author, in the persona of Montesinos, and the ghost of Sir Thomas More, recently returned from the dead. While the simplicity of this device in no way approaches the complexity of Carlyle's re-presentation of Jocelin and his text, Southey's attempt certainly marks a blatant, if crude, attempt at "revivalist" historiography; Sir Thomas More "comes alive," if you will, to narrate a history of loss: the loss of mutual interdependence, of monastic and aristocratic beneficence, and of a pervasive faith in religion. "A trading spirit thus gradually superseded the rude but kindlier principle of the feudal system," says More, and thus "profit and loss became the rule of conduct; in came calculation, and out went feeling."[24]

In "Colloquy VII: The Manufacturing System," this loss of feeling is quickly extended to a metaphor of petrifaction, accompanied by a mythological analogy familiar to readers of Carlyle. The "servants of Mammon," says Montesinos,

> pursue their object with steadiness and singleness of purpose, and rewarded they are abundantly with what they covet. Yet their power of creating wealth brings with it a consequence not dissimilar to that which Midas suffered. The love of lucre is one of those base passions which
>
> harden all within
> And petrify the feeling.
>
> He who, at the beginning of his career, uses his fellow-creatures as bodily machines for producing wealth, ends not unfrequently in becoming an intellectual one himself, employed in continually increasing what it is impossible for him to enjoy. (*STM*, 1:171)

The first chapter of the Proem to *Past and Present* is, of course, entitled "Midas," and there Carlyle expands the metaphor Southey introduces above, mapping it across class boundaries and onto the terrain of the entire nation:

> In the midst of plethoric plenty, the people perish; with gold walls, and full barns, no man feels himself safe or satisfied. Workers, Master Workers, Unworkers, all men, come to a pause; stand fixed, and cannot farther. Fatal paralysis spreading inwards, from the extremities, in St. Ives workhouses, in Stockport cellars, through all limbs, as if towards the heart itself. Have we actually got enchanted, then; accursed by some god? (11–12)

If the industrialists were the ones initially rewarded with the Midas touch, as in Southey's metaphor, in Carlyle we see an England in which everyone has been touched by Midas. The pervasiveness of this "enchanted" condition of England, and particularly its movement throughout the national body as if it were a disease, also has its roots in Southey's "Colloquy VII," where the manufacturing system figures as a particularly virulent, inextricable Cobbettian Wen: it is "a fungous excrescence from the body politic. . . . [I]ts nerves have branched so widely, and the vessels of the tumour are so inosculated into some of the principal veins and arteries of the natural system, that to remove it by absorption is impossible, and excision would be fatal" (*STM*, 1:171).

While Southey seems to believe that this figurative use of the body overstates the case—"Happily," says Montesinos, "this is but a metaphor; and the body politic, like its crowned head, never dies" (*STM*, 1:171)—for Carlyle, the diagnosis of the body politic is so dire it necessitates "a total change of regimen, change of constitution and existence from the very centre of it; a new body to be got, with resuscitated soul—not without convulsive travail-throes, as all birth and new-birth presupposes travail!" (41). The body here encompasses many forms: the body politic, the body before and of the law (the citizen and the written constitution), the physical body, spiritual body, and the textual body. The violence of this creation of a new body through work (*travail* has its etymological root in *torture*), Carlyle tells us, comes "from the very centre of it." And the key to the creation of this new body lies, significantly, in Carlyle's representation of an old textual body—Jocelin's *Chronicle*—a text he represents as a corpse: "And so, in a word, the *Chronicle of Jocelin* is, as it professes to be, unwrapped from its thick cerements, and fairly brought forth into the common daylight, so that he who runs, and has a smattering of grammar, may read" (48). Though Carlyle means to suggest that the Camden Society's publication of the chronicle has effected this exhumation, it is really *Past and Present* that unwraps (through incorporation and translation) the corpus of Jocelin's text for us. Nevertheless, I will argue that Carlyle metaphorically connects the body of history and the body of a corpse in order to underscore the paradoxical nature of any historical investigation: on the one hand, the past will always remain, by its very definition, utterly remote and unrecoverable; on the other hand, the practice of historiography struggles against this inaccessibility, striving to represent—indeed, maybe even to "revive"—the dead. As Michel de Certeau asserts in *The Writing of History*, this paradox lies at the very heart of the historiographic enterprise:

> Historiography tends to prove that the site of its production can encompass the past: it is an odd procedure that posits death, a breakage everywhere reiterated in discourse, and that yet denies loss by appropriating to the present the privilege of recapitulating the past as a form of knowledge. A labor of death and a labor against death. (7)

Within the text of *Past and Present*, this paradoxical historiographic practice is "embodied" in Carlyle's translation of Jocelin's twelfth-century narrative. But as we will see, Carlyle's "unwrapping" of the body of Jocelin's text leads us only to another dead body—the corpse of St. Edmund—which in turn becomes subject to the same forensic process of exhumation and translation. And it is Jocelin's account of the "translation" of the saint's body that provides Carlyle with his most vivid (and misunderstood) metaphor for the paradoxical relationship between the past and the present. At the same time, two key metaphors—the magical speculum and the camera lucida—structure Carlyle's initial approach to the body of Jocelin's text. Each metaphor offers us, seemingly, the means to apprehend directly what is utterly dead and other, but simultaneously denies us those means, substituting instead a mediated translation based on a logic of displacement and virtual representation. Carlyle's writing of history thus participates self-consciously in this paradoxical mode, but toward a specific end—for the death against which Carlyle labors, ultimately, is not the loss of an idealized past, but the imminent death of the present social body, now "dying of inanition" (7).

Most commentators on Carlyle's historiographical enterprise in *Past and Present* have neglected this metaphoric interplay between writing and the body that both grounds the logic of his social vision and structures the unfolding of his narrative. Gordon Hirsch and Joseph Childers, for example, agree that Carlyle's understanding of historiography begins with the notion of "history as a text."[25] While both critics also agree that Carlyle's relationship to Jocelin's text is one of "interpretative rewriting,"[26] Hirsch finally encapsulates Carlyle's historiography as a "dialectic of reciprocal interpretation" between past and present (230), while Childers suggests that Carlyle's text oscillates between "recitative and dialogic exegeses" of Jocelin's chronicle (254). Childers and Hirsch each view Carlyle, then, as *interpreting* history by rewriting it, but as Michel de Certeau suggests, the "practice of history" (i.e., writing) "is not content with a hidden 'truth' that needs to be discovered; it *produces* a symbol through the very relation between a space newly designated within time and a *modus operandi* that fabricates 'scenarios' capable of organizing practices into a currently intelligible discourse" (6). This project, for de Certeau, is the project of the "making of history." The narrative of Carlyle's text may be understood in this way, then, as a *production* of "truth," an attempt to intervene into what Carlyle perceives as a culture rapidly degenerating into simulation.

This paradoxical process of "making history" begins as Carlyle first introduces his readers to Jocelin of Brakelond:

> Here he is, and in his hand a magical speculum, much gone to rust indeed, yet in fragments still clear; wherein the marvellous image of his existence does still shadow itself, though fitfully, and as with an intermittent light! Will not the reader peep with us into this singular *camera lucida*, where an extinct species, though fitfully, can still be seen alive? (49)

Despite the rather rousing "Here he is," an introduction meant to conjure Jocelin's very presence, Carlyle's description clearly foregrounds the fragmentary, shadowy nature of that presence, and his deployment of scientific instruments as metaphors for Jocelin's writing increases the ambiguity of our relationship as readers to the text of the chronicle. Even given their magical and singular qualities, both the speculum and the camera lucida, as we shall see, reveal certain difficulties in arriving at the "truth" of a text. A speculum is, of course, a mirror, and Jocelin's relationship to his own text is thus one of reflection and representation. When we gaze at this speculum, the mirror attains its "magical" qualities, reflecting not our own image, but the remnants of Jocelin's world, fragmented by the cultural differences in the six-and-a-half-century gap between Jocelin's time and Carlyle's, as well as by the initial production of the text (Jocelin chose to record some things and not others). As a historical chronicle, Jocelin's text may be all we have left as a record of his existence, but the image of that existence is still discernible only as a "fitful shadow" of itself, twice removed from its originary experience. The chronicle is thus a shadow of the image of the monk's existence, a representation of a representation of a "truth" that is now ultimately unrecoverable.

Even so, if the text of Jocelin's chronicle is now laid open before us like an uncovered dead body, as Carlyle suggests, we may proceed to view this corpse/corpus with another kind of speculum—a body-probe. This particular definition of speculum, certainly available to readers of the nineteenth century, refers to an array of instruments designed to dilate various bodily orifices, especially the vagina, mouth, and eye.[27] The eye, of course, is not exactly an orifice; in fact, it is an organ that fills a cavity, rather than the cavity itself. Nonetheless, the eye is grouped with the other orifices because of its relative inaccessibility, a result not of the constraints of space, but rather the propensity the eye has to close upon probing. The eye must be forced open to facilitate a gaze, just as the vagina, mouth, and anus must be dilated to allow the probing vision of the physician, or the penetration of surgical instruments.

"We will," writes Carlyle, "in this Second Portion of our Work, strive to penetrate a little, by means of certain confused Papers . . . into a somewhat remote Century; and to look face to face on it" (45). If Jocelin holds in his hand a "magical speculum," then, allowing us to gaze at the image of his medieval abbey, Carlyle's text, the very process of his writing, is another kind of speculum, a probing of Jocelin's corpus that offers us the illusion of direct inspection. Significantly, though, the speculum metaphor also suggests the fragmentary nature of that inspection; just as the speculum facilitates the gaze of the physician on only several relatively inaccessible or "remote" body parts, so too does the text of Jocelin's chronicle (and Carlyle's representation of that text) afford only a fragmentary inspection of "the image of his existence."

Carlyle's method throughout *Past and Present,* then, reflects his desire to foreground the paradoxical task of the historiographic enterprise: the representation of the past as a labor of death and a labor against death. In practice, Carlyle's incorporation of Jocelin's text mirrors this paradox; his efforts to animate or resuscitate the dead letters of the chronicle bring his audience seemingly "face to face" with the twelfth-century monastery, while at the same time those efforts foreground the illusory nature of such a "direct inspection." A prime example of this rhetorical effect occurs toward the end of the Abbot Hugo chapter in Book 2. Jocelin's chronicle opens with an account of the troubled leadership of Abbot Hugo, and we have learned, up to this point, that the ineffectual Hugo has allowed the coffers of the Abbey to fall into a seemingly endless spiral of debt. Carlyle then warns his audience:

> But let any reader fancy himself one of the Brethren in St. Edmundsbury Monastery under such circumstances! How can a Lord Abbot, all stuck over with horseleeches of this nature,

> front the world? He is fast losing his life-blood, and the Convent will be as one of Pharaoh's lean kine. Old monks of experience draw their hoods deeper down; careful what they say: the monk's first duty is obedience. Our Lord the King, hearing of such work, sends down his Almoner to make investigations: but what boots it? Abbot Hugo assembles us in Chapter; asks, "If there is any complaint?" Not a soul of us dare answer, "Yes, thousands!" (66)

The opening sentence of this passage makes explicit the difference (in time, in place, in substance) between the contemporary reader of Jocelin's text and the actual characters (the monks) of that text itself, a difference that can be bridged only by imagination. Nevertheless, the explicitness of this difference occurs in the context of a warning against that very act of imagination; a warning that underscores the degree of financial peril that plagues the monastery under Abbot Hugo, but also presents itself as *a challenge* to the reader, a dare to make that leap, as it were, from the present into the past. But before we decide whether or not to follow, Carlyle's text rhetorically enacts the very movement that it first warned us against, the movement of the reader *into* the text. The imagery draws us in at first, as surely as the veteran monks draw their hoods deeper, until the phrase "Our Lord the King" both marks and obscures the shift into the twelfth century. Because no punctuation or contextual cues tell us that the moment we read the possessive plural pronoun "our" we are now hearing the voice of Jocelin rather than Carlyle, this indeterminacy forces us to include ourselves, as readers of *Past and Present*, as possible referents for the pronoun. Although the rest of the sentence provides the context by which we can establish the time period as the twelfth century, rhetorically we have now been written into the text, and it is here we find ourselves standing "in Chapter" (inside the text and in the midst of the Brethren) before Abbot Hugo, who issues "us" the second rhetorical challenge of this passage: do we dare voice any complaints? And like good monk-readers, whose first task is obedience to the text, we remain silent, despite our objections.

But were we to dare raise a complaint, we might remark that it is Carlyle who has broken the conventional historiographer's vow of obedience to "real History," to the letter of the original text. A quick comparison of Carlyle's rendering of Hugo's defensive challenge to his monks with a "true" translation of Jocelin's chronicle reveals that Carlyle has indeed wholly rewritten this passage, condensing it to a few lines. The text has been trans-formed, moved from the dead letter past and given a new body for "direct inspection." And it is this movement of the text, its transformation through re-presentation, that Carlyle's second metaphor, the *camera lucida*, embodies in a manner that first seems akin to the visual component of the speculum, but that also allows Carlyle to foreground *graphically* the production of representation itself, in the form of writing or tracing.

"Will not the reader peep with us," writes Carlyle, "into this singular *camera lucida* . . . ?" (49). While we have seen how the speculum functions primarily as a specular metaphor, even when read as a body-probe, the camera lucida links the visual to writing itself, to the production of a corpus. A camera lucida is literally a light chamber, a device that generates a "virtual image" of an object, projecting that image onto a flat surface so that it may be traced. The resultant graphic image is itself thus the trace of a displaced image, one that at once simulates and mediates a direct correspondence with its originary object. As an instrument of graphic (re)production and (re)presentation, then, the camera lucida functions according to a logic of virtual images and displaced signs—the origin remains inaccessible. As a metaphor for Jocelin's chronicle, the camera lucida thus repeats the process of division and suture that underpins the historiographic logic of *Past and Present*. Like Jocelin's "magical speculum," the camera lucida seems to offer us the means to apprehend directly what is utterly dead and other (the past) and simultaneously denies us those means, substituting instead the possibility of writing a new corpus, a translation based on the logic of displacement and virtuality.

If Carlyle's project can thus be characterized as a "translation" or movement of this twelfth-century body/text, that metaphor has its literal basis in the section of Jocelin's chronicle titled "Concerning the Translation of the Body of St. Edmund," a portion of which appears in the "St. Edmund" chapter of *Past and Present*.[28] While the cadaver-like text of Jocelin's chronicle appears to lie at the "center" of *Past and Pre-*

sent (though its very presence remains "translated" and thus displaced), at the center of the *Chronica Jocelini de Brakelonda*, in turn, lies the translated body of the martyred St. Edmund. Himself the object of bodily violence at the hands of the "Ultra-Chartist" Danes (59), Edmund was a beneficent landlord, the very embodiment of justice and humility. The St. Edmundsbury monastery is built quite literally around the remains of his body. The sacred corpse here generates its own sacred embodiment; as Carlyle tells us: "In one word, St. Edmund's Body has raised a Monastery round it" (61). Around the monastery, of course, grew the town of St. Edmundsbury, itself "properly the Funeral Monument of Saint or Landlord Edmund" (62). Just as the historiographer must posit a past to establish the present place of writing, so too does the topography of the town repeatedly divide itself from the corpse of the saint (all the more other for its sacredness), only to suture that division by circumscribing itself geographically, and centering itself spiritually and historically, upon a dead body. A labor of death and a labor against death.

The translation of Edmund's body, its movement to a place of higher prominence within the abbey, necessitates the exhumation of the corpse, and its unwrapping. The procedure is conducted by Abbot Samson, the living saintly subject of Jocelin's hagiography, and the one who comes face to face, as it were, with the sacred body. Two events foreshadow the need for a "translation" of St. Edmund's body. First, a fire engulfs the shrine of St. Edmund, damaging part of its exterior but leaving the interior intact. Jocelin tells us that St. Edmund himself willed the fire "to terrify our monastery, and to teach us that his body should be more reverently and carefully guarded."[29] Shortly thereafter, a naked and distraught St. Edmund appears to "a certain great person" in a dream (172). Abbot Samson then addresses his interpretation of the dream to the monks: "St. Edmund proclaims himself naked, because ye defraud the naked Poor of your old clothes, and with reluctance what ye are bound to give them of meat and drink. . . . Well might our Holy Martyr seem to lie cast out from his Shrine, and say with groans that he was stript of his garments, and wasted with hunger and thirst!" (*PP*, 121). This image of St. Edmund, denuded and displaced, mirrors the rupture Carlyle documents earlier in *Past and Present* between "eternal inner Facts" and "temporal outer Appearances" (14). Although this rupture is represented by the displacement of St. Edmund, the realignment itself must begin with the displacement or recentering of the *inner*, rather than with a modification of the outer. In Jocelin's chronicle, this realignment literally takes the form of the movement of St. Edmund's shrine, and thus the "translation" of the corpse of the martyr within, to the high altar where it would be "placed more securely and splendidly in a prominent position" (170). The panels of the shrine are moved first, followed by the coffin. The actual translation, though, entails the opening of the coffin itself, the unwrapping and "inspection" of the body, then the rewrapping of the body, re-covering of the coffin, and finally the sealing of the shrine.

Significantly, the process of uncovering the corpse of St. Edmund does not reach the naked flesh of the body. Upon removing several layers of silk and cloth, "they now found the Sacred Body all wrapt in linen; and so at length the lineaments of the same appeared" (*PP*, 124). The meeting between Abbot Samson and St. Edmund is not so much face-to-face, then, as it is face-to-trace. All that unwrapping and uncovering has led not to the originary center, but to the *lineaments* of that center, to its traceable outline. Because the corpse, as the embodiment of the past and of death, is so wholly (and in this case, holy) other, any complete return to that other would transgress the very division that generates meaning and history. The untouchableness of the corpse is a sign of its heterogeneity, of the otherness and utter irretrievability of the past. Nevertheless, just as the historiographer marks that otherness by tracing (through the writing of history) the absent place of the past, so too may the sacred body of St. Edmund be traced—and trace it Abbot Samson does, touching first the eyes, then the nose, breast, arms, fingers, and feet. The privileged proximity of Abbot Samson to St. Edmund's body—their fingers entwined (divided only by the cerements), touching, but not flesh-to-flesh, looking, but not face-to-face—in the final instance, this moment of privileged proximity, both tactile and visual, captures precisely the historiographical operation Carlyle himself is engaged in. The near transgression of the law that separates the living from the dead, the profane from the sacred ("he durst not proceed further, or look at the sacred flesh naked" [124]), in this sense this near transgression *authorizes* Carlyle's project as surely as it underwrites and strengthens, within the *Chronicle*'s narrative, the authority of Abbot Samson.

This authority, based as it is on the privileged proximity of one (living) man to another (dead) one, is clearly also a masculine authority. In *Past and Present,* Abbot Samson functions as the embodiment of the Carlylean masculine Hero, successfully completing the "Herculean Labours" necessary to reform a corrupt and inefficient monastery.[30] Yet it is not the completion of these labors but the translation of the body of St. Edmund that marks the "culminating point of his existence" (127), according to Carlyle, because this is the moment Abbot Samson comes into contact (specifically, a *mediated* contact), with the otherwise inaccessible and unknowable truth embodied in the corpse of the martyred St. Edmund. As Carlyle explains,

> on the whole, who knows how to reverence the Body of Man? It is the most reverend phenomenon under this Sun. For the Highest God dwells visible in that mystic unfathomable Visibility, which calls itself "I" on the Earth. "Bending before men," says Novalis, "is a reverence done to this Revelation in the Flesh. We touch Heaven when we lay our hand on a Human Body." And the Body of one Dead;—a temple where the Hero-soul once was and now is not: Oh all mystery, all pity, all mute *awe* and wonder; *Super*naturalism brought home to the very dullest; Eternity laid open, and the nether Darkness and the upper Light-Kingdoms;—do conjoin there, or exist nowhere! (126)

Here, Carlyle underscores the paradoxical significance of the encounter between the living and the dead. The male corpse ("where the Hero-soul once was") figures as the visible embodiment of truth and meaning, yet as a dead body it retains its otherness, its mystery, its unknowability. The corpse conceals meaning as if veiled; its visibility is "unfathomable," impossible to penetrate, even with a "magical speculum." But this masculine mystery *need not* be penetrated, only posited and revered, in order to legitimize the transfer and exercise of power in its name. Thus Abbot Samson does not need literally to view or touch St. Edmund's body; indeed, he cannot—he *must not*—because to do so would violate the decorum of reverence that ritually ensures the corpse's mysterious significance, and thus jeopardize the corpse's status as a transcendental guarantor of history, meaning, and truth.[31]

Though Carlyle's retelling of the exhumation of St. Edmund has such a clear relationship to his own approach to Jocelin's text (inasmuch as the *Chronicle* has already been metaphorically linked to a corpse), this scene rather mysteriously has been neglected by recent commentators interested in problems of historiography and intertextuality in *Past and Present*. Among those scholars who do "touch" on the exhumation scene, nearly all *misread* the moment that Abbot Samson traces the body of St. Edmund as a moment of unmediated physical and visual contact.[32] We can combine two of the more recent instances of this misreading by citing Stephen Bann's essay, "The Sense of the Past: Image, Text, and Object in the Formation of Historical Consciousness in Nineteenth-Century Britain," which appears in the anthology *The New Historicism* edited by H. Aram Veeser.[33] In his essay, Bann acknowledges John D. Rosenberg's *Carlyle and the Burden of History* as a significant contribution to a new wave of critical texts on nineteenth-century historiography that have followed in the wake of Hayden White's *Metahistory* (103). And what Bann finds most significant about Rosenberg's approach to Carlyle is his interpretation of St. Edmund's exhumation:

> Rosenberg's discussion of "The Ancient Monk" details the stages by which Carlyle converts a potent visual metaphor into an even more potent tactile metaphor as he begins to describe the exhumation of the embalmed corpse of King Edmund by the medieval Abbot Samson. First he promises us, in overtly biblical language, that we shall look "face to face" upon an ancient century. Then he follows the process by which Samson "strips away layer upon layer of outer cerements" until he comes to the body itself, finally touching the eyes, the nose, the breast, the arms, and the toes. As Rosenberg puts it, "the reader senses the presence of the double miracle, the one palpable to Abbot Sam-

> son's touch, the other performed by Carlyle, through the medium of Jocelin, of bringing 'that deep-buried Time' back to effulgent life. A 'laying on of hands' takes place on the page, Samson touching the long-buried Edmund, Carlyle touching us through the freshly unearthed words of Jocelin." (105)

Bann then adds that he "certainly agree[s] that Carlyle's account works in the way that Rosenberg describes." This passage from Bann's essay merits quoting at length, for it foregrounds the desire of cultural critics like Bann and Rosenberg to come to "the body itself," a desire that seems based on the faith that somehow, when properly executed, the "miraculous" power of language will enable a bodying forth or *presentation* of that which seemed heretofore utterly remote, untouchable, and unrecoverable.[34] And not only does the above passage foreground this almost fundamentalist faith in the power of the word, it also reveals the interpretative service into which this magical "laying on of hands" is pressed—namely, the resurrection or revival of the dead past, the bringing of "that deep-buried Time," in Rosenberg's words, "back to effulgent life."[35] This "thick description" of Carlyle as an amalgam of both faith healer and Frankenstein, touching (and perhaps converting?) us through the reanimation of the past, gives the lie to Carlyle's status as a medieval revivalist, and to *Past and Present* as "the most remarkable fruit" of that genre. For it is not the past that Carlyle seeks to revive, but the *present:*

> It is this Editor's clear opinion, accordingly, that we must learn to do our Hero-worship better; that to do it better and better, means the awakening of the Nation's soul from its asphyxia, and the return of blessed life to us,—Heaven's blessed life, not Mammon's galvanic accursed one. To resuscitate the Asphyxied, apparently now moribund, and in the last agony if not resuscitated: such and no other seems the consummation. (*PP,* 39)

The translation of the social and textual body is thus also, for Carlyle, a resuscitation (literally, a stirring or movement) of the present place of that body, and *not* a Frankensteinian "galvanic accursed" resuscitation of the "unearthed." Recent commentators have unwittingly mystified this exhumation scene by characterizing it as a moment of *unmediated* contact, a moment that illustrates, metaphorically, the resuscitation of the past that a romanticized historiography would posit as its object. Far from bringing back the dead, Carlyle offers us instead the past as utterly remote and other, examinable in parts, through the speculum of Jocelin's text, and partly representable, through the displaced graphics of the camera lucida metaphor. Carlyle's writing of history participates self-consciously in this paradoxical mode, but the death against which Carlyle labors is the imminent death of the present, not the loss of an idealized past.[36] In response to this situation, Carlyle's "translation" of Jocelin's corpus functions as the theoretical ground for the later sections of *Past and Present*, where a further "translation"—the symbolic movement or reinscription of Labor into the center of all social and productive relations—will also serve as an anchor or fulcrum around which (and in relation to which) social meaning will be authorized.

4

Resisting the Abyss

The Reinscription of Labor in Carlyle's *Past and Present*

THOMAS CARLYLE'S *PAST AND PRESENT* IS GENerally regarded as a topical text, a response to the Condition-of-England question. Less well known, though, is the extent to which Carlyle characterizes this condition as utterly unfamiliar and historically unprecedented: as "one of the most ominous, and withal one of the strangest, ever seen in this world" (7). Again and again in the opening pages of *Past and Present*, Carlyle turns to the metaphor of "enchantment" to describe this strange world and to denote the following contradiction: that England is among the most productive and wealthiest of nations, but at the same time "England is dying of inanition" (7), of a "hollowness" resulting from a lack of food, work, morals, and spirit. Objects produced are seemingly enchanted (untouchable), and idle workers sit in "workhouses" as if enchanted (immobile). Wealth itself here takes on the character of a simulacrum; it seems to belong to no one, to signify nothing. "It is," says Carlyle, "an enchanted wealth" (10).

Carlyle's use of the word "enchantment" is interesting for its double implication: that the people of England are the passive victims of some power exercised through language (by incantation, for example) and/or that the people of England are seduced by a particular system of representation, and are thus, in a certain sense, complicit with the current condition of the country. Although *Past and Present* testifies to Carlyle's acute awareness of class difference (the opening chapter includes a brief firsthand account of the St. Ives Workhouse, and secondhand reports of the streets of Glasgow and the cellars of Stockport), the "enchanted" condition of England elides and transcends this difference. As we have seen, Carlyle describes this enchanted condition as affecting all members of English society as if it were laid on them like a curse, or transmitted among them like a virus:

> Workers, Master Workers, Unworkers, all men, come to a pause; stand fixed, and cannot farther. Fatal paralysis spreading inwards, from the extremities, in St. Ives workhouses, in Stockport cellars, through all limbs, as if toward the heart itself. Have we actually got enchanted, then; accursed by some god? (11–12)

Carlyle maps the course of this paralytic disease onto two terrains: the physiology of the human body and the geography of England. The metaphorical description of the disease and its movement here reiterates the spatial aspect of the enchantment metaphor; its power originates from without, enters the most extreme parts of the body (the limbs) and of the country (cellars near Manchester, workhouses in East Anglia), and "spreads inward," following the blood, perhaps, to the "heart" itself, to London.[1] Though enchantment also clearly transgresses the boundaries between the classes, Carlyle does not map its trajectory from one class to another; instead, we are offered the effect of that trajectory, the unifying "fixity" of its totality. The condition of enchantment, therefore, is not only pervasive, but also beyond the control of any one class or individual. While "laissez faire" may name the ideology that started this whole business, that ideology is no longer capable of containing the virus of enchantment as it proceeds to ossify even its proponents.

Carlyle's analysis of this social crisis here differs markedly from the position Karl Marx and Friedrich Engels were developing at approximately the same time.[2] Their version of "enchantment" concerns the mystification of the masses through a historically determined nexus of bourgeois ideology and economic oppression. The Marxist position, of course, readily identifies the agents of that oppression and ideology as belonging to a particular class, with interests that are coterminous with a specific political formation: the State. Collective revolutionary action, on the part of a historically conscious proletariat, is thus provided with a clear target for the expenditure of its energy. In this way, theory and analysis become closely linked to "concrete" praxis, in what Marx and Engels hoped would be a dialectical rather than dogmatic relation.[3]

In his review-essay of *Past and Present*, written while he was living in Manchester in 1844, Engels parts company with Carlyle precisely over the notion of praxis:

> As I have said, we too are concerned with combating the lack of principle, the inner emptiness, the spiritual deadness, the untruthfulness of the age; we are waging a war to the death against all these things, just as Carlyle is, and there is a much greater probability that we shall succeed than that he will, because we know what we want.[4]

Engels's assertion here marks the difference between the *telos* of his *ideologikritik* and Carlyle's position, which might be said to go *beyond* the critique of ideology, to the very edge of a precipice Carlyle likens to an abyss (142). The untruthfulness of the age, for Carlyle, does not mask an immanent historical truth; instead, it masks the absence of any truth. In *Past and Present*, therefore, Carlyle seeks to address (and redress) this situation, calling for a reanchoring of social discourse (and the social body) through the construction of a central, transcendental signifier: namely, *Labor*. As we shall see, by representing labor as "sacred," Carlyle underwrites its transcendent status, a status mirrored in a particular code of labor relations—the Chivalry of Work—that Carlyle offers as an ideological justification for a recentering of the workplace around the all-penetrating gaze of the Captains of Industry. In so doing, Carlyle would thus bring the structural relations of commodity production in line with his vision of the centralized structure of symbolic production, the production of meaning. The relation he proposes in each case is hierarchical, centralized, and orderly, and functions as a last-hope symbolic effort to intervene in what he perceives as society's imminent descent into meaninglessness.

In his initial attempt to describe this "crisis of representation" facing England in the 1840s, Carlyle begins by returning to a dichotomy familiar to readers of "Signs of the Times": a dichotomy between "eternal inner Facts" and "transient outer Appearances," between "the right Inner True" and "the outer Sham-true" (14). Though this second chapter of his *Proem* is titled "The Sphinx," Carlyle returns to the Midas analogy of the first chapter to narrate the "hidden" moment of the country's disavowal of the truth:

> The secret of gold Midas, which he with his long ears never could discover, was, That he had offended the Supreme Powers; —that he had parted company with the eternal inner Facts of this Universe, and followed the transient outer Appearances thereof; and so was arrived *here*. Properly it is the secret of all unhappy men and unhappy nations. . . . They have become enchanted; stagger spell-bound, reeling on the brink of huge peril, because they were not wise enough. (14)

The secret of Midas, and of the condition of England's "enchantment," it would seem, lies in this transgression of divine law, in the pursuit of appearances. But where does this transgression occur in the tale of "gold Midas"? Midas, after all, was kind to the satyr Silenus, and Dionysus in turn offered to reward Midas, not punish him, with whatever Midas desired.[5] Midas chose the ability to turn whatever he touched into solid gold, which is to say, to confer value on any object outside himself, and simultaneously to possess that newly created wealth. Midas quickly discovers, of course, that the conversion into gold of any object he touches, including his food, effectively stymies his ability to *consume* that wealth, as surely as it immobilizes the world around him. No longer able to sustain himself, in a world full of wealth (and potential wealth), Midas begins to die of inanition.

Midas's transgression, and England's as well, therefore, proves to be nothing other than pursuit of the sham-true, of appearance, itself. "Enchantment" may thus denote both the punishment for the offense, and the very nature of the transgression. Like Midas, whose wish contains its own built-in punishment for the base material motivations of his desire, the people of England, "because they were not wise enough," have in a sense brought this condition upon themselves—thus the passive construction of the phrase "They have become enchanted." Though we have already remarked that Carlyle's deployment of the term "enchantment" differs from the classical Marxist conception of ideology, particularly in its expression of a "fixity" that crosses traditional class boundaries, at first reading the bipolarity of the terms "truth" and "sham-truth" seems analogous to a similar assumption that underlies much of the post-Marxist theorizing of ideology. In a famous elaboration of the forms and functions of capitalist ideology, for example, Louis Althusser offers the following thesis: that "ideology represents the imaginary relationship of individuals to their real conditions of existence," and that "while admitting that they [ideologies] do not correspond to reality, i.e., that they constitute an illusion, we admit that they do make allusion to reality, and that they need only be 'interpreted' to discover the reality of the world behind their imaginary representation of that world."[6] While Althusser's elaboration of the subtle machinations of ideology is indeed a sophisticated one, relying heavily on Gramsci's insistence on the various ways ideology operates at the macro- and micro-political levels, its theorization is still essentially based on a bipolar assumption: that there exists a reality ("the real conditions of existence") that those who control the means of representation willfully *misrepresent*, in order to entrench more fully the existing order of society. Ideology, in this sense, is equivalent to a "false representation of the real,"[7] while the real itself, according to Althusser, may be recovered hermeneutically, through the "proper" interpretation of the signs that constitute a particular ideology.

The Carlylean enchanted condition, at first glance, appears homologous to the Althusserian "imaginary relation," especially in its double implication of being under the spell of a greater power and of offering a Gramscian consent, if you will, to be placed in such a state. However, Carlyle's vision of the progress of industrial capitalism and its effect on both the "real conditions" of the working class and the manner in which those conditions are represented goes beyond the thesis that a gulf exists between the lived materiality of everyday life and the representation of that life, toward the possibility that laissez-faire policies are leading the country beyond ideology itself, to the hyperreality of a logic-without-grounds, an abyss of simulation. Writing in *Chartism*, just four years before the publication of *Past and Present*, Carlyle described the situation this way:

> [I]n such times it grows to be the universal belief, sole accredited knowingness, and the contrary of it accounted puerile enthusiasm, this sorrowfulest *dis*belief that there is properly speaking any truth in the world; that the world was, has been or ever can be guided, except by simulation, dissimulation, and the sufficiently dextrous practice of pretence. The faith of men is dead: in what has guineas in its pocket, beefeaters riding behind it, and cannons trundling before it, they can believe; in what has none of these things they cannot believe. Sense for the true and false is lost; there is properly no longer any true or false.[8]

While Marx and Engels bear witness to this "upside down" world of bourgeois ideology in the 1840s, Carlyle testifies to more than an inversion—to a world of representation that has broken away from any allusive reference to truth, indeed, to the very erosion of reference itself. In a society where "there is properly no longer any true or false," whose members "work no longer on Nature and Reality" but "on Phantasm, Simulation, [and] Nonentity,"[9] the condition-of-England question is no longer one of a "false representation of the real," or of the gulf between the "Two Nations" (as Disraeli asserts in his novel *Sybil*), but "a question of substituting the signs of the real for the real itself."[10]

In her influential study *The Industrial Reformation of English Fiction*, Catherine Gallagher reaches a similar conclusion about the ultimate end of what she refers to as Carlyle's analysis of "the ironic degradation of the symbol"—namely that, for Carlyle, these "symbols may devolve into meaninglessness" (195, 198). She describes this process of devolution as taking place in three stages: from the divinely meaningful sign (akin to Coleridge's notion of the "tautegorical"); through the corrupted, ironic sign; and finally to the empty, meaningless sign. While Gallagher asserts that for Carlyle "the whole realm of the political is stuck in the ironic stage of devolution," that claim is somewhat mitigated by her citation of Teufelsdröckh's anecdote in *Sartor Resartus* concerning the "Champion of England" as evidence that "the state has become an emblem of the evaporation of meaning from society itself" (198). Indeed, as is clear from the reappearance of the Champion of England in Book 3 of *Past and Present,* the only thing ironic about this "Champion" is his obliviousness to the shift from the ironic to the meaningless. As Carlyle asks: "Does not this Champion too know the world; that it is a huge Imposture, and bottomless Inanity, thatched over with bright cloth and other ingenious tissues?" (143).

While Gallagher would confine Carlyle's analysis of the "devolution" of the symbol to "the realm of the political," it is precisely here in Book 3 of *Past and Present* that Carlyle extends his investigation of this degradation to the realm of civil society. In the first chapter of Book 3, ironically titled "Phenomena," Carlyle offers his readers two memorable and compelling examples of this erosion of reference: the spectacle of an "amphibious Pope" and a "seven-foot Hat." The "amphibious" Pope refers to a contraption designed to alleviate the physical discomfort Pope Gregory XVI experienced during extended periods of continuous kneeling. Essentially, this structure, made of wood with an iron frame, *simulates* the form of a kneeling pope, and "to this stuffed rump he, sitting at his ease on a lower level, joins, by the aid of cloaks and drapery, his living head and outspread hands: the rump with its cloaks kneels, the Pope looks, and holds his hands spread; and so the two in concert bless the Roman population on *Corpus-Christi* Day, as well as they can" (140–41). As John Rosenberg has noted, the irony of the appearance of this amphibious Pope on *Corpus-Christi* Day, a feast-day that celebrates the Eucharist, marks "a transubstantiation not into the Sacred Body but into a stuffed rump"—an irony, we may assume, that did not escape Carlyle.[11] Still, Carlyle deduces more than irony from this "phantasmic" Pontiff; he deduces, in fact, an entire system of religious spectacle he terms the "Scenic Theory of Worship" (142), which asserts that "all worship of God is a scenic phantasmagory of wax-candles, organ-blasts, Gregorian Chants, mass-brayings, purple monsignori, wool-and-iron rumps, artistically spread out,—to save the ignorant from worse" (141).

Carlyle's objection here to Catholic iconography (that the worship of God has degenerated into a worshipping of appearances, of *scenes*), reflects his more generalized fear that the foundation of *all* meaning is being eroded, (d)evolving into a simulated system of signification in which "there is properly no longer any true or false." At the root of this shift, as Baudrillard notes, is the disappearance of God:

> All of Western faith and good faith was engaged in this wager on representation: that a sign could *exchange* for meaning and that something could guarantee this exchange—God, of course. But what if God himself can be simulated, that is to say, reduced to the signs which attest his existence? Then the whole system becomes weightless, it is no longer anything but a gigantic simulacrum.[12]

It is precisely this disappearance of God into the realm of simulation that Carlyle designates as "the centre of the Social Gangrene" (139): "You touch the focal centre of all our disease, of our frightful nosology of diseases, when you lay your hand on this. There is no religion; there is no God; man has lost his soul, and vainly seeks antiseptic salt" (140). The issue for Carlyle here, though, is not a theological one. For Carlyle, the concept of God functions as a "guarantor" of meaningful exchange; God is "real" only as a transcendental signifier (a reality that for Carlyle is more than adequate). "God" thus functions as an anchor for the system of representation, an anchor Jean-Joseph Goux has likened to Marx's positioning of money as the "universal equivalent" in relation to all other commodities. The deployment of the universal or general equivalent, writes Goux, "is a (legal) process whereby the established domination of the universal and normative equivalent (money, father, phallus, word) centers or anchors all products of exchange in a single point, such that their multiple, heterogeneous relations swivel around a single, unilateral fulcrum."[13] For Carlyle, the Scenic Theory of Worship does not constitute an affront to this fulcrum, but is rather *an effect* of the absence of such a center or reference. Moreover, the Scenic Theory of Worship does not pretend to be something other than what it really is—a simulacrum, that which conceals (rather transparently, Carlyle would add) that there is no truth. Ask the Pope himself, writes Carlyle, and he will tell you:

> Under this my Gregorian Chant, and beautiful wax-light Phantasmagory, kindly hidden from you is an Abyss, of Black Doubt, Scepticism, nay Sansculottic Jacobinism; an Orcus that has no bottom. . . . The Bottomless of Scepticism, Atheism, Jacobinism, behold, it is thatched over, hidden from your despair, by stage-properties judiciously arranged. (142)

A "thatched-over" abyss is more than just an inadequate job of simulation; it is a perilous trap sprung by the very inability of the "thatch" to serve as a (logical) ground to (make a) stand on.

Lest his readers think the pursuit of such appearances occurs only in the streets of Rome, Carlyle turns swiftly to the streets of London, where he finds not a parade of amphibious kneeling Popes, but a "great Hat seven-feet high" being wheeled around the city with somewhat less solemnity, but just as much pomp, as the Pope on Corpus-Christi day. This "hat," of course, is really nothing more than a clever advertisement for a hatter, but for Carlyle its appearance signifies more than "the vanity of mid-Victorian capitalism";[14] in fact, it marks an important shift in the direction industry seems to be taking, inasmuch as this hatter "has not attempted to *make* better hats . . . but his whole industry is turned to *persuade* us that he has made such!" (144). Though akin to Rome's Scenic Theory of Worship, this enormous hat points to a development perhaps even more disastrous, something we might call, by analogy, the Scenic Theory of Labor.

Just as the religious spectacle in Rome has shorn itself of the need for the "reality" or "fact" of God, so too has the advent of spectacular advertising in London ruptured the relationship between the signifier of a commodity and the very substance or "fact" of that commodity itself. With a critical flourish that presages some postmodern analyses of the commercial image in the age of advanced capitalism, Carlyle detects a vital shift in human productive activity, from the constructive and useful practice of "making" to the rhetorical and representational practice of "persuading." In other words, Carlyle here marks the shift from the production of material goods to the circulation of signs—from an industry based on production to one based on consumption and reproduction. In such a society, writes Carlyle, "the symbol shall be held sacred, defended everywhere with tipstaves, ropes and gibbets; the thing signified shall be composedly cast to the dogs" (194). And while the Scenic Theory of Worship rather ineffectively "thatches-over" the bottomless pit of the absence of meaning, the Scenic Theory of Labor is pushing England to the very brink of that precipice, as its people "advance incessantly towards the land's end . . . and the next step now is lifted *not* over land, but into air, over ocean-deeps and roaring abysses" (146). The people of England are, writes Carlyle, "literally enough 'consuming the way'" (146). And it is the mammoth seven-foot hat itself, the quintessentially absurd figure of the circulating sign (as it is literally wheeled around London), that sounds, in this context, "too surely like Doom's-blast!" (141).[15]

With the erosion of God and production as "universal equivalents" (guarantors of meaningful exchange), Carlyle thus sees industrial capitalism accelerating toward the realms of consumption, reproduction, and simulation, toward an abyss in which "there is properly no longer any true or false." Nevertheless, the "weightlessness" of such a system, as Baudrillard would put it, is a condition those in control of the means of (re)production wish to keep *unrepresentable*. As the discourse that accompanies industrial capitalism, for example, laissez faire establishes a logical, rational ground for capitalism's implementation and growth, a ground ironically and literally expressed as a "letting alone," allowing capital and its interests to proceed by laws "inherent" in a free market economy. And it is precisely such a discourse that seeks to normalize economic fluctuations and the resulting (and thus "inevitable") hardship for the working class. In this way, laissez faire functions as more than mere economic policy; as Carlyle well knew, its ideology of freedom of choice and competition attempts its own "thatching-over," in this case of the true nature of social relations:

> We call it a Society; and go about professing openly the totalest separation, isolation. Our life is not a mutual helpfulness; but rather, cloaked under due laws-of-war, named 'fair competition' and so forth, it is a mutual hostility. We have profoundly forgotten everywhere that *Cash-payment* is not the sole relation of human beings; we think, nothing doubting, that *it* absolves and liquidates all engagements of man. (148)

While Carlyle here contextualizes laissez-faire ideology in the familiar bipolar relation between the real conditions of existence and the false representation of those relations, he implies that that relation is itself undergoing a kind of erosion, a "forgetting" that marks a society's entry into the spectacular.

The agent of this movement, more than any other for Carlyle, is "cash-payment," the pursuit of money not merely as a commodity to be accumulated, but as a sign to be circulated. The fear of the "modern English soul," as Carlyle puts it, is the "Hell" of "'Not succeeding'; of not making money, fame or some other figure in the world" (148). As the "sole nexus" of social relations, money has in this sense supplanted "God" or "production" as a universal equivalent, as that unilateral axis in reference to which meaning and value are established. Thus the world subscribes to a "Gospel of Mammonism," rather than to a Gospel of God or Work. But money, in Carlyle's view, like its deity-form Mammon, can only function as a false god, a false idol or symbol, and thus as a false (or better, empty) sign that merely simulates (rather than guarantees) social cohesion.

To re-anchor this "weightless" system of simulation, and to combat the laissez-faire ideology that masks its groundlessness, Carlyle seeks the reinscription of a new symbol to function as Goux's "fulcrum" for meaning. It is this fulcrum or anchor that Carlyle connects metaphorically to the soul of the human/social body. As we have seen earlier, he designates the disappearance of God and the loss of the soul as the "focal centre of all our disease" (140). Now that the progress of this Social Gangrene has "spread inwards . . . toward the heart itself" (11–12), eroding the center (ironically) in the name of "progress" and "freedom," it has become imperative that this center be reestablished, reinscribed, and reanchored:

> For all human things do require to have an Ideal in them; to have some Soul in them, as we said, were it only to keep the Body unputrefied. And wonderful it is to see how the Ideal or Soul, place it in what ugliest Body you may, will irradiate said Body with its own nobleness; will gradually, incessantly, mould, modify, new-form or reform said ugliest Body, and make it at last beautiful, and to a certain degree divine!—O, if you could dethrone that Brute-god Mammon, and put a Spirit-god in his place! One way or other, he must and will have to be dethroned. (191)

Here Carlyle expresses metaphorically what was enacted literally in the translation and re-enshrinement of the corpse of St. Edmund in Book 2. Just as the St. Edmundsbury abbey must realign itself, physically and morally, by a reedification that proceeds from the inside out, so too must the social body recenter itself around a new "Spirit-god," an axis that would guarantee the "proper" and "truthful" exchange of meaning and value.[16] *Past and Present* thus seeks to intervene in the (d)evolution of representation; the terrain of battle, for Carlyle, is at the level of the sign. While Carlyle describes this crisis of representation by asserting that "there is no God; man has lost his soul," the figure Carlyle offers as the new "focal centre" is not the Christian god, but *labour:*

> Giant LABOUR, truest emblem there is of God the World-Worker, Demiurgus, and Eternal Maker; noble LABOUR, which is yet to be the King of this Earth, and sit on the highest throne,—staggering hitherto like a blind irrational giant, hardly allowed to have his common place on the street-pavements; idle Dilettantism, Dead-Sea Apism, crying out, "LABOUR Down with him, he is dangerous!"
>
> Labour must become a seeing rational giant, with a *soul* in the body of him, and take his place on the throne of things. (170–71)

As the "focal centre" of a new body of representation, labor here takes on the character of a god—not the tripartite Christian god, as we have noted, but a god-like universal equivalent, an axis that stabilizes (indeed generates) meaning. It is precisely as a productive force that this "noble Labour" becomes the "truest emblem" of the divine task of "making" meaning and value. For Carlyle, this symbolic reinscription of labor into the heart of the social body will, in a sense, reestablish the divinity of work as expressed in the monastic motto, "*Laborare est Orare*, Work is Worship" (201).[17]

The process of this symbolic reinscription proceeds on two levels: first, as we have remarked above, Carlyle will emphasize the divine (and therefore transcendent) character of Labour as the stabilizing force of a meaningful system of representation; and second, in terms of social organization, Carlyle will advocate as the foundation of human interaction (and especially the conditions and relations of productive activity) a model of beneficent governance that conforms to a code he will term the "Chivalry of Work" (270). At each level, Carlyle must confront the ideological apparatus that both props up and defends the policies of laissez-faire economics, an apparatus that has crowned Mammon as the fulcrum of meaning and value, and reduced human interaction to the perfected separation of individuals "at liberty" to exchange their labor for wages according to the terms of the "free" market.

It is in direct opposition to the alienated commodification of labor, for example, that Carlyle offers "the perennial nobleness, and even sacredness" (196) inherent in work. Though he adopts the "Laborare est Orare" slogan of the medieval monks, and even asserts that "all true work is Religion" (201), for Carlyle the divine character of labor precedes the formal organization of worship; its source lies in an essentialist thesis concerning human energy and the imperative of its expenditure:

> Older than all preached Gospels was this unpreached, inarticulate, but ineradicable, forever-enduring Gospel: Work, and therein have well-being. Man, Son of Earth and Heaven, lies there not, in the innermost heart of thee, a Spirit of active Method, a Force for Work; and burns like a painfully smouldering

> fire, giving thee no rest till thou unfold it, till thou write it down in beneficent Facts around thee! (201)

By asserting that the divine character of work lies within the "innermost heart" of the human body, Carlyle at once preserves the transcendental significance of labor, and avoids what might otherwise be construed as a paradoxical contention: that the activity of work, because of its sacredness, somehow *exceeds* the human. On the contrary, the sacredness of labor derives from the manner in which the energy of labor is expended, a condition that, for Carlyle, bears directly on the organization of human social relations. Under laissez-faire capitalism, either this energy is directed toward the meager wages necessary to survive (as in the case of the working poor) or toward the accumulation of capital (as with the burgeoning class of industrial factory owners), or it sits idle (among the unworking poor and the game-preserving aristocracy).

For Carlyle, the "true" practice of labor (and hence its "divine" character) is founded on a sacrificial economy of energy, as an expenditure or "giving" of one's life energy as an end-in-itself, rather than as a commodity to be exchanged for wages, or as an investment for a greater return. The wages of labor, writes Carlyle, are not found "in Bank-of-England bills, [or] in Owen's Labour-bank"; there cannot be an "adequate" monetary reward for "noble" labor, because the value of that labor is nothing less than the value of human life itself (204). Instead of a reified labor, brought to market as a commodity to be sold, Carlyle offers an alternative form of exchange, a unilateral "giving": "My brother, the brave man has to give his Life away. Give it, I advise thee;—thou dost not expect to *sell* thy Life in an adequate manner? What price, for example, would content thee?" (204). And later, "Thou wilt never sell thy Life, or any part of thy Life, in a satisfactory manner. Give it, like a royal heart; let the price be Nothing: thou *hast* then, in a certain sense, got All for it!" (204).[18] I use the word *sacrifice* here in its most literal sense, as a "making" or production of something sacred; the sacred product, from Carlyle's perspective, is not the commodity-fetish that reifies the true nature of social relations, but the social relations themselves, here based on an economy of mutual obligation and sacrifice.

Carlyle's notion of the sacred here approaches a similar conception forwarded by Georges Bataille nearly a century later; for Bataille, "the sacred is only a privileged moment of communal unity, a moment of the convulsive communication of what is ordinarily stifled," a communication that is "not directed toward a personal and transcendent being (or beings), but toward an impersonal reality," in other words, toward a social relation that transcends the separateness of individual identity.[19] While Bataille's primary sociological interest lies in the various ways this "communication" was produced or invoked through ritual sacrifice and ceremony, Carlyle's formulation of the sacredness of labor also stresses the centrality of this kind of communication: "For there is a perennial nobleness, and even sacredness, in Work. . . . Work, never so Mammonish, mean, *is* in communication with Nature; the real desire to get Work done will itself lead one more and more to truth" (196).

Although Bataille is especially concerned with separating the "transcendental substance" that Christianity imposed on experience of the sacred (i.e., the positing of God as the object of religion) from the "impersonal reality" of social relations that sacred rituals of so-called primitive societies claimed as their object, Carlyle's "Work in communication with Nature" bears directly on relationships both intrapersonal and interpersonal, even if, at times, he overlays those relationships with monotheistic rhetoric. For example, Carlyle writes: "Labour is Life: from the inmost heart of the Worker rises his god-given Force, the sacred celestial Life-essence breathed into him by Almighty God; from his inmost heart awakens him to all nobleness,—to all knowledge, 'self-knowledge' and much else" (197). It is important to remark here that Carlyle's invocation of God as the source of life does not entail the positioning of God as the object of work. As Walter Houghton has quite correctly remarked, "Carlyle places this life of earnest endeavor in a religious context. But he does not say, work because it is the will of God. He says, work and you will end your misery and forward the progress of civilization."[20]

As the above passage from Carlyle indicates, the "true" object of work is the production of knowledge, a knowledge that is "in communication with Nature" as well as with the self. But Nature also holds the key to human communication, to the social relations that the ideology of laissez faire has eroded into an organization of mutual isolation:

> Supply-and-demand is not the one Law of Nature; Cash-payment is not the sole nexus of man with man,—how far from it! Deep, far deeper than Supply-and-demand, are Laws, Obligations sacred as Man's Life itself: these also, if you will continue to do work, you shall now learn and obey. . . . He that will not learn them, Nature is against him; he shall not be able to do work in Nature's empire,—not in hers. Perpetual mutiny, contention, hatred, isolation, execration shall wait on his footsteps. (187)

These "sacred obligations," which Carlyle characterizes elsewhere as bonds of "mutual helpfulness," form the foundation of what he will call, in his chapter on the "Captains of Industry," a "Chivalry of Work" (270). This appeal to a chivalric order was, of course, a common trope among those "feudal socialists"[21] who offered the social organization of the medieval past (or at least the literary representation thereof) as a corrective to the increasing entrenchment of laissez-faire ideology. In fact, many twentieth-century commentators on Victorian culture characterize this invocation of a chivalric code as a strategic deployment in direct opposition to Benthamite utilitarianism.[22]

This view has become particularly common among commentators on Carlyle, whose opposition to Bentham's social theory is as pervasive as it is legendary.[23] Catherine Gallagher, for example, notes Carlyle's sharp objection to "the Benthamites' stress on the isolated individual," in opposition to which, she says, he "emphasizes and exalts the social nature of man, partly by locating the sources of value and meaning there. In his concept of society, meaning is produced collectively, not by the self-interested exchanges of competitive individuals, but by 'sacred' combinations of men."[24] It is precisely these "sacred" combinations that, for Carlyle, form the basis of a chivalric social order. And while the polar opposition between "sacred combinations of men" and the Benthamite "isolated individual" is offered by critics like Gallagher as practically self-evident, this dichotomy leaves unexamined Carlyle's scheme for instituting these "chivalric" social relations, especially with regard to the organization of labor. What it neglects specifically is the distribution of power relations in the Carlylean model; as we shall see, far from offering a mutually beneficent alternative to Benthamite utilitarianism, this Chivalry of Work in fact *reproduces* the very machinations of internalized surveillance first forwarded by Bentham in his architectural design known as the panopticon.

To better grasp Carlyle's understanding of the forms of chivalry and its function in the medieval past, it is perhaps best to start with his definition of the term *chivalry*. Writing more than a decade before the publication of *Past and Present*, Carlyle defined chivalry as "a translation into Practice of whatever was noblest in the sentiments of mankind," for it was in the twelfth century, he asserts, that "for the first time the grand principles of order, or subjection to rule were universally inculcated, and the maintenance of them made a habit and a social duty."[25] Of particular interest to us here is the implied movement from a process of "inculcation" to one of "maintenance." The two forms of maintenance Carlyle offers, "a habit and a social duty," suggest that this shift from inculcation to maintenance moves in the direction of an internalization of the law—not, in this case, of a rule codified in the legal system, but one codified ideologically, as a "social duty." And by his own definition, this social duty is nothing other than a "subjection to rule," an imperative to obey the law. As Frederick William Roe approvingly remarks in his chapter "The New Chivalry of Labor":

> Freely will he [the worker] subject himself to the guidance, nay, even the authority, of his master, to whom he will be attached by bonds quite other than the bonds of servitude. He will be bound by the strong force of good-will and justice, the only powers that can keep men together. Social progress, in other words, could not be effected, Carlyle held, unless men, leaders and workers alike, could be gradually transformed into a fuller and richer humanity.[26]

This internalized subjection to rule (and its ideologically "humanist" intentions) is also the aim of Bentham's panopticon, and its maintenance, of course, hinges on the possibility of continuous scrutiny from the central tower—the very indeterminacy of when one is *not* under surveillance produces the effect of *perpetual* surveillance. The power relation, as Michel Foucault remarks, is thus internalized: "He who is subjected to a field of visibility, and who knows it, assumes responsibility for the constraints of power; he makes them play spontaneously upon himself; he inscribes in himself the power relation in which he simultaneously plays both roles; he becomes the principle of his own subjection."[27] While Carlyle's definition of chivalry cited above does not itself hinge on "visible and unverifiable" power,[28] this self-incorporation of the gaze *is* central to his translation of chivalry into a model for the organization of labor.

"All men," writes Carlyle, "if they work not as in a Great Taskmaster's eye, will work wrong, work unhappily for themselves and you" (207). For proof of the effectiveness of the "taskmaster's eye," we need only turn to the example of Abbot Samson himself, who upon becoming Abbot of the St. Edmundsbury monastery, was faced with labors of heroic proportions. As Carlyle explains:

> His troubles are manifold: cunning *milites*, unjust bailiffs, lazy sockmen, he an inexperienced Abbot; relaxed lazy monks, not disinclined to mutiny in mass: but continued vigilance, rigorous method, what we call 'the eye of the master,' work wonders. The clear-beaming eyesight of Abbot Samson, steadfast, severe, all-penetrating,—it is like *Fiat lux* in that inorganic waste whirlpool; penetrates gradually to all nooks, and of the chaos makes a kosmos or ordered world! (95)

Carlyle's simile here, that the powerful effect of Abbot Samson's "all-penetrating" eyesight resembles the effect of God's command "Fiat lux," provides us with the foundation of Carlyle's link between labor and the gaze. Just as Abbot Samson "ordered" his monastery by bringing all of its subjects into a field of perpetual visual scrutiny, so too did God "order" the universe with a command that engenders visibility itself. "Fiat lux" functions here as a kind of originary scene, a staging of the first moment energy was expended in the direction of productive labor. In this case, of course, the labor is of a divine nature, its product nothing less than the creation of life itself, the transformation of chaotic waste into organic order. It is this assertion of the divine character of labor, of *all* labor, that authorizes Carlyle's reinscription of labor as a transcendent universal equivalent: "Genuine WORK alone, what thou workest faithfully, that is eternal, as the Almighty Founder and World-Builder himself" (136). God here becomes the originary laborer, and "fiat lux" the originary labor.

As Sharon Aronofsky Weltman has asserted in her essay, "Female and Maelstrom: The Gender Vortex in Carlyle and Ruskin," Carlyle sometimes explicitly genders this confrontation between chaos and order. For example, writes Weltman, "In *Sartor* Carlyle's male God and hero defeat the powers of whirling chaos often characterized as feminine; in this Carlyle joins a long tradition in Western philosophy, going all the way back to the Greeks, in which masculine forms impose order on female formlessness."[29] While Carlyle's "inorganic waste whirlpool" in *Past and Present* is not explicitly marked as feminine, in the passage cited above we do have Abbot Samson deploying "the eye of the master," clearly a male gaze that "penetrates" all the recessed, hidden "nooks" of the thus implicitly passive and feminine chaos.[30] And indeed, this passage is bookended by explicitly feminized representations of particularly dangerous elements of this chaos: the "Jew and Christian creditors" who "pounc[e] on him like obscene harpies," and "the Female Chartism of St. Edmundsbury," which threatens "to explode into the streets" (95).[31]

However, the most recalcitrant forces of disorder are not these that lie external to the monastery, but *within* it—that is, the monks themselves, who are variously described as lazy, unjust, drunken, and self-indulgent, but also rebellious and potentially violent. In this respect, Abbot Samson's "all-penetrating gaze" may be said to function as the instrument through which masculinity (of the Carlylean, heroic variety) is policed and enforced. Samson's immediate task within the monastery is to bring the monks "to order" as they submit to his manly authority. As Herbert Sussman has noted, the monks' "consequent submission to the stronger male, to the father (the etymological root of 'abbot' is, of course, 'father'), indicates their progress toward manliness."[32] Such submission, then, in Carlyle's view, is not tantamount to feminized passivity, but the first step toward an heroic masculinity.[33] "To learn obeying," writes Carlyle, "is the fundamental art of governing," (90) and governing itself "is man's highest work, done *well*" (91). And Samson himself is the very embodiment of manly governance: "There is in him what far transcends all apprenticeships; in the man himself there exists a model of governing, something to govern by! There exists in him a heart-abhorrence of whatever is incoherent, pusillanimous, unveracious,—that is to say, chaotic, *un*governed; of the Devil, not of God. A man of this kind cannot help governing!" (91–92).

As Carlyle makes clear at the outset of his "Captains of Industry" chapter, however, we should not imagine that this ordering of chaos was enabled by simply "shedding light" on the matter, as if the command "fiat lux" came from a point outside the chaos. On the contrary, the chaos must be illuminated and ordered from *within*; as Carlyle writes, "A Human Chaos *in* which there is no light, you vainly attempt to irradiate by light shed on it: order never can arise there" (267). This is precisely why, when translating this metaphor of illumination and scrutiny to the terrain of the labor question, Carlyle designates the "captains of industry" as best suited to accomplish this God-like task of organization, because of their central position *within* the chaos: "The main substance of this immense Problem of Organising Labour, and first of all of Managing the Working Classes, will, it is very clear, have to be solved *by those who stand practically in the middle of it*; by those who themselves work and preside over work" (267, my emphasis). What is needed, according to Carlyle, is "light *in* the Human Chaos, glimmering, shining more and more" (267), and it is the captains of industry who will be the source of that centralized, illuminating gaze.

Carlyle would return to this metaphor of the penetrating gaze seven years later in his critique "Model Prisons" in *Latter-Day Pamphlets* (1850). Though he objects to the comfort and relative idleness of the inmates of the model prison, Carlyle praises

> the Captain of the place, a gentleman of ancient Military or Royal-Navy habits. . . . A man of real worth, challenging at once love and respect: the light of those mild bright eyes seemed to permeate the place as with an all-pervading vigilance, and kindly yet victorious illumination; in the soft definite voice it was as if Nature herself were promulgating her orders, gentlest mildest orders, which however, in the end, there would be no disobeying, which in the end there would be no living without fulfilment of.[34]

Though this model prison[35] does not itself appear to be of panoptic architectural design, clearly its internal organization and governance belong to that "chivalric" order exemplified practically by Abbot Samson and potentially by the captains of industry. In a significant Carlylean critical twist, it is precisely on the grounds that this Captain of the Model Prison is himself the very embodiment of the chivalric *aristio* that Carlyle claims this prison system *fails*. For Carlyle, the beneficent governance of this model prison, where "substantial wholesome comfort reigned everywhere supreme" (*LDP*, 52), is in fact nothing more than a wasteful misapplication of a chivalric code better suited to the law-abiding working class, to the "Seven-and-twenty Millions of neglected mortals who have not yet quite declared for the Devil" (*LDP*, 59). The Captain of the Model Prison is therefore a sort of displaced Captain of Industry, charged with the visionary governance of a marginal class of "scoundrels," none of whom, in Carlyle's view, merit such honorable treatment. It seems Carlyle would thus reserve the operation of "discipline," to borrow Foucault's terminology, solely for the realm of workplace, and retain "punishment," preferably corporeal, for transgressors of the law.

For Carlyle, the model prison offers a concrete example of the government misreading the true nature of these "base-natured beings, on whom in the course of a maleficent subterranean life of London Scoundrelism, the Genius of Darkness . . . had now visibly impressed his seal," and then generating a solution that addresses the "falsest of problems" (*LDP*, 55, 56). In other words, the prison system treats these inmates as if they are capable of being rehabilitated, when in fact, asserts Carlyle, they are not. Thus, the Prison-Governor is forced into what for Carlyle is a gross absurdity: the Captain of the Model Prison must not "command good men to do something, but bad men to do (with superficial disguises) nothing" (*LDP*, 56).

In his fifth lecture on heroes and hero-worship delivered in 1840, Carlyle diagnosed Benthamism itself as suffering from a similar problem of *misreading:* "Benthamism has something complete, manful, in such fearless committal of itself to what it finds true; you may call it Heroic, though a Heroism with its *eyes* put out! . . . [H]e who discerns nothing but Mechanism in the Universe has in the fatalest way missed the secret of the Universe altogether."[36] Carlyle is primarily concerned here with remarking on Bentham's principle of utility and its corresponding pleasure/pain index, rather than the panoptic plan for prison reform, but his deployment of the *eyeless* metaphor captures concisely the central difference between the Benthamite and Carlylean systems for organizing labor, as far as Carlyle is concerned. Carlyle's Chivalry of Labor depends entirely on the centrality of a scrutinizing authority underwritten by an allusive code of feudal ethics, while Bentham's "gross, steamengine Utilitarianism" depends solely on the blind assumption that social organization itself can be reduced to a calculus of pain and pleasure (*OH*, 172).

As *Past and Present* makes clear, it is precisely by (re)centering Labour that Carlyle proposes to organize it; the center exists now, in the form of the "captains of industry" themselves, but that center is at present a "virtuality" rather than an "actuality" (268). And the blueprint for this "translation into Practice" of humanity's noblest sentiments, this movement from the virtual to the actual, is the chivalric code. "No Working World," writes Carlyle,

> can be led on without a noble Chivalry of Work, and laws and fixed rules which follow out of that,—far nobler than any Chivalry of Fighting was. As an anarchic multitude on mere Supply-and-demand, it is becoming inevitable that we dwindle in horrid suicidal convulsion, and self-abrasion, frightful to the imagination, into *Chactaw* Workers. With wigwams and scalps,

> —with palaces and thousand-pound bills; with savagery, depopulating chaotic desolation! Good heavens, will not one French Revolution and Reign of Terror suffice us, but must there be two? (270)

In this passage Carlyle clearly situates his Chivalry of Work as a system in opposition to, even redemptive of, laissez-faire economics, here depicted as the agent of social devolution. "Chactaw Indians" (and elsewhere "Bucaniers") signify both the desire for the accumulation of wealth (through "fighting") and the *primitive*, even savage, nature of that desire. Supply-and-demand, as the basis of economic organization, has produced a "fighting" society—an aggregate of parasitic competitors, preying on their "work-hosts" (270) and "world-hosts" who are themselves, as a result, "on the eve of fiery wreck and madness" (272).

Fighting and laboring are linked metaphorically for Carlyle because they both involve the expenditure of energy in the direction of domination and mastery—over Nature, the Enemy, or even the false beliefs of others: "It is forever indispensable for a man to fight: now with Necessity, with Barrenness, Scarcity, with Puddles, Bogs, tangled Forests, unkempt Cotton;—now also with the hallucinations of his poor fellow Men" (191). The true fighter prevails over his enemy in the same way a successful laborer prevails over the object of his work. Thus, writes Carlyle, a battlefield

> is a kind of Quintessence of Labour; Labour distilled into its utmost concentration; . . . Here too thou shalt be strong, and not in muscle only, if thou wouldst prevail. Here too thou shalt be strong of heart, noble of soul; thou shalt dread no pain or death, thou shalt not love ease or life; in rage, thou shalt remember mercy, justice;—thou shalt be a Knight and not a Chactaw, if thou wouldst prevail! (192)

While Carlyle throughout Books 3 and 4 aligns Chactaw warriors and "Bucaniers" with Mammon-worshiping capitalists (in Carlyle's view, the actions of all three groups are predicated on a logic of accumulation —of scalps, gold, and paper money, respectively), the Chactaw warrior is here opposed to the Chivalric Knight in the terms of an ethical code, inscribed in the "thou shalt" language of the ten commandments. This passage is the closest Carlyle comes in *Past and Present* to specifying the universal code that would comprise a Chivalry of Work, but that code seems as vaguely stated here as elsewhere, appealing to "noble souls" and "strong hearts." Though he insists on opposing this Chivalry of Work to laissez-faire economic organization, Carlyle fails to elaborate upon the codes of honor that would accompany, indeed *underwrite*, the mechanism of the "Taskmaster's eye." Instead he relies fully (and solely) on the allusions that the concept "Chivalry of Work," based on "sacred obligations," suggests: knighthood and feudalism, with their romantic connotations of selflessness, order, mercy, and justice.

But to dismiss completely Carlyle's Chivalry of Work as "either feudal nonsense or too paltry to do more than scratch the surface of the problem" (as E. P. Thompson and countless others have done), *or* to excuse the vagueness of Carlyle's plan by placing the burden for its development and implementation on the capitalists and workers themselves (as Roe attempts), is to neglect Carlyle's own understanding of his medium (writing), to obfuscate the power relations Carlyle's "chivalry of work" seeks to codify, and to reduce the complexity of *Past and Present*'s engagement with the social discourse of crisis circulating around the "Condition-of-England question."[37]

Instead, Carlyle offers what I have been terming a "reinscription" of labor, a recasting of the role of labor as an anchor for England's system of social signification, a system now in crisis, and fast approaching an abyss of meaninglessness. As we have seen, this anchoring is authorized by an appeal to the divine character of labor, to its central position as the vital, productive form of the expenditure of human energy; moreover, Carlyle's translation of this centralized hierarchy of labor onto the terrain of the labor question itself, via the penetrating male gaze of the "Taskmaster's eye," in turn reproduces that centralized hierarchy within the workplace. In this way, Carlyle's ideal relations of commodity production would thus mirror his ideal relations of symbolic production. In calling for a Chivalry of Work, Carlyle at once alludes to the "spirit" according to which the workplace will be organized and to the codification that would underwrite the implementation of that organization. In so doing, Carlyle appropriates the (albeit heterogeneous) discourse of the medieval revivalists as surely as he interferes with it, translating that discourse's rhetoric of loss (of "authentic" labor relations and "authentic" class relations) onto the level of the sign, and attempting a reinscription of the hierarchy of symbols and the stability of their meaning.

This reinscription is thus the "work" of *Past and Present;* its "labor" is one of representation and writing. But its rhetorical strategy allows for the reversibility of that relationship. Labor too, for Carlyle, is a kind of writing. Thus, Carlyle exhorts the productive (and technological and imperial) powers of English society this way: "Nature alone knows thee, acknowledges the bulk and strength of thee: thy Epic, unsung in words, is written in huge characters on the face of this Planet,—sea moles, cotton-trades, railways, fleets and cities, Indian Empires, Americas, New-Hollands; legible throughout the Solar System!" (162).[38] Carlyle's representation of labor in *Past and Present* may thus be characterized as its own reversion, as a labor of representation. And just as the national body "writes" its character upon the surface of the earth, so too is the individual human body compelled to "write it down in beneficent Facts around thee!"—that is, to make legible that "Force for Work" that "lies in the innermost heart" of the human body (201). For Carlyle, it is this reinscription of labor into the heart of the social and individual body that enables the production of meaning and value, and the stabilization of that process will ensure the legibility of that "heroic" production, its inscription as an *epic*.

5

The "Recovery" of the Past

History and (Self-)Representation in Benjamin Disraeli's *Sybil; or, The Two Nations*

The History of the world is but the Biography of great men.
—Thomas Carlyle, "Hero as Divinity" (1840)

Read no history, nothing but biography, for that is life without theory.
—Benjamin Disraeli, *Contarini Fleming: A Psychological Romance* (1832)

IN THE PREVIOUS CHAPTER, WE HAVE SEEN Thomas Carlyle advocate the deployment of a transcendental signifier that would function as a center or fulcrum around which, and in relation to which, social signification would be organized. Faced with a society that he believes is losing its ground, morally and economically, Carlyle calls for "the giant LABOUR" to serve as this anchor of signification. As we have also seen, in *Past and Present* Carlyle offers us the seeming embodiment of this anchor in the person of the "heroic" Abbot Samson, whose all-penetrating gaze brings order to the chaotic, degraded monastery of St. Edmundsbury, and who serves, in turn, as a model for those modern-day Abbots who stand "practically in the middle" of the contemporary chaos of the 1840s: the Captains of Industry.

Carlyle's emphasis on "great men" as the necessary embodiment of authorial (indeed, authoritarian) meaning received its fullest articulation just three years prior to *Past and Present* in his lectures on heroes and hero-worship, delivered over the course of several weeks during May 1840, and published together in a single volume as *On Heroes, Hero-Worship, and the Heroic in History* the following year. In those lectures Carlyle acknowledges that the status and efficacy of a "great man"—his very identity as "great," in fact—depend upon his ability to secure the consent of others, his "worshippers." Hero-worship, writes Carlyle, is nothing less than the "submissive admiration for the truly great" (*OH*, 12), and it is this quality, a fundamental and natural one, according to Carlyle, that serves as the "eternal corner-stone" that will survive the devolution of society: "That man, in some sense or other, worships Heroes; that we all of us reverence and must ever reverence Great Men: this is, to me, the living rock amid all the rushings-down whatsoever;—the one fixed point in modern revolutionary history, otherwise as if bottomless and shoreless" (15).

And yet clearly it is the Hero himself who plays the crucial role here; without his presence, without an object of worship, the times will "go down to confusion and wreck" (13). The Great Man is "the indispensable savior of his epoch," writes Carlyle, an assertion notoriously encapsulated in his oft-cited phrase, "the History of the world is but the Biography of great men" (29). The famous phrase itself lays bare Carlyle's myopic elitism, his unabashed authoritarianism, and his gender exclusivity. With good reason some critics have pointed to the lectures on heroes and hero-worship as a kind of warning sign, a precursor to the fully blown antidemocratic rantings of *Latter-Day Pamphlets* and *Shooting Niagara*.[1]

By juxtaposing as dual epigraphs Carlyle's famous "great men" statement and an obscure line from an obscure early novel by Benjamin Disraeli, it may seem as though my intention is to assert an affinity between them, perhaps even to claim that the young Disraeli, twenty-eight at the time of *Contarini Fleming*, anticipated Carlyle by nearly a decade. As I intend to show, however, these two statements do not have an affinitive relationship so much as an ironic and paradoxical one, given the multiple contexts in which Disraeli's quotation has appeared. For example, the line from *Contarini Fleming*, Disraeli's third novel, also appears as the rather provocative epigraph for William Flavelle Monypenny's *The Life of Benjamin Disraeli*. And because the epigraph (there, as here) does not attribute this line to a particular character, only to the novel itself, the voice would seem to be Disraeli's own. The voice behind the *Contarini Fleming* quotation is not Disraeli's, however, but that of the eponymous protagonist's father, the Baron Fleming. Significantly, his advice "Read no history," when read in the context of the chapter in which it appears, is completely and utterly discredited.[2] As Contarini Fleming tells us, with hindsight:

> I pursued the system which my father had pointed out with exactness, and soon with pleasure. I sacredly observed my hours of reading, and devoted myself to the study of the lives of what my father considered really great men [among them, Cardinal de Retz, Richelieu and Napoleon];[3] that is to say, men of great energies and violent volition, who look upon their fellow-creatures as mere tools, with which they can build up a pedestal for their solitary statue, and who sacrifice every feeling which should sway humanity, and every high work which genius should really achieve, to the short-sighted gratification of an irrational and outrageous selfism.[4]

As a result of following this course of study and the rest of his father's maxims concerning the proper method to enter society, Contarini admits "that at the age of fifteen I had unexpectedly become one of the most affected, conceited, and intolerable atoms that ever peopled the earth" (112).

Given that the epigraph to the Monypenny biography is clearly taken out of context, the quotation thus ironically distorts, even reverses, Disraeli's attitude toward history, a subject he takes very seriously. Far from dismissing history as overburdened by "theory," Disraeli himself advances, through analyses of political history such as the *Vindication of the English Constitution* (1835–36) and through historically minded novels like *Coningsby* (1844), *Sybil* (1845), and *Tancred* (1847), a specific interpretation of the course of English history, insisting that important events and personages have been suppressed and distorted by the dominant "Whig" historical opinion of his day. As we shall see, because Disraeli believes that political ideology largely determines the way in which history is recorded and narrated, he consistently foregrounds the disjunctive interrelation between textual representation and historical truth. This foregrounding serves a twofold purpose: on the one hand, the disjunction reveals the extent to which textual representation can usurp and displace historical truth, appearing to the unwary reader as an almost self-evident representation of historical events; on the other hand, the assertion of such a disjunction opens up the possibility of restoring the relation between textual representation and historical truth, through a process of rewriting that would correct the effects of historical marginalization and dispossession.

By engaging this dual aspect of historical representation within the context of the debates surrounding the condition-of-England question, Disraeli's fiction of the mid-1840s—especially his novel *Sybil*—seeks what I term a historical "recovery," one that Disraeli offers not just as a correction to historical displacement in the written history of England, but also as a solution to the political and social crises facing the England of his time. Moreover, it is precisely these crises, grouped under the general question of "the condition of England," that Disraeli, echoing Cobbett (one of his primary sources in this regard), represents as having their collective roots in the major material and cultural displacements of the English past, particularly the displacement of the Catholic Church and the monastic-centered community.

As "political" novels, then, Disraeli's trilogy (*Coningsby*, *Sybil*, and *Tancred*) engages questions of political and historical representation not only as a commentary on those ongoing debates, but also as a force (no matter how limited) for promoting the Disraelian prescription for social change. In addition to this broad political dimension, however, Disraeli's fiction addresses questions pertinent to matters of representation at the personal level. To draw correspondences between Disraeli's novels, especially his political novels, and his life, especially his role as a politician, is not new. In general, though, these connections have been drawn primarily between Disraeli and his main characters. Richard Weeks, for example, asserts that "whatever the story line, whatever the configuration of main characters, the ambitious Disraeli, hungry for recognition, can be found somewhere inside. His psychology, his values, his objectives all can be discovered with greater or lesser facility in his novels."[5]

Although such a relationship has been firmly established by Weeks and others as far back as Monypenny, the relation between Disraeli's view of English history and his perception of his own place in that history has been taken up only in a very limited way—in the sense that the views of history offered by the narrator of a novel like *Sybil*, for example, are indeed the opinions of Disraeli himself. As Peter Jupp has noted, though, "[o]ne of the principal ways in which Disraeli fashioned an identity and a role for himself in public life was by constructing a particular interpretation of the past and giving it repeated publicity through a steady stream of writings."[6] Whereas Jupp focuses primarily on Disraeli's work from the 1820s and 1830s, I focus here on the 1845 novel *Sybil*, written while Disraeli was a member of Parliament and actively seeking to further his career. I attend first to the relationship between Disraeli's political life and his view of English political history in order to understand more clearly how Disraeli views himself *within* history, and *in relation to* history, before examining his novel's project of historical "recovery" itself.

With respect to historiography, Disraeli's assertion that written history is largely a misrepresentation, a product of prevailing political ideology, is made explicit in the opening chapters of *Sybil*, and will be accompanied by several gestures on Disraeli's part toward the recovery of *actual* historical figures whose "true" role has been distorted or marginalized by the existing historical record. This historical effacement, as it were, parallels a similar fate Disraeli recognized as potentially his own during the turbulent political seasons immediately preceding the writing of *Sybil*. His view of history, then, is precisely what bridges the topical (the condition-of-England question) and the personal (especially the future of his own career as a politician); Disraeli recognized very early in his career that his theory of history, which holds that written history distorts the record and marginalizes its key players, explains his own initial political marginalization, a significant impediment, from Disraeli's perspective, to the fulfillment of his own desire for "greatness." For Disraeli, the history of England is thus not the biography of great men, but the systematic suppression of the truly "great," and the corresponding elevation of lesser, but politically fortunate, men.

It is Disraeli's vision of a true or corrected history, one that would *recover* that which has been obscured or denied, that is represented in the fiction of *Sybil* itself, among invented characters set in a "historical" field of "real" events, namely the Chartist agitation of the late 1830s and early 1840s. As we shall see, though, the recovery of that past does not restore the full rights and entitlements to those who have been wronged. Rather, the text will perform a recovering of that history, remapping the condition-of-England question onto the terrain of gender and calling for a solution that looks quite a bit like Carlyle's hero-worship, as Sybil, the self-described "daughter of the People," submits to the authority of Egremont, her heroic savior and the budding "great man" of Parliament.

As Gary Handwerk has accurately noted, recent trends in the interpretation of Disraeli's fiction suggest that his work is undergoing a reassessment of sorts, with increasing attention being given in particular to Disraeli's complicated use of irony.[7] Although such readings have indeed generated a more complexly textured *Sybil*, all too often their authors have beaten a hasty retreat when faced with the admittedly problematic subject of Disraeli's view of history and historiography. Generally speaking, it has become a critical commonplace to avoid interrogating Disraeli's view of history by dismissing it as merely eccentric. Robert O'Kell's otherwise cogent and persuasive reading of *Sybil* as an allegorical romance, for example, falls back on the pejorative when characterizing the third chapter of the novel as a "short revisionist and conspiratorial 'history' of England."[8] In his appendix to the Penguin edition of *Sybil* entitled "Disraeli's View of History," Thom Braun takes this appraisal one step further, arguing for the almost complete critical dismissal of Disraeli's theory of history. "Disraeli's view of history, as expressed in *Sybil*," writes Braun, "is inordinately distorted, and . . . notably illiberal, despite his obvious lofty intentions as far as the future of the social well-being of the classes is concerned. In the light of this it is best that we do not take these historical views too seriously."[9]

Among recent critics, only Catherine Gallagher has attempted to extend her reading of Disraeli's deployment of irony to include the novel's representation of history.[10] Toward this end, and significant for my purposes here, Gallagher attacks the notion that Disraeli establishes a binary relation between present and past systems of social organization; in so doing, Gallagher contrasts *Sybil* with a work often cited as one of its primary influences—Carlyle's *Past and Present:*

> But whereas that book [Carlyle's *Past and Present*] simply juxtaposes the two terms, drawing in its turn on Pugin's *Contrasts*, *Sybil* concentrates on the process that leads from the past to the present, a process of necessary and continual displacement that wears away the absolute Puginesque distinctions: medieval-modern, sacred-profane. . . . Disraeli's political position is actually dependent on this vision of history as perpetual displacement, a realm without origins or stable values.[11]

Disraeli's view of history, as Gallagher represents it, performs a doubled displacement; by describing the progression of history as a series of displacements, Disraeli's view of history displaces the very bipolarity (and thus the meanings) of the terms "past" and "present," and in the process displaces other views of history contemporaneous with Disraeli's but dependent on (in Gallagher's view) the past/present bipolar relation, namely the Puginesque and Carlylean.[12]

Gallagher's description of this "continual displacement" here recalls Richard Levine's earlier characterization of Disraeli's view of historical progress as "a type of forward, *spiraling* motion."[13] While a spiral does indeed track a progression of perpetual displacement, that displacement occurs only with reference to an organizing center, to a point of origin. Gallagher rejects the concentricity of Levine's spiral metaphor (in the sense that a helical history would presuppose a principle or fulcrum around which meaning might be organized) in favor of a process of displacement that functions in a "realm without origins or stable values."[14] "Most importantly," she writes, "as long as one inhabits the realm of history, one encounters nothing but displacement and usurpation; one never reaches the origins that confer legitimacy. In *Sybil*, history and displacement are synonymous."[15]

Though Gallagher persuasively describes Disraeli's view of the progress of English history, her assertion that "one never reaches the origins that confer legitimacy" when "inhabiting" Disraelian history applies only to Disraeli's critique of the current and accepted *representation* of that history. Part of the confusion here stems from Gallagher's tendency to collapse the past and the historiographical representation of that past into a single category like "the realm of history." Disraeli, in fact, distinguished between the two, as any nineteenth-century historiographer would—between that aggregate of events usually termed historical and the narrative representation of those events. And if the course of history could accurately be described as a series of displacements, then for Disraeli the current and accepted representation of that history constitutes a displacement of the history of displacements, a *misrepresentation* of that history:

> If the history of England ever be written by one who has the knowledge and the courage, and both qualities are equally requisite for the undertaking, the world would be more astonished than when reading the Roman annals by Niebuhr. Generally speaking, all the great events have been distorted, most of the important causes concealed, some of the principal characters never appear, and all who figure are so misunderstood and misrepresented, that the result is a complete mystification. (*Sybil*, 39–40)

Disraeli clearly locates the displacement of history here at the level of writing, in the sense that current (and past) representations of history have misled the public through a deliberate process of concealment, omission, and misrepresentation. But because such a displacement does not constitute a complete erasure of history, Disraeli asserts that it is still possible to recover that history, to represent it accurately, through writing. The displacement would thus be re-placed, corrected by a narration that would be the first step toward a rediscovery of "the origins that confer legitimacy," and, theoretically, a restoration of the rights of the disenfranchised.

By speculating that the reaction to such a "true" history of England might exceed the "astonishment" with which Barthold Niebuhr's *History of Rome* was greeted, Disraeli at once highlights the gulf between accepted historical truth and the "real" history of England. By association, he aligns the recovery of such truth with the writing of a historiographer like Niebuhr, who is often cited as one of the precursors to a "scientific" historiography, one who (at the very least) subjects his sources to critical analysis.[16] In his seminal study *Metahistory*, Hayden White cites Niebuhr as an important source for all subsequent "palingenetic" historians (i.e., those who seek, according to White, "the pious reconstruction of the past in its integrity"), as evidenced by Niebuhr's feeling that one gains historiographical pleasure, as it were, through the restoration of "forgotten and overlooked greatness to a position where it can be recognized. He to whom fortune grants this enters into a relation of the heart with spirits long departed, and he feels himself blessed."[17] Niebuhr's sentiment here is also clearly that of the Disraelian historiographer, "one who has the knowledge and the courage" to bring such "overlooked greatness" out from under the obfuscatory discourse of English "history."

It might suffice to "write off" Disraeli's hypothetical historiographer as a purely speculative invention were it not apparent that this reference to the possibility of a "true" written history is also self-referential —that in a very problematic way Disraeli here refers to himself as the one (perhaps the only one?) "who has the knowledge and the courage" to recover the true meaning of English history. The self-referentiality of the above passage is immediately evident from its context. Appearing almost midway through Book 1, chapter 3 of *Sybil*, this passage is really only a digression within a chapter now notorious for containing (albeit in a concentrated manner) Disraeli's own retelling of English history, from the reign of Henry VIII to the Tory administration of Wellington. As Gallagher has noted, Disraeli views the true history of these three centuries as one of displacement: the Anglican Church displaces the Catholic Church; the Whig Oligarchy displaces the Monarchy; the Venetian Constitution displaces the English Constitution; and a feeble

Toryism displaces the Old Toryism. An even earlier displacement becomes important in subsequent chapters: the Norman displacement of the Saxons.

While it is true, as Gallagher says, that within this history one does not reach the "origins that confer legitimacy" on the *present* distribution of power—the origins that would legitimate the present aristocracy, for example—that is precisely Disraeli's point. The accepted version of history masks, or omits, legitimate origins, origins that, if recognized, would confer legitimacy precisely on what is now dispossessed (the Saxon aristocracy, the Catholic Church, the Monarchy, the English Constitution, and the Old Toryism). A gesture toward just such a Niebuhrian recognition, though on a much smaller scale, occurs in the paragraph immediately following Disraeli's call for a "true" history of England:

> Not one man in a thousand for instance has ever heard of Major Wildman: yet he was the soul of English politics in the most eventful period of this kingdom, and one most interesting to this age, from 1640 to 1688; and seemed more than once to hold the balance which was to decide the permanent form of our government. But he was the leader of an unsuccessful party. (40)

That Disraeli should think Wildman, a radical antimonarchist and former "Leveller," worthy of historical "recovery" (and possibly even reverence) seems politically inexpedient, to say the least, especially given Wildman's post-Leveller career.[18] From about 1654 to practically the end of his life, Wildman was alleged to have been involved in an astonishing variety of conspiracies and assassination plots against a series of English rulers including Cromwell, Charles II, and James II. Much of that time Wildman spent imprisoned—1655–56, 1661–67, and again in 1683—until he finally fled the country in 1685, and spent the next two years in exile.[19]

In *Oliver Cromwell's Letters and Speeches with Elucidations*, published in the same year as *Sybil*, Thomas Carlyle's editorial voice merges with Cromwell's narrative voice in a more general (and memorable), but equally negative assessment of Wildman's character: "A stirring man;

very flamy and very fuliginous; perhaps . . . the noisiest man in England. The turning of the key on him in Chepstow will be a deliverance to us henceforth."[20] On just what basis Disraeli proposes to convert this "noisiest man in England" at the margins of English history into "the soul of English politics" from 1640 to 1688 remains unclear. Disraeli offers no accounting of Wildman's career, and though he implies that Wildman is at best extremely marginalized by the historical record ("not one man in a thousand" has heard of him), he does not detail the manner in which Wildman's "story" has been distorted or omitted. What Disraeli does tell us, though, is *why* Wildman has been marginalized—because "he was the leader of an unsuccessful party." And it is here that Disraeli's Niebuhrian gesture toward recovering "overlooked greatness" begins to look increasingly self-referential. Just as Disraeli's earlier reference to a hypothetical historiographer ("the one who has the knowledge and the courage") takes on a self-referential character from its very context (the call for such a "true" historian appears in the midst of a chapter in which Disraeli purports to be offering a "true" history), so too does Wildman's historical position, his marginalization at the hands (literally) of hostile historians, mirror what Disraeli may have imagined his own historical position and fate to be during the months leading up to and during the composition of *Sybil*.

In his "General Preface" to the 1870 collected edition of his novels, Disraeli situates the advent of his political dissension from the accepted version of historical truth practically at birth: "Born in a library, and trained from early childhood by learned men who did not share the passions and the prejudices of our political and social life, I had imbibed on some subjects conclusions different from those which generally prevail, and especially with reference to the history of our country."[21] Disraeli then asserts that his initial efforts to enter Parliament in the mid-1830s only highlighted his singular perspective:

> When I attempted to enter public life, I expressed these views, long meditated, to my countrymen, but they met with little encouragement. He who steps out of the crowd is listened to with suspicion or with heedlessness: and forty years ago there prevailed a singular ignorance of the political history of our

> country. I had no connection either in the press or in public life. I incurred the accustomed penalty of being looked on as a visionary, and what I knew to be facts were treated as paradoxes.[22]

Significantly, it is Disraeli himself who singles out his view of English history as the primary locus of his disagreement with the prevailing opinion of his potential political constituents and colleagues. Though he claims in the following paragraph that "ten years afterward [i.e., in the mid-1840s] affairs had changed," that change really occurred only gradually, and on a limited scale (at least until the 1845 session), since he was now listened to and respected by a small group of Parliamentary friends and political allies, the core of which (John Manners, George Smythe, and Alexander Baillie Cochrane, along with Disraeli) came to be known as Young England.

Young England was active in Parliament only from 1842 to 1846, and while its members constituted, as Robert Blake remarks, a "small and rebellious section" of the Tory Party, occasionally voting against the government as a block, they achieved no concrete political results.[23] Although Blake deems their legacy significant only for "incurable romantics" (168), the editors of the fourth volume of *Benjamin Disraeli Letters* offer a more positive assessment of the Young England group:

> Like Carlyle, in *Past and Present*, they saw in the mediaeval past an organic concept of society, a chain of coherent responsibility *uniting* all classes, and an idealism springing from a common belief in the primacy of moral law. This ostensible romanticism (like Disraeli's) was therefore not based on nostalgia for its own sake, but on a concrete sense of the ways in which these qualities had been lost as part of the price paid for the industrial revolution, and for the extension of the franchise. Their emphasis was not on turning back the clock, but rather the advocacy of a type of moral rearmament to cope with the present and future.[24]

Although Carlyle himself recognized that Young England exhibited tremendous potential for political accomplishment, he did not see

Young England as focused on the present and future, as the editors of the *Benjamin Disraeli Letters* suggest. In fact, Carlyle believed that it was precisely their glorification of the past that undermined their political potential. In an 1844 letter to Monckton Milnes, Carlyle writes:

> On the whole, *if* Young England would altogether fling its shovel-hat into the lumber-room, much more cast its purple stockings to the nettles; and honestly recognizing what was dead, and leaving the dead to bury that, address itself frankly to the magnificent but as yet chaotic and appalling Future, in the *spirit* of the Past and Present; telling men at every turn that it knew and saw forever clearly the *body* of the Past to be dead (and even to be damnable if it pretended to still be alive, and go about in a galvanic State),—what achievements might not Young England perhaps manage for us! Whatsoever was noble and manful among us, in terrible want of a rallying-point at present, might rally there, and march. But alas, alas![25]

Carlyle's articulation here of the past as utterly dead and other (and of the damnable nature of false, "galvanic" resuscitations of the past) is consistent with the position he takes in *Past and Present* (as discussed in chapter 3), and thus reflects his overriding concern that social and political discourse focus its attention on the condition of England, present and future. In Carlyle's view, the outmoded dress of Young England (clothed in the vestments of religion and royalty) signifies its backward-looking politics, championing old aristocracy—especially old Toryism—and a powerful monarchy. Shorn of these vestments, and infused with "the *spirit* of the Past and Present," Young England might function as a much needed fulcrum or "rallying-point," a way of organizing and strengthening the flagging manliness of society.

Though never quite reaching the status of "rallying-point," Young England did achieve notoriety and a degree of fashionability, especially after the 1844 publication of *Coningsby; or, The New Generation*, with its eponymous protagonist based on George Smythe and its relentless attack on the policies and character of Peel. The Young England years from 1842 to 1846 were thus extremely significant in the shaping of

Disraeli's oppositional status; it was in September of 1841 that Disraeli's request to serve in Peel's government was denied, and Blake marks that refusal as crucial to Disraeli's positioning himself as an outsider within the Tory party, a position that would ultimately lead him to be in "open rebellion against Peel" by 1845.[26] Blake is careful, though, not to reduce the course of Disraeli's disputes with the Tory leaders to his "rebuff" by Peel. However, Blake does describe Disraeli as being "mortified" and "bitterly disappointed" at being passed over, and suggests that his subsequent psychological state—"bored, restless, vaguely discontented"—is what led him to align himself with Young England.[27] Monypenny goes even farther, asserting that Disraeli's "exclusion" from office by Peel, along with Stanley's, "led to *Coningsby* and *Sybil* and the creation of the political novel."[28]

Monypenny, however, overstates the case, at least if we take him to mean that Peel's rebuff of Disraeli led *directly* to the writings of Disraeli's political novels. An argument can be made, though, that Disraeli's exclusion from office contributed to his increasing dissatisfaction with his role as a mere "supporter of administration," and that this dissatisfaction led directly to his fashioning himself as an "outsider" within the Tory party, as a Tory in opposition to his own party's leadership.[29] As Paul Smith has noted, Disraeli's "immediate response to [Peel's] neglect was to act as pied piper to a handful of aristocratic young hopefuls in the Young England group, harassing the leader who had refused him office with what Peel explicitly recognized as a version of the 'patriot' opposition tactics of the previous century."[30] In Disraeli's view, then, if the role of "supporter" and the exercise of political power become mutually exclusive, a new role would seem to be in order.

Richard Weeks draws a careful distinction between the desire to obtain power and the desire to exercise power, with respect to Disraeli's ambitions: "The evidence suggests that, regardless of Disraeli's political principles, he acted on the political stage out of ambition for personal recognition, and that obtaining power (recognition) was far more important to him than the exercise of power."[31] While I am sympathetic to the distinction, and find the metaphor "political stage" appropriate, if Disraeli were solely interested in personal recognition, he might simply have become, like Carlyle's Wildman, "the noisiest man in

England." But Disraeli was also interested in *historical* recognition, even "greatness," and such recognition could not be attained without the exercise of political power; even then, that recognition would remain uncertain, contingent on future changes in the political landscape. Weeks bases his distinction upon the oft-cited discontinuity between Disraeli's political program of the 1840s (Young England's agenda), and the policies of his later Prime Ministry. But Weeks is mistaken to seek ideological consistency here; rather, both Disraeli's association with the Young England faction and his political novels are better seen as strategies of self-representation, as attempts to secure political survival and mobility. Formerly (since the mid-1830s, in fact), the Tory party served as a way for Disraeli to represent himself publically and politically, as would any party with respect to its members. When the role of "a supporter of administration" became, for Disraeli, a misrepresentation of his political present and future, he embarked (though not immediately) on the fashioning of a different, oppositional way of representing himself politically.[32] All of this maneuvering, then, from 1841 to 1846, was in the service of *personal* recognition, which served as a precursor or a stepping stone to a position of power (and its exercise), and thus *historical* recognition.

In a speech before his Shrewsbury constituents in 1844, Disraeli made plain his desire for personal and historical recognition: "There is no doubt, gentlemen, that all men who offer themselves as candidates for public favor have motives of some sort. I candidly acknowledge that I have, and I will tell you what they are: I love fame; I love public reputation; I love to live in the eyes of the country; and it is a glorious thing for a man to do who has had my difficulties to contend against."[33] We have already seen Disraeli link historical recognition to political success. The name of Wildman has been relegated to obscurity, says Disraeli, "because he was the member of an unsuccessful party." And although the rhetorical thrust of that passage from *Sybil* (indeed the very fact that Wildman's name is mentioned at all) calls for an active recovery of such "overlooked" figures, the conduct of Disraeli's political life in the early to mid-1840s would seem to *capitulate* to the injustice of historical oversight, rather than agitate against it. In other words, if Disraeli sees himself in 1844 as a potential Wildman, at least with respect to the future historical record, his call for historical demystification translates into a rather direct, and even contradictory political strategy: do not become a member of an unsuccessful party. Or to put it yet another, but more accurate way, if your successful party will not have you, seek to make that party unsuccessful. Thus we have, in May of 1845, the publication of *Sybil* (complete with an unflattering portrait of Peel himself), the famous Corn Law debates of 1845–46, and the fall of Peel's government in the latter year.

This is not to say, of course, that *Sybil* directly contributed to the downfall of the Peel government. However, *Sybil* does belong to a larger strategy on Disraeli's part to position himself apart from the Tory leadership, to publicize his own views, including those with respect to his theory of English history, and, with luck, to further his own political career. In this respect, *Sybil* did not contribute to the crisis in the Tory government so much as it further defined, in a way designed for mass consumption, Disraeli's representation *of himself*.[34] As Paul Smith puts it in his introduction to the volume *The Self-Fashioning of Disraeli*, "Disraeli's novels are autobiographical, not in the sense that they furnish a simple record of feelings and events, but in the sense that they exhibit a process of self-fashioning of which they themselves form a vital part."[35] This self-representation, as Weeks notes, does not precisely correspond to the political agenda Disraeli would actually put into practice later in his career; however, it does correspond to his political agenda *at that moment*, if we understand that agenda to be focused primarily on personal and political ambition. Rather than succumb to marginalization because of his "difference," Disraeli inscribes that difference in a fictional direction, attempting to, in his own way, define himself and define the issue of the day, while historicizing both. The result, as Raymond Williams has noted, expresses "the generalized anger of an outsider making his way."[36]

IN the passage from Book 1 chapter 3 of *Sybil* in which Disraeli labels the whole of English history as "a complete mystification," he illustrates his assertion with reference to four rather disparate texts: Plato's *Republic*, More's *Utopia*, the Inquisition testimony of Gaudentio di Lucca, and Robert Paltock's *The Life and Adventures of Peter Wilkins*.

The "perusal of the narrative" of English history, writes Disraeli, "is about as profitable to an Englishman" as seeking historical truth would be in any of these four texts (40). By alluding to texts that do not claim to bear any relation to historical truth, or whose claims to historical accuracy are transparently fictional, Disraeli seems to be asserting a strong and clear division between history and fiction. And yet, if the whole of English history is misrepresented, mystified, and thus a fiction as far away from the historical truth as Disraeli believes Plato, More, di Lucca, and Paltock are, how is the novel *Sybil*, which draws on "historical" fact but employs imaginary plots and characters, any different? Or, to put it more directly, of what *use* is *Sybil*, with respect to Disraeli's own view of history?

The answer lies in Disraeli's claim that *Sybil*, though a fictional narrative, remains historically accurate. In his "General Preface" to the collected novels, for example, he describes *Sybil* "as an accurate and never exaggerated picture of a remarkable period in our domestic history"; as such, writes Disraeli, "the pages of SYBIL may, I venture to believe, be consulted with confidence" (xiv). Anticipating that the accuracy of this novel, its usefulness as history, would be subject to criticisms of exaggeration and embellishment, Disraeli states that

> [the author] believes there is not a trait in this work for which he has not the authority of his own observation, or the authentic evidence which has been received by Royal Commissions and Parliamentary Committees. But while he hopes he has alleged nothing which is not true, he has found the absolute necessity of suppressing much that is genuine. For so little do we know of the state of our own country that the air of improbability that the whole truth would inevitably throw over these pages, might deter many from their perusal. (*Sybil*, 24)

Deftly, Disraeli reverses the potential criticism. Here the truth is not that which must be told, as if by inherent imperative, but that which must be held in abeyance. The very writing of the novel thus repeats the process of omission and suppression that Disraeli impugns conventional historiography for employing, but by asserting that the narrative actually *withholds* the truth, and that its plot bears only a partial relation to its historical referent ("the state of our own country"), Disraeli makes the "displaced" character of historical representation work in his favor. His novel represents itself, then, as a kind of counter-displacement, one that self-consciously calls into question the relation between historical truth and historical representation on the one hand, while simultaneously participating in (and correcting) the very medium it decries as a "mystification." In a world in which "sense for the true and false is lost,"[37] Disraeli chooses to negotiate such terrain by blurring the engagement of his fiction with the historical, in an effort to "recover" the truth of English history.[38]

In Book 1 chapter 3 of *Sybil*, this engagement is particularly keen. Though the chapter itself both presents Disraeli's view of English history and puts that theory to use (by narrating the "real" version of English history, and by recovering, in the process, such "suppressed characters" as Wildman), this representation of history intersects with the "history" of the fictional Egremont family, whose youngest son, Charles, is *Sybil*'s protagonist. The family patriarch, one Baldwin Greymount, rose from a humble position as a "confidential domestic" in Henry VIII's household to that of a commissioner in charge of overseeing the seizure of monastic property. After seventy years of faithful service and the discreet but ample accumulation of abbey lands and wealth, a Greymount descendant ascended to the aristocracy as Baron Marney (33–34). And it is here that the historical mystification begins, a mystification that parallels, and that indeed, for Disraeli, is in many ways inextricably intertwined with, the political history of England:

> The heralds furnished his pedigree, and assured the world that although the exalted rank and extensive possessions enjoyed at present by the Greymounts, had their origin immediately in great territorial revolutions of a recent reign, it was not for a moment to be supposed, that the remote ancestors of the Ecclesiastical Commissioner of 1530 were by any means obscure. On the contrary, it appeared that they were both Norman and baronial, their real name Egremont, which, in their patent of peerage the family now resumed. (35)

In the case of the "Egremont" family, the authority for their peerage, their nobility, has been completely fabricated. So complete is this history of false origins, that the *real* origin, the fact that Baldwin Greymount procured his wealth and power through the dispossession and displacement of others, here appears as a brief *interruption* of what is otherwise supposed to be a coherent narrative; thus, the family need only "resume" its rightful name, in order to signify that its origins are indeed Norman and baronial. This "interruption" is thus based upon and at the same time conceals another, more permanent "interruption": the seizure of monastic lands. The Egremont family history displaces this displacement, substituting false (and conveniently remote) origins for their relatively recent ones. No one believes that history more than the Egremonts themselves; though "descendants of the old gentleman usher of one of King Henry's plundering vicar-generals," they "counted themselves nobility; and turned up their noses at the Pratts and the Smiths, the Jenkinsons and the Robinsons of our degenerate days" (37). Their situation then is doubly ironic: the Egremonts believe themselves to be a family with origins in Norman nobility when they are not; and even though they have risen to a position from which a more ambitious family might reach for even higher status and influence, the Egremonts have "never said anything that was remembered, or done anything that could be recalled" (37).

The Egremonts, of course, are not alone in their false origins. They are joined by Lord Fitz-Warene, now Earl de Mowbray, whose family origins are purported to be, like the Egremonts', Norman and baronial, but whose real origins begin only in the mid-eighteenth century, with the lowly John Warren, a waiter at a club frequented by government officials. He is subsequently taken on as a valet to an official for His Majesty's government in India, and made a private secretary; then, through prudence and faculties superior to his master's, he profits from the settling of his master's estate, returns a "nabob," purchases a "close borough" and enters Parliament, marries the daughter of an Irish earl, and through alliance and ingratiation, begins his ascent through the peerage (107–11). Though Lord Fitz-Warene was at first the object of derision when his true origins were discovered and circulated, such talk soon passed, and with the family name thus "resumed," Lord Fitz-

Warene's son, Altamont Belvidere, begins the process of obliterating his family's true origins: "The new Lord Fitz-Warene was the most aristocratic of breathing beings. He most fully, entirely, and absolutely believed in his pedigree; his coat of arms was emblazoned on every window, embroidered on every chair, carved in every corner" (111). Here Disraeli makes clear the extent to which aristocratic authority depends upon inscription; the emblazoning of the Fitz-Warene heraldry at once underscores and underwrites that authority. It both represents the aristocratic origin of the family, and serves as *proof* of—literally seals—that origin. As with the Egremonts, the Fitz-Warene name and coat of arms refers not to an illustrious and noble past, but only to itself.[39]

As Catherine Gallagher has noted, the ironic truth about the aristocratic origins of the Egremonts and Fitz-Warenes "devalues" or "destabilizes" their claim to power and rule. Given the pervasiveness of this irony, Gallagher further asserts (as we have seen earlier) that "as long as one inhabits the realm of history, one encounters nothing but displacement and usurpation; one never reaches the origins that confer legitimacy."[40] While this statement certainly holds true for the Egremont and Fitz-Warene family histories, and, more generally, for any historical narrative that for Disraeli qualifies as a "mystification," to assert that such narratives result in the *absolute* obfuscation of origins is rather misleading. While false genealogies and doctored narratives do indeed dominate the "realm of history" in Disraeli's world, fragments and traces of these "origins that confer legitimacy" still remain. Sometimes these fragments are little more than ruins, as in the case of Marney Abbey, but sometimes the trace is embodied in a perfect, pristine form, as in the case of Sybil Gerard herself. Whatever their form, enough remnants of these "origins" exist for a disaffected yet sensitive pseudo-aristocrat like Charles Egremont to assemble the pieces into a coherent counter-narrative, one that does not seek necessarily to restore the entitlement to those who have been dispossessed, but instead to "re-present" those forgotten claims and narratives by reconfiguring the present form of (political) representation.

In Book 2 chapter 4, Charles Egremont makes his first visit to the ruins of the medieval Marney Abbey since the days of his youth.

Disraeli quickly establishes the significance these ruins already hold for Egremont:

> [H]e had been almost born amid the ruins of Marney Abbey; its solemn relics were associated with his first and freshest fancies; every footstep was as familiar to him as it could have been to one of the old monks; yet never without emotion could he behold these unrivalled remains of one of the greatest of the great religious houses of the North. (86)

On the surface, Egremont's kinship, as it were, with the abbey's ruins is clearly ironic. It was his own ancestor, Baldwin Greymount, who seized possession of the abbey and its acreage in the name of Henry VIII; one of its towers still stands unfinished, its incompleteness signifying that very moment of "usurpation." But Disraeli's purpose here lies beyond the ironic. Egremont's affinity for these ruins predisposes him to question the received version of historical events. As the narrator tells us, these ruins do indeed testify to a particular historical moment of the dissolution of church property, but they also narrate a history of the past that counters the received historical opinion: the history of the monastic-centered community.

The ruins are spread over ten acres of land, and on the outer fringe the most decayed remnants stand as "mouldering memorials that told where once rose the offices and spread the terraced gardens of the old proprietors" (86). From these markers "might still be traced the dwelling of the lord abbot; and there, still more distinctly . . . the capacious hospital . . . where all the rights of hospitality were practiced" (86). At the center of these ruins the abbey church itself still rises, "with a strength that had defied time, and with a beauty that had at last turned away the wrath of man" (87). What remains of the abbey church reiterates the words of the farmer Bingley, who told Egremont as he began his ride to the ruins, "You wunna find them much changed. They have seen a deal of different things in their time!" (85).

All this strength and beauty, this permanence in the face of the passage of time and human destruction, contributes to Egremont's seemingly instinctual reverence for the medieval abbey. Above all, the ruins offer him "a silence so profound" that "there was that stirring of the mind of Egremont which rendered him far from indisposed for this loneliness" (88).[41] As Egremont begins to reflect, his questions open up the issue of historical representation, particularly as it pertains to the social and economic effects of the monastic dissolution:

> He stood among the ruins that, as the farmer had well observed, had seen many changes: changes of creeds, of dynasties, of laws, of manners. . . . His own house, his own order, had established themselves on the ruins of that great body, the emblems of whose ancient magnificence and strength surrounded him. And now his order was in turn menaced. And the People—the millions of Toil, on whose unconscious energies during these changeful centuries all rested—what changes had these centuries brought to them? Had their advance in the national scale borne a due relation to that progress of their rulers, which had accumulated in the treasuries of a limited class the riches of the world; and made their possessors boast that they were the first of nations; the most powerful and the most free, the most enlightened, the most moral, and the most religious? Were there any rick-burners in the times of the lord abbots? And if not, why not? And why should the stacks of the Earls of Marney be destroyed, and those of the Abbots of Marney spared? (88–89)

It is in this passage that *Sybil*'s political theme converges with its theory of history. Echoing Cobbett's insistent emphasis on the greater social cohesiveness of the medieval past, Disraeli's rhetoric here implies the existence of just such a mutually beneficent pre-dissolution relation between the People and their "superiors," a historical relation subsequently breached by the seizure of monastic property. The result of this breach may be understood in two related senses: as a breaking or betrayal of the traditional historical relation of beneficence and mutual obligation, and as a breaching or separation of the People from their social superiors, forming two mutually exclusive orders—the "Two Nations" of the novel's title.

Though Charles Egremont does not yet realize in what direction the implications of these political and historical reflections will take him, in the following chapter, still set in the abbey ruins, Egremont meets (though unbeknownst to him) one of the dispossessed, face-to-face, in the person of Walter Gerard, who just happens to be a descendant of the last Abbot of Marney Abbey; it was this ancestor who commissioned the unfinished tower and who presided over the abbey at the moment Egremont's ancestor, Baldwin Greymount, seized the abbey and its lands.

Most of Book 2 chapter 5 consists of a conversation between the two men, along with Gerard's companion Stephen Morley, about the medieval past and its relation to the present. While Egremont repeats briefly, and as if by rote, the received narrative of monastic corruption and sloth, his "master" narrative is countered by Gerard's alternative narrative of the dispossessed, a narrative that begins with an assertion that encapsulates the thesis of Book 1 chapter 3: "their history [the Monastics'] was written by their enemies" (91). In a passage cribbed directly from Cobbett's *A History of the Protestant "Reformation,"* Gerard's counter-narrative illustrates the reciprocity of the monastic-centered community through the beneficence of the abbot "landlords," the local distribution of wealth, and the relative state of "comfort" in which all members of the community lived: "The Monastics could possess no private property; they could save no money; they could bequeath nothing. They lived, received, and expended in common."[42] Within this argument the ruins themselves function primarily as signifiers of violent usurpation. "They are the children of violence," says Gerard, "not of time. It is war that created these ruins, civil war, of all our civil wars the most inhuman, for it was waged with the unresisting" (91). Gerard further characterizes the injustice committed during the monastic dissolution as the violation of property rights, rather than the persecution of a particular religion. As he tells Egremont, "you had no right to deprive men of their property, and property moreover which under their administration so mainly contributed to the welfare of the community" (91).

Gerard's focus on property rights reflects his own interest in reclaiming his familial inheritance.[43] While Egremont returns to the ruins of Marney Abbey because of a vague spiritual kinship with that place that began in his youth, Gerard's visit has a more specific purpose—to view with his own eyes the tomb of the last abbot of Marney Abbey. Like the ruins themselves, the tomb represents the "truth" about the past, but because the tomb has inscribed upon it the name "Gerard," this gravestone is also a sort of historical document, marking incontrovertibly (and indelibly) the nobility of Gerard's ancestral lineage.

Though the truth here is written in stone for all to see, this truth has been "papered over" by the process of political and genealogical mystification. On one level, Disraeli thus represents the competing claims to the land through a kind of symbolic dichotomy between "rock" (with all its attendant qualities of permanence and strength that the ruins of Marney Abbey embody) and "paper" (with its connotations of impermanence and flimsiness exemplified by the false paper-based family genealogies of the Egremonts and Fitz-Warenes). When each is further considered as a medium for writing, the dichotomy seems equally clear; inscriptions in rock, like the last abbot's tombstone, would seem to carry more "weight," as it were, to convey with more authority the meaning of that inscription, than would paper, which, after all, might be subject to erasure, forgery, destruction, and so on. Of course, this dichotomy is itself ironized by the fact that paper appears to have won here, and won *historically*, in the very pages of history for which paper supplies the medium.

Similarly, there is some indication throughout the first two books of *Sybil* that the historical triumph of a paper-based society could also be traced economically, with the emergence and domination of capitalism. In Book 1 chapter 3, Disraeli singles out what he terms "Dutch finance" (imported, allegedly, by William III himself) as responsible for the introduction of a credit-centered economy and the creation of a national debt, and thus, in general, for the mismanagement of the economy and the suffering of the millions of working poor (44–45). In Book 2 chapter 1, the self-educated radical Devilsdust reiterates this theme as he reminds his companion Mick Radley that "Labour may be weak, but Capital is weaker. . . . Their capital is all paper" (134). The fact that Devilsdust becomes a capitalist in the end, of course, undermines this position, as does his name change from Devilsdust (the waste-product of commodity production) to Mowbray (his place of birth, a "decorous appellation," we are told, "adopted in due homage to the social decencies" [495]). In the last instance, Devilsdust is taught the power of paper; he receives the trickle-down benefits of Mick Radley's safe delivery of the papers that prove the Gerard family entitlement, and has joined a business firm that "will probably furnish in time a crop of members of Parliament and Peers of the realm" (495).

In focusing on the consequences of society based on the medium of paper, Disraeli ultimately foregrounds the way in which the struggle against historical obfuscation and displacement must proceed at the level of writing. Though Gerard was already aware that his family had a claim to the land (now under the dominion of the Earl de Mowbray), the "Gerard" tombstone confirms for him the nobility of his lineage, and thus the full scope of the injustice committed against his family. While the tombstone records this historical fact, it does not carry any legal authority; that authority exists elsewhere, *on paper*, in the form of land deeds and other documents.

Though the papers themselves establish that the Gerards are the rightful owners of the land now held by the Earl de Mowbray, mere existence of the papers proves nothing. So convoluted has the peerage system become, that only a heraldry expert like Baptist Hatton is capable of pursuing such a claim successfully. Hatton originally worked on the writ of right brought by Gerard's father; the process exhausted the elder Gerard's finances, and upon his death the opportunistic Hatton, also economically insecure, sold the papers to Lord Mowbray himself. Though the pursuit of the Gerard papers drives one of the novel's primary subplots (several characters join the ensuing "paper chase," including Gerard, Morley, and Hatton himself, each with rather different objectives), the papers themselves do not embody, within the fiction of *Sybil*, the entire "truth" about the past.[44] The papers, after all, refer only to a specific displacement, signifying the entitlement of one dispossessed family. While the usurpation of the Gerard claim to the land represents the more general historical condition of "the People"—estranged from the land and wholly separated from the aristocracy—the full representation of that condition, one that incorporates not only the fact of the dispossession itself, but also, seemingly, the spiritual and communal qualities of the past (divinity and "the People"), may be found embodied in Sybil Gerard.

Sybil first appears in the novel at the end of the scene between Egremont, Gerard, and Morley, at the ruins of Marney Abbey, singing "the evening hymn to the Virgin" in a voice "of almost supernatural sweetness" (96). As the "divine melody" ends, Egremont catches a glimpse of Sybil "apparently in the habit of a Religious" (97). Her beauty is nothing short of ethereal; her fair, "radiant" hair, the "brightness of her complexion," and "a character of almost divine majesty" combine to create the effect of an apparition—"the fair phantom of some saint haunting the sacred ruins of her desecrated fane" (97).[45]

Framed by one of the empty arches of the church ruins, and backlit by the setting sun, Sybil's entrance into the novel is as contrived as it is idyllic. With this entrance, Disraeli represents the past as god-centered and devotional, and establishes Sybil as a living emblem of that past, a symbol that, as we shall see, provides an important link between that past and the present. Her description mirrors that of the "fair and serene" Queen Victoria at the moment of her ascension to the throne, "a maiden" who also "has the blood and beauty of a Saxon" (67).[46] At this initial moment, though, Sybil's "ghostly" form, like "some saint haunting the sacred ruins of her desecrated fane," testifies both to the divinity and to the "otherness" of the past, to its utter remoteness and seeming inaccessibility.

Much of Sybil's embodiment of the past rests on this repeated use of religious associations to describe her appearance. In *The Industrial Reformation of English Fiction*, Catherine Gallagher calls her, using Coleridge's adjective, "a tautegorical symbol of the sacred"; in other words, writes Gallagher, "Disraeli tries to make her mean nothing more nor less than she appears to mean." Drawing on the way in which Sybil is depicted throughout as isolated from the "outside" world, in the sense that she is both holy and naive, Gallagher thus sees her as the "embodiment of pure value," which she explains as "a kind of value that is not socially produced, . . . [but] produced by its removal from the social process of exchange." Ultimately, Gallagher sees this value as put to symbolic use with Sybil's marriage to Egremont, "which represents the Coleridgean union of the sacred with its rightful representative, the state."[47] Only in this way, says Gallagher, is Disraeli able to ground the political in the symbolic.

While the symbolic significance of Sybil's character certainly functions tautegorically with respect to what Gallagher rather vaguely terms "the sacred" (if we take that term to mean simply "holiness" or "divinity"), Gallagher's use of that word accounts for only half of what Sybil's character represents. As she herself says to Egremont: "I have lived under two roofs, only two roofs; and each has given me a great idea; the Convent and the Cottage. One has taught me the degradation of my faith, the other of my race. You should not wonder, therefore, that my heart is concentrated on the Church and the People" (220). Though her "otherness" signifies her proximity to the sacred, it also indicates her status as a representative of the People. That otherness —she is a woman, Catholic and a virgin—allows her to stand in for both the remote, displaced past, and for the great masses of the lower class who are themselves positioned as "other" to the aristocracy and the wealthy capitalists. Within Sybil, then, are merged these two principles, and *both* principles, not just the Church, might thus be thought of as grounded in the idea of "the sacred." The degradation of the two principles has resulted from the dispossession of the sacred cause of the Church, and from the dispossession of the sacred rights of labor. In terms of the working classes, this dispossession is coterminous with their lack of political representation and the increasingly alienated (and brutalizing) conditions of work.

Throughout the novel, various characters (including Sybil and Egremont) appeal to the sacred character of labor as a way of authorizing a modification of political representation.[48] However, it is precisely on this issue of political representation that the views of Sybil (and thus her significance as a symbol) are called into question. Although several critics of the novel, Gallagher included, have equated Sybil's symbolic significance with her "sacredness" or "innocence" (and thus interpreted her marriage to Egremont as divine authorization of his political agenda), the matter of Sybil's relation to "the People" and to her faith becomes, long before the marriage, a vehicle for the critique of her contention that the "gulf" between the "Two Nations" is "utterly impassable" (300).[49] In fact, the revision of her opinions early in Book 5 (partly due to her own experiences in London and partly due to the active lobbying of Egremont), reveals Sybil to be not so much a "tautegorical symbol of the sacred" as a kind of medium through which Egremont might represent his message, so that the gulf between the so-called "Two Nations" may in fact be bridged. We need not refer to the marriage to "seal" this union of the message and its medium; Sybil herself embodies this link between the two terms (medium and message, disenfranchised and enfranchised, past and present), and the process of encoding Sybil as that link entails a kind of conversion, beginning with Egremont's revelation of his true identity, and ending with Sybil's reading of his speech before Parliament. In the process, her own understanding of her symbolic (and symbiotic) relationship to "the People" is undermined by her experiences, then reinscribed by Egremont, while the matter of her Roman Catholicism no longer seems to matter; the subject quietly vanishes just prior to their marriage.

Michael McCully also stresses the importance of Sybil's changing convictions as central to the novel's ideological message, asserting that the novel is thus tantamount to a kind of *Bildungsroman*, tracing Sybil's growth from an innocent, childlike believer in the cause of the People to "an enlightened aristocrat" who "must outgrow her view of herself as an angelic daughter of the working class so that she can acknowledge what the author believes to be her true relation to the poor, that of a protective 'queen' who can save them from future hardship with the aid of her future 'kingly' husband, Egremont."[50] While I share McCully's emphasis on the importance of Sybil's ideological transformation, in the discussion that follows I will foreground the way in which Sybil's "conversion" marks the convergence of Disraeli's gender politics with his class politics, a convergence much more trenchantly hierarchical than McCully's protective queen/kingly husband image suggests. For example, when Sybil tells Egremont that her "heart is concentrated on the Church and the People," he suggests, in response, that "there are other ideas . . . that might equally be entitled to your thought." Sybil replies, "I feel these are enough . . . too great, as it is, for my brain" (220). While this sentiment is meant, assuredly, to highlight the import of these two great principles, Sybil's reply also emphasizes her own limitations, limitations that, according to the gender politics of the novel, are characteristically feminine. Compare Egremont's own developing political awareness as a result of his encounter with Gerard, Morley, and Sybil at the ruins of Marney Abbey:

> It seemed to Egremont that, from the day he met these persons in the Abbey ruins, the horizon of his experience had insensibly expanded; . . . He could not resist the conviction that from the time in question, his sympathies had become more lively and more extended; that a masculine impulse had been given to his mind; that he was inclined to view public questions in a tone very different to that in which he had surveyed them a few weeks back, when on the hustings of his borough. (169–70)

Here, the willingness to question received opinion, to open one's mind to alternative possibilities (including, for Egremont, narratives of history that counter his own family's historical narration), is equated with a *masculine* impulse. Indeed, what is marked here is Egremont's transformation from a limited, implicitly feminized position as an ineffectual, minor aristocrat to a masculinized position as a broad-minded, potentially "heroic" politician. In this hierarchy of gender-based traits, then, it is the "masculine impulse," defined over and against the limited capabilities of the "feminine," that accounts for Egremont's ability to see "beyond" his preconceived notions of class and history. In the end, it is precisely Egremont's "masculine impulse" that will seek to structure and colonize the limited, feminine vision of Sybil, according her a proper, narrowly circumscribed place within the novel's symbolic economy. As we will soon see, this process involves nothing less than the wholesale "conversion" of Sybil to Egremont, a conversion that necessitates her submission, both personal and political, to his masculine, "heroic" authority.

It should be noted here, also, that at two key moments in his life, an encounter with a woman turned Egremont's mind in a "progressive," expansive direction. The initial moment occurred when Egremont was twenty-four, and fell in love with Lady Arabella, who, as Egremont would later put it, was "stolen" from him by his brother Lord Marney.

This experience of dashed expectations, common to us all, says our narrator, provided for Egremont just the sort of "shock . . . which first makes us think" (60). Indeed, from then on, his "awakened curiosity led him to investigate and read," and as a result, "the great system . . . in which he had been born and nurtured began to tremble" (60). Even so, "he was now conscious he wanted an object" (61); enter Sybil, radiant and haunting, at the ruins of Marney Abbey. As Christina Crosby has argued in *The Ends of History*, "[s]elf-consciousness is no innocent achievement, and if middle-class Victorian men become aware of themselves by means of 'the other,' then otherness is conceivable only as a means to an end."[51] Such a situation, contends Crosby, is part of a more general tendency in Victorian novels to establish men as universal subjects via the exclusion of "the other," especially women. Though her discussion focuses on the positioning of middle-class men as the privileged subject of history, Crosby's argument is applicable to Egremont and his perception of Sybil as well. It is precisely the extreme "otherness" of Sybil's character—not only her gender, religion, and self-identified class position, but also (and to a certain extent, even more crucially) her radical political call for direct political representation—that Egremont must overcome in order to achieve his inextricably intertwined political and sexual goals, an achievement that will be consummated upon the eradication of Sybil's radical politics, and her subsequent offering of hegemonic consent to her conquering hero.

In addition to her position as a woman, a Catholic, and a self-declared "daughter of the People," Sybil's political convictions (including her call for direct political representation of the People and the "restoration" of the Catholic faith) constitute the most troubling aspect of her "otherness" for Egremont, and function as the most serious obstacle to the progress of their romantic relationship. Although from the time of their encounter at the ruins of Marney Abbey "the form of Sybil Gerard was stamped upon his brain" (168), and he declares to her later that "from the moment I first beheld you in the starlit arch of Marney has your spirit ruled my being" (335), Egremont's true agenda with respect to Sybil is thus the erasure of these political convictions, which are founded upon her understanding of the past, specifically on the idea that the Church and the People are now degraded. "I have had the happiness and the sorrow of knowing you too well to doubt the convictions of your mind, or to believe that they can be lightly removed," says Egremont, "and yet I would strive to remove them" (333). Though Egremont's initial efforts at erasure and conversion have little immediate impact on Sybil, his statements systematically attack her convictions at their base—namely, the extent to which she grounds her view of the present on her understanding of the past. He tells her, for example, that "you have formed your opinions upon tradition, not upon experience," that "the world that exists is not the world of which you have read," and that "the class that calls itself your superior is not the same class as ruled in the time of your fathers" (333–34). Though this initial attempt at the conversion of Sybil does not succeed (clumsily followed, as it is, by Egremont's declaration of love), it does contribute, along with various other elements (including the factionalism of the Chartist movement, its increasingly violent activity, and her growing understanding of her father's role in that violence), to Sybil's abandonment of her conviction that the gulf between the Two Nations is "impassable."

Reflecting on the way in which her two guiding principles, "the oppression of her church and the degradation of her people . . . had resolved themselves into one profound and gloomy conviction, that the world was divided only between the oppressors and the oppressed" (348), Sybil now realizes that "she had raised up two phantoms which with her represented human nature" (349). In the place of these convictions Egremont had earlier submitted the following: that the "natural leaders of the People" are none other than the "new generation of the aristocracy of England" (334). In this assertion lies the secret of the Egremont/Sybil relationship; it will symbolically mirror, at the interpersonal level, what Egremont seeks to achieve on a political level. The conversion of Sybil finally succeeds when, still in St. James's Park, she reads Egremont's recent speech to Parliament, a speech that "dared to express immortal truths," including "his conviction that the rights of labour were as sacred as those of property" (350). This speech, though represented only in summary, completes Sybil's conversion to a new organizing principle: Egremont. Her conversion serves as a microcosm of what would be a national conversion of the People, converted to offering their consent to a new leadership, and thus to a new form of representation.[52]

From this point on, Egremont will be to Sybil "what man should be to woman ever—gentle, and yet a guide" (362). Sybil's subjection to Egremont here has a dual effect: it enables Egremont to assume the role of "representative" (legitimated here through the patriarchal logic of romantic desire), while simultaneously silencing Sybil's own previously articulated political convictions. Sybil's disappearance from the scene of *Sybil,* ironized by her presence in its title, supports Crosby's observation that when Victorian fiction portrays "history as the realization of Man," this gendered representation necessitates that "[w]omen are thus either rendered invisible or seen only as the immanent matrix of historical progress and fulfillment."[53] In the case of *Sybil,* this formula ("gentle, yet a guide") has its parallel in the Disraelian vision of parliamentary representation; the gender politics of the Egremont/Sybil relationship thus functions as the symbolic mode through which Disraeli articulates his desired political relationship between the "new aristocracy" and "the People."[54]

With the "recovery" of the papers that prove the Gerards to be the rightful owners of the Mowbray lands, and the untimely death of Walter Gerard himself (while valiantly defending the People), it is perhaps easy to say that the rights of Sybil, now married to Egremont and the heiress of the Gerard estate, have been fully "restored."[55] However, throughout the novel Sybil pronounced the claims of the dispossessed, and her political position called for the pressing of those claims upon the present social system, in the form of *direct* representation. To Egremont's claim that the "new generation" of aristocrats are the "natural" leaders of the people, Sybil contends (at the end of Book 4) that leaders of the People will be, like her father, "Those whom the People have also chosen; and from a like confidence in their virtues and abilities" (334). Egremont, as we have seen, seeks to convert Sybil from this position of direct representation to a position of *symbolic* representation. The fact that Sybil's "conversion" to Egremont necessitates the muting of her voice and thus the complete revolution of her political convictions suggests that her "restoration" may be only a literal "re-covery," in the sense that the past and its legacy (and Sybil herself) are now represented anew.

Though Sybil's call for direct representation mirrors Disraeli's call in Book 1 chapter 3 for a "true" history, one that would correct the misrepresentations and replace the omissions, Sybil and *Sybil* both opt, ultimately, for what I have been calling a "re-covery" of history, a symbolic re-presentation that simulates a "natural" correspondence between the signifier and the signified—between the present and the past, between the leaders and the people, between men and women. In each pair the latter term is subject to "recovery," to a kind of representation that purports embodiment and offers restoration, but seeks, in reality, only hegemonic consent.[56] This symbolic recovery itself mirrors, as we have seen, an attempt at personal and political recovery on the part of Disraeli himself during the years leading up to the writing of this novel; Disraeli, in fact, asserts in *Sybil*'s penultimate paragraph that for the last fourteen years he has had to combat the "misrepresentation" (497) of his political convictions. Ironically, *Sybil* thus offers the correction of that misrepresentation through the "conversion" of a title character from the very position Disraeli himself felt he occupied (as politically and racially "other" with respect to the established system of representation) to a position of mediation and silence. In the process, history appears "recovered" and its claims "restored"; however, *Sybil*'s narrative instead authorizes a "new" form of representation—one that seeks an entitlement to the present (and future) through the recovery of the past.

6

"With the shuttle and spindle we may redeem our race"

Labor, Redemption, and the Working-Class Body in Disraeli's *Sybil*

DURING THE 1830S AND 1840S, FROM THE passage of the first Reform Bill and the New Poor Law Amendment Act to the rise of the Chartist movement and the Plug Plot riots, the question of the condition of England was inevitably a question of the condition of labor. While that condition, for the working class, might best be described as one of *lack* (the lack of humane working conditions, the lack of political power, the lack of employment itself), the question of how to redress such conditions ultimately rested on some notion of how labor should be represented. By "representation" I mean not only political representation, as in the Chartists' call for the enfranchisement of working-class men, but also textual representation, the kind that is employed in the very process of embodying the "condition" of labor itself, a description inseparable, really, from the ideological underpinnings of the "solution" to that condition.

In writing of this kind of "representation of labor" in Carlyle's *Past and Present*, I chose the term "reinscription" to describe his project because it seemed to capture best the way in which Carlyle sought to rewrite or resituate labor into the very heart of the degraded social body, a reinscription that is intended to resuscitate that nearly asphyxiated body and to enable the (re)production of meaning and value. For Carlyle, the need for this symbolic reinscription is made imperative by a historical shift away from the signified and toward the signifier, away, that is, from the solid ground of truth (even if that truth is only posited and not fully accessible), toward the meaningless abyss of simulation, "where there is no longer, properly speaking, any true or false."[1]

Although there are numerous affinities between Disraeli's project and Carlyle's with regard to the question of labor, the laboring body, and its representation, Disraeli does not share Carlyle's ambivalence regarding the representation of history. As we have seen in the discussion of Disraeli's interpretation of history, he begins with the thesis that the truth has been displaced and misrepresented, and therefore must be recovered if the condition of England is to be repaired. Ultimately, as we have also seen, this project of recovery really entails yet another displacement of that which was lost, a "re-covering" that passes itself off as the restitution of lost rights. How, then, does the representation of labor and the laboring body figure in this ideology of recovery? The answer lies in a particular kind of recovery also predicated on loss and degradation, but one that seeks to redress that loss according to the logic of a moral economy that necessitates the exclusion of self-representation. This "recovery" of labor proceeds, in short, according to a logic of redemption.

To redeem literally means "to buy back"; the process necessitates a kind of exchange, a balancing of accounts. In certain religious discourses (Christianity, for example), the action that initiates the redemption is itself an act of loss, a sacrifice that redeems and thereby elevates that which had been degraded. In this sense the redeemed's participation in the act of redemption remains limited to an acceptance of the terms and conditions of the redeemer. This relation implies, of course, that those who are degraded and in need of redemption are incapable of redeeming themselves, and thus that redemption can be initiated only from without—or more precisely, from *above*. However, in its more general sense of being saved or otherwise rescued from a state of degradation, the term "redemption" does not itself inherently preclude the meaning of being able to "redeem oneself." Indeed, as we shall see, much of the working-class rhetoric in Disraeli's *Sybil* revolves around the very possibility of self-redemption, a possibility that the narrative seeks to negate, substituting instead the redemption of labor from above, a redemption that would (re)solve the question of labor and the laboring class in terms that will necessitate not only the disappearance of working-class politics, but also, ironically, the disappearance of "the People" themselves.

Disraeli's *Sybil* maps the terrain of the political struggle of the working class in the late 1830s and early 1840s in terms of a particular polarity—redemption versus self-destruction—that draws on terms already circulating in the condition-of-England debate, a debate in which the notion of redemption in particular may be found across the full spectrum of political ideologies.[2] Andrew Ure's *The Philosophy of Manufactures* (1835), for example, advocates the use of Christian indoctrination as part of the factory system's "moral machinery."[3] For Ure, the Christian education of factory workers has both a practical and philanthropic motive: practical, because he perceives Christian doctrine as instilling the moral discipline that goes hand-in-hand with factory productivity; philanthropic, because the laborers themselves are in need of such elevation, subject as they are to the depravities of their own degraded condition. As Ure warns:

> Persons not trained up in moral and religious nurture, necessarily become, from the evil bent of human nature, the slaves of prejudice and vice; they can see objects only on one side, that which a sinister selfishness presents to their view; they are readily moved to outrage by crafty demagogues, and they are apt to regard their best benefactor, the enterprising and frugal capitalist who employs them, with a jealous and hostile eye. (407)

As E. P. Thompson has noted, alluding to the passage quoted, "the unredeemed operative was a terrible creature in Ure's sight . . . capable of any atrocity against his masters."[4] To rescue both the capitalists and the laborers, then, from this "evil bent," Ure asserts that "the first and great lesson—one inculcated equally by philosophy and religion" must be taught to the working-class "operatives": namely, "that man must expect his chief happiness, not in the present, but in a future state of existence."[5]

It is this principle that forms the core of Ure's "moral economy" of the factory system, and this principle derives its "moral force," says Ure, from the "transforming power" of the crucifixion (424). Significantly, for Ure this "transforming power" is precisely the power of the cross to command submission: "it excites obedience; it purchases strength for obedience; it makes obedience practicable; it makes it acceptable; it makes it in a manner unavoidable, for it constrains to it; it is, finally, not only the motive to obedience, but the pattern of it" (425). Ure's emphasis on obedience here echoes his earlier description of the worker's relationship to the factory system as a whole. Just as the attainment of redemption "in a future state of existence" might be thought of as a union with the "body" of Christ (ritualized in the present through the sacrament), so too does Ure envision the factory system as an enormous mechanical body, "a vast automaton, composed of various mechanical and intellectual organs, acting in uninterrupted concert for the production of a common object, all of them being subordinated to a self-regulated moving force" (13). This communion with the machine necessitates the "training [of] human beings to renounce their desultory habits of work, and to identify themselves with the unvarying regularity of the complex automaton."[6] As Ure makes clear throughout his argument, the factory worker remains, *by nature*, incapable of self-improvement; in fact, it is only through a paradoxical deferral of redemption itself (to take place only in the future, across the boundaries of both time and "existence") that the factory worker may be "redeemed" in the present, stripped of unfulfilled wants and desires, and "transformed" into a productive and, above all, a *disciplined* member of the factory system.

Ure's thesis—that laborers exist only in a passive relation to their own redemption, as objects to be "transformed" by a higher authority through submission, rather than as subjects capable of redeeming themselves—strongly contrasts with John Francis Bray's *Labour's Wrongs and Labour's Remedy* (1839), in which Bray insists that the laboring classes can improve their condition only by changing "that social whole which keeps them poor."[7] Though Bray's call for social transformation diverges radically from Ure's "transforming power of the cross," he too situates both the urgency and the scope of his proposal in terms of redemption, choosing Luke 21:28 as the epigraph to his introduction: "And when these things begin to come to pass, then look up and lift up your heads; for your redemption draweth nigh."[8] In his opening paragraph, Bray asserts that what will be redeemed are the injustices of the past:

> If it were ever possible to predict what shall be, from a consideration of what has been—if ever the signs of the times gave warning of great troubles or changes—there is that in the present which tells us, in a manner not to be misunderstood, that the hour for the final conflict between Right and Might cannot be far distant. That it is time the event took place, let the wrongs of man for forty centuries testify—that it is time to put an end to the bondage of labour, let the sufferings of the millions of her martyred children bear witness![9]

For Bray, the redemption of labor will come as a fulfillment of what the "signs of the times" portend, as an *end* to the present circumstances of injustice and as a repayment for the past sufferings of the laboring class. In *Sybil*, Disraeli's rhetoric is similar to Bray's; he too asserts, in the end, that "The claims of the Future are represented by the suffering millions," and that "We must prepare for the coming hour" (497). Although the rhetoric imitates the radical urgency of Bray's tone, Disraeli will seek to mediate the relation between the "suffering millions" and "the claims of the future" in a way that brings him much closer to Ure's advocation of the use of "moral machinery" to elevate the masses into more productive, and more docile, members of society. Though he does not subscribe to Ure's "transforming power of the cross," Disraeli will advocate instead a structurally similar but more secular redemption, one that specifically necessitates the abandonment—indeed, the destruction—of working-class bodies and working-class politics, deploying in its stead a homogenizing system of moral obligation that renders self-redemption untenable.

The task that Disraeli sets for himself in *Sybil*, then, remains inherently paradoxical. On the one hand, he must depict the full extent of the physical and moral degradation of the masses in order to establish that they stand in need of elevation. Given the fact that Disraeli has derived (and in more than a few cases actually transcribed) many of the words, actions, and especially the living circumstances of working-class characters from the reports of various commissions and Parliamentary committees, it would seem Disraeli has a stake in making audible and visible, as it were, the condition of everyday life for much of the English laboring class.[10] On the other hand, the political thrust of the novel, as we have seen in the previous chapter with the Sybil/Egremont relationship, seeks the muting of such voices, their "conversion" through representation, through the effacement of working-class politics by a new generation of signifiers.

As a result, although Disraeli intends the plight of the working poor to be "heard" or "aired" in this novel, he also seeks to redress that plight by discrediting much of what we hear. As Patrick Brantlinger comments, "Disraeli is not much interested in making us feel sorry for the poor; he is much more intent on proving the poor to be mistaken."[11] Brantlinger bases his conclusion in part on what he terms "the failure of logic" in Disraeli's representation of the poor, which Brantlinger reads as producing an irreconcilable dichotomy between "the good ones (who are aristocrats anyway in the case of the Gerards), and the riffraff." Thus we have Sybil, the self-proclaimed "daughter of the People," constantly contrasted with (and very often endangered by) the People themselves.[12] What Brantlinger's reading overlooks, though, is precisely the means by which Disraeli links all the heterogeneous working-class elements together, the Gerards included. All the working-class characters, in fact, are in need of redemption, yet none has the power to achieve such "elevation" without assistance. What distinguishes "good" members of the working class from the "riffraff," then, is not their hidden class affiliations, but their willingness to "buy into" a logic of redemption-from-above. Disraeli's novel thus transforms the condition-of-England question into a question of redemption, and seeks to displace the politics of class difference with a system of moral difference, a system grounded in the irreconcilable opposition between redemption and destruction. And the working model for "buying into" such redemption from above is none other than Sybil herself.

Prior to her conversion to Egremont's political position in Book 5, Sybil asserts the utter impassibility of the gulf between the "Two Nations," rejecting Egremont's initial claim that the aristocrats of the "new generation" are the "natural leaders" of the masses, and favoring instead the working-class leadership offered by men "of the People," like her father (334). By advocating the organization of the masses according to a system of direct (male) representation, with its leaders "supported by the sympathy of millions" (334), Sybil's envisioning of political struggle clearly positions the laboring class on the road to self-improvement. Their movement on that road is represented as a force driven by the utter righteousness of both their method and cause. As Sybil tells Egremont, the assembly of Chartist delegates "is a sublime spectacle, these delegates of labour advocating the sacred cause in a manner which might shame your haughty factions. What can resist a demonstration so truly national! What can withstand the supremacy of its moral power!" (334–35).

What resists that power, as Sybil learns, is nothing other than its very absence; her discovery that the Chartist movement is itself beset by the very factionalism she attributes to Parliament unravels her naive faith in the unity of the people in their struggle, and this revelation in particular prepares her to seek that power somewhere other than in the masses themselves—in, of course, Egremont (349–51). What Sybil might be said to lose in this process, then, is the conviction that moral force is identifiable with, indeed inextricable from, the laboring body. As early as Book 3, when Gerard remarks to Sybil that he "could not help fancying that [his] maker had fashioned these limbs rather to hold a lance or draw a bow, than to supervise a shuttle or a spindle" in Trafford's Mill, Sybil replies: "Yet with the shuttle and the spindle we may redeem our race . . . if we could only form the minds that move those peaceful weapons. Oh! my father, I will believe that moral power is irresistible, or where are we to look for hope?" (211).

Setting aside for a moment the contingency on which this redemption rests, Sybil's appeal to "the shuttle and the spindle" here as the means to that redemption clearly functions as a metonym for labor itself. Sybil's position on the redemptive power of labor might be described as Carlylean (even Calvinist) in its assumption that physical labor—the expenditure of bodily energy in the act of working—is inherently *morally* beneficial, to the individual and to society.[13] Sybil reiterates this position (and ties it not to Calvinism but to Catholicism) in her questioning of Baptist Hatton in Book 4, after Hatton invokes the maxim "Qui laborat, orat" (301) as the source of his success:

> "Qui laborat, orat," said Sybil with a smile, "is the privilege of the people."
>
> "Of whom I am one," said Hatton bowing, well recollecting that he was addressing the daughter of a chartist delegate.
>
> "But is your labour, their labour," said Sybil. "Is yours that life of uncomplaining toil wherein there is so much of beauty and of goodness, that by the fine maxim of our Church, it is held to include the force and efficacy of prayer?" (302)[14]

Although Hatton ducks the question with a compliment ("I am sure that I should complain of no toil that would benefit you" [302]), had he a mind to challenge her on this point, he might ask, in reference to "the people": Is "that life of uncomplaining toil wherein there is so much beauty and goodness" really *their* labor? Are these the terms in which the members of the laboring class understand the relation between their bodies and their work?

The contingency Sybil herself attaches to her earlier comment about the redemptive power of the shuttle and spindle reveals that the answer is clearly No. That contingency—"if only we could form the minds that move those peaceful weapons"—suggests that for Sybil the moral power inherent in labor and the laboring classes exists only as an unrealized potential, and that potential remains unrealized precisely because the laborers themselves exist in an un(in)formed state, one in which they do not recognize the redemptive "power" latent in their bodily work.

Sybil elsewhere refers to this condition as "degradation" (220), and from such a condition Sybil is confident the people will one day be delivered. As is evident from her questions directed to Hatton, Sybil closely identifies the "redemption" of her people through "the shuttle and spindle" with the redemption offered by "our Church"—that is, by the Roman Catholic Church. She even offers, shortly after her comment to her father about the redemptive character of labor, a kind of corollary to that potential, as she tells a disguised Egremont that the only thing that "engages" her thoughts in addition to the condition of the masses is her desire "to see the people once more kneel before our blessed Lady" (214). Given her religious convictions, it is not surprising, then, that when faced with the daunting task of "forming the minds" of the degraded laboring class, Sybil turns to a higher redemptive power: "It sometimes seems . . . that nothing short of the descent of the angels can save the people of this kingdom" (215).

What follows reveals this comment to be no idle musing on Sybil's part. Her father responds by alluding to Stephen Morley, a man Gerard credits with the articulation of a more practical (at least by comparison) political project, one that offers remedies:

> "But Stephen Morley does not believe in angels," said Sybil with a sigh; "and I have no faith in his plan."
>
> "He believes that God will help those who help themselves," said Gerard.
>
> "And I believe," said Sybil, "that those only can help themselves whom God helps." (215)

Although Sybil's statement may at first seem to contradict her earlier contention that "with the shuttle and spindle we may redeem our race," the contingency attached to that contention here finds its larger context—offered, ironically, as yet another contingency. This time, though, the contingency produces a paradox; by reversing the temporal relation between self-improvement and God's help, Sybil characterizes self-improvement as absolutely dependent upon an outside agency (the grace of God), a contingency that would seem to undermine the sense in which such improvement is really *self*-improvement. Sybil's position here resembles a similar view of the relation between self-improvement and divine grace found in Wesleyan Methodism, according to which, as E. P. Thompson states, "It would be presumptuous to suppose that man might save *himself* by an act of his own will," but which also acknowledges that in "labour itself . . . undertaken for no ulterior motives but (as Dr. Ure has it) as 'a pure act of virtue' there is an evident sign of grace."[15]

For Sybil, though, the necessity of "God's help" does not contradict her faith in the self-improving "moral power" of labor, at least not yet; indeed, the former appears to function as a condition that *enables* the latter, as the very source from which that power flows. Sybil's mistake lies not in the way she assigns this divine contingency to the possibility of self-improvement, but rather, as she comes to learn, in her assumption that such "moral power" might be directly represented through the Chartist convention of 1839: "She thought that the People, calm and collected, conscious at last of their strength and confident in their holy cause, had but to express their pure and noble convictions by the delegates of their choice, and that an antique and decrepid [*sic*] authority must bow before the irresistible influence of their moral power" (349).

Her error is precisely a problem of representation and embodiment; Sybil assumes the relation between the convention delegates and the People is a direct relation, that "moral power was embodied" in that assembly (353), when in fact that assembly of bodies misrepresents the People—or rather, represents them all too accurately. "The People," Sybil discovers, "was not that pure embodiment of unity of feeling, of interest, and of purpose, which she had pictured in her abstractions" (349), and thus the Chartist delegation actually reproduces that disharmony of interest in its factionalist tendencies, particularly in its split between those in favor of "physical force" and those against.[16] In a sense, we might say that Sybil's recognition of the utter degradation of the People (as evidenced now by their inability to unite on a political front, rather than by their historical dispossession and continuing exploitation), confirms her worst fears, that "nothing short of the descent of angels can save the people of this kingdom." As the "one voice that . . . had dared express immortal truths" (350) concerning the sacred rights of property and labor, Egremont becomes a medium through which such a "descent" is made possible; such a position, in turn, lends credence to his assertion that the members of the "new generation of the aristocracy" are the "natural leaders of the People" (334). Ironically, in the process of becoming conscious of the extent of this degradation of "her" People, Sybil also realizes that she had been wrong to assume that "the People" shared her perspective: "I thought the People all felt as I feel" (353). Instead, she now sees herself as alienated from that very "body" in relation to which she previously defined her identity.

This alienation is represented by a series of events that separate or distance Sybil from those closest to her, especially from her father, and that lay the groundwork for her "conversion" to Egremont's position.[17] In the chapter immediately following the one in which Sybil admits to Egremont that she "was but a dreamer of dreams" (353), she and her father argue heatedly over the proper method for political action. She reminds Gerard that "you and Stephen once taught me . . . to prove to our rulers by an agitation, orderly and intellectual, that we were sensible of our degradation; and that it was neither Christianlike nor prudent, neither good nor wise, to let us remain so" (359). Given her father's turn toward the necessity of physical confrontation, Sybil accuses him of allowing "this great moral power . . . [to] escape from your hands" (359). Knowing that Gerard intends to meet with a small group of Chartist leaders that night, Sybil insists, in an attempt to keep her father close to her (literally and figuratively), "You shall not leave me" (359).

Though their separation is not permanent, Gerard's commitment to political action necessitates his departure, and their resultant physical separation reflects their widening ideological differences. As such, Sybil's subsequent trek through Seven Dials to warn her father of the imminent danger he faces at the hands of the government not only reiterates her increasing alienation from the People,[18] but also represents the extent to which the metaphoric terrain that separates Gerard's political position from Sybil's is nearly "impassable," filled as it is with "scenes of terror," as Sybil will later put it (394). There are really two such scenes, both of which hinge on Sybil's bodily proximity to the decidedly repulsive, threatening, degraded bodies of the underclass. In the first, after Sybil's cab breaks down, she is immediately surrounded by "young thieves . . . a dustman, a woman nearly naked and very drunk, and two unshorn ruffians" (377), who are subsequently dispersed by a policeman. In the second, a stranger who Sybil believes is escorting her to 22 Hunt Street, where her father and his comrades are meeting clandestinely, instead attempts to lead her into a brothel.

"Overwhelmed with shame and terror," Sybil cries out, "O holy Virgin aid me!" (379), and is rescued once again, this time by a sympathetic bystander, identified only as an Irishman. Robert O'Kell calls this latter scene a "paradigmatic encounter," and remarks that Sybil is here "both a victim rescued and an agent of redemption."[19] While this association of Sybil with the promise of redemption may be found as far back as Monypenny ("She stands for the people, for the nation of the poor, for pity of their sufferings, for their hopes of redemption"),[20] describing Sybil as an "agent of redemption" remains misleading, given the extreme limitations of her power in the larger context of the "real world." Sybil also intends, of course, to "rescue" her father from arrest. Arriving exhausted and near collapse, but with the appearance of a "holy messenger" (390), Sybil nonetheless arrives too late, and is herself imprisoned. Her predicament sets the stage for Sybil's first appeal to Egremont as *her* redeemer, as the concluding language of her desperate letter to him makes clear: "You are powerful; you know all; you know what I say is truth. None else will credit it. Save me!" (394).

Egremont, true to form, comes to Sybil's rescue, and his intervention results in an "enrapturing situation" for Sybil, as she finds herself "pressed to the throbbing heart of Egremont" (400). Although the scene clearly invokes sexual desire, as Jennifer Sampson puts it, "The violent image of the woman forcibly held against the throbbing body of a man dissolves with the chaste Sybil's acceptance of the gesture and the assurance of Egremont's 'tenderness' and 'devoted love.' Disraeli emphasizes that Egremont acts as a loving protector, not a man with a bedchamber plot."[21] In other words, the violent sexuality of this "pressing" and "throbbing" is quickly displaced onto a more palatable dichotomy of protection and submission. This is the first of two such scenes with Egremont in the role of savior, and both of them hinge on Sybil's bodily proximity to her manly hero, and thus inversely mirror her Seven Dials encounters with the degraded bodies of the underclass. The second scene occurs at the end of the novel, as Egremont rescues Sybil from an unruly mob outside Mowbray Castle: "One ruffian had grasped the arm of Sybil, another had clenched her garments, when an officer [Egremont] covered with dust and gore, sabre in hand, jumped from the terrace, and hurried to the rescue. He cut down one man, thrust away another, and placing his left arm around Sybil, he defended her with his sword" (491). Having thus dispatched her attackers, Egremont "turned around and pressed Sybil to his heart" (492). As overdrawn and melodramatic as these scenes are, these bodily embraces might be read as symbolic of the "union" of Egremont and Sybil (or at least as prefiguring that union); however, the sense of transcendent selflessness implicit in such a reading misses the power relation embodied in these gestures. In each scene, it is Egremont who appears as the deliverer, and it is he who embraces Sybil, while Sybil merely gives herself up, so to speak, to the "enrapturing" moment.[22] Of particular interest in the second scene is the fact that Egremont is covered with "gore," presumably the bodily remains of those unruly members of the underclass whom he has summarily eviscerated. It is to this body that Sybil is pressed; her "union" with Egremont is thus predicated on, even literally marked by, the bodily destruction of the violent mob of working-class agitators.

In June 1840, Charles Attwood, chairman of the Northern Political Union, wrote to Disraeli informing him of a recent mass meeting described in the *Newcastle Journal*, and added that he desired to correspond with Disraeli "because your Parliamentary course induces me to regard you as one of those whose efforts must & will & essentially contribute to the redemption of your country, in unison with a new party of Conservatives—which *shall* embrace the radical Masses."[23] It is in response to this letter that Disraeli famously replied, "I entirely agree with you that 'an union between the Conservative party and the Radical Masses' offers the only means by which we can preserve the Empire. Their interests are identical; united they form the Nation; and their division has only permitted a miserable minority, under the specious name of the People, to spoil all rights of property and person."[24] This "embrace" or "union" never became, of course, a political reality. And while it is tempting to assert that this embrace does achieve a literary, rather than literal, reality in the conclusion of *Sybil*, to do so would erroneously equate Sybil with the "radical Masses." In fact, as we have seen, before Sybil can be embraced at all, it is precisely her radicality that must be purged.

Although embraced and thus assimilated by Egremont, Sybil's status as a model of political and moral consent to a more powerful, yet "natural" authority remains beset by problems. Of all the characters associated with "the People," Sybil remains (from the very beginning) the most atypical, the one whose life experience bears the least resemblance to the everyday lives of the laboring class as represented elsewhere in the novel. Indeed, by the end of the novel her very status as a "daughter of the People" has come into question, by virtue of both her moral proximity to Egremont and her secret class affiliation. If Sybil at the conclusion of the narrative might be said to have been redeemed, elevated, or restored, the reason is paradoxical; she is, in a sense, the only working-class character—from the outset—who appears, in body and in mind, not to be degraded in any way.

However, it would be a mistake to read Sybil's aristocratic heritage with its attendant attributes (her "noble" nature, her religious conviction, and so on) as the primary aspect of her character that authorizes her redemption. As Gary Handwerk notes, "The historical legitimacy of [Sybil's] reestablishment counts for far less than the fact that she merits the position. Her representative willingness to transcend class boundaries, born of native sympathy and fostered by Egremont's arguments, makes her worthy of aristocratic inheritance."[25] Handwerk here correctly identifies Sybil's willingness as the primary condition for her "elevated" status, and more significantly, reassigns her aristocratic inheritance as a *reward*, rather than a prerequisite, for that elevation. Although I read Sybil's willingness more ironically than Handwerk does (in the sense that the effect of her "willingness" is essentially the displacement of her will as it falls in line—in love—with Egremont), it is indeed this willingness, more than her aristocratic heritage, her Catholicism, her beauty, or her irreproachable moral character, that distinguishes Sybil from the masses themselves, simultaneously (and ironically) disassociating her from those she supposedly "represents."

As we have seen, Sybil's increasing alienation from "the People" is also apparent in her ideological estrangement from her father. Gerard's character is very nearly as unimpeachable as his daughter's; given his aristocratic heritage, his leadership abilities, his unmatched oratory, his integrity, and his selfless dedication to the Chartist cause, Gerard would be a prime candidate for redemption, were it not for his "fatal specific of physical force," as Sybil calls it (210). Sybil uses the word "fatal" here in a doubled sense, representing physical force (to put it another doubled way) as a "dead-end." She deems direct, violent, bodily confrontation unviable because it is ultimately futile (and thus "fatal"), but more importantly, its futility derives from its deadliness, from its inherent and inevitable self-destructive character. It is on this latter basis that Sybil tries to convince her father that moral power and physical force are mutually exclusive, as she perceives him gravitating increasingly toward putting his "fatal specific" into practice.

From Gerard's perspective, however, the moral power/physical force opposition is not mutually exclusive; in fact, they form two successive parts of one whole. For Gerard, the difference between moral power and physical force is analogous to the difference between words and action, and thus, ultimately, to the difference between Stephen Morley's politics and his own. As Gerard says, "Stephen is a scholar; I have no pretensions that way; but I can feel the pulse of a people, and can comprehend the signs of the times, Sybil. Stephen was all very well talking in our cottage and garden at Mowbray, when we had nothing to do; but now we must act, or others will act for us" (358–59).[26] Here then is the practical, materialist conviction of Gerard laid bare, as it were. In touch with "the pulse of the people," Gerard has a priviliged proximity to the social body that allows him to measure that body's level of agitation. Coupled with his ability to read "the signs of the times" (and the People's pulse is surely one of those signs), Gerard is in a much better position than the more theoretically minded Morley to act decisively. Although Gerard's participation in physical force receives its practical expression only after Parliament's rejection of the Charter in 1839 and the subsequent split within the Chartist movement itself (and even then his participation, interrupted by police action, remains limited to drawing up a plan to arm the masses), his commitment to physical force is evident as early as Book 3. Sybil's full comment—"*There is ever* your fatal specific of physical force" (210, emphasis mine)—suggests that Gerard's advocacy of physical struggle has long been a part of his political agenda. Gerard himself confirms this longstanding belief when he tells Sybil in Book 5: "I came here [to London] to do the business that was wanting, and, by the blessing of

God, I will do it. I am no changeling, nor can I refine and split straws, like your philosophers and Morleys; but if the people will struggle, I will struggle with them; and die, if need be, in the front" (359).

It is clear from this statement that Gerard views his participation in violent confrontation as a kind of sacrificial duty consistent with his unwavering political commitment to the People, and also consistent with his firm sense of his own identity. This selflessness of Gerard's, especially with regard to risking his own life, would, under any other circumstances, render his character "redeemable." However, in this latter part of the novel, Gerard's selflessness is constantly contrasted with Sybil's, with the only difference between the two lying in the different ends this selfless activity serves. Gerard *thinks* his participation in violent action serves a just cause, and that his methods are necessitated by historical circumstance, all other political options having been exhausted. Even so, his understanding of the efficacy of mass political struggle, as the novel is at pains to show, does not accurately reflect the "reality" of the nature of the People themselves—a nature that is fundamentally degraded, not just in terms of class, education, and morality, but to such an extent that any articulation of working-class politics *from below* is already compromised by that degradation. In other words, the degraded condition of the People can only produce a degraded, disorderly articulation of the needs and desires of the working (and unworking) class. As Sybil herself warns her father, "The people are not disciplined; their action will not be, cannot be, coherent and uniform; these are riots in which you are involved, not revolutions; and you will be a victim, and not a sacrifice" (357).[27]

Sybil's words are prescient. Her father dies not in a heroic struggle against capitalist tyranny, but in a clash rife with the irony of chance encounter and mistaken perceptions. As he leads a large group of people across Mowbray Moor "for purposes of peace" (488), Gerard's "multitude" is confronted by armed troops headed by Lord Marney, who intends to aid the yeomanry (led by his brother Egremont) already engaged in defending Mowbray Castle. Mistaking Gerard's group for part of the violent mob assaulting the castle, Marney orders his troops to attack. Gerard, his "indignant spirit" aroused, personally dispatches one of Marney's men, and while attempting to rally those around him, "the real friend and champion of the People" is killed (489). Gerard's death reverses the course of the violence. Prior to his demise the People "were in general scared and dispersing," but with Gerard's death, they attack the troops in a "frenzy" (489). Lord Marney himself is singled out and killed by "a shower of stones" that "seemed never to cease" (489). Given the circumstances leading up to these "disastrous events" (489), the deaths of Gerard and Marney (as well as the others) are clearly offered as senseless and needless products of class prejudice, of a rhetoric of fear and loathing that assumes violent confrontation to be inevitable.[28] Both Gerard and Marney are victims, then, of the very prejudice that grounds their belief in the "impassability" of the gulf between the Two Nations, and in this case, that prejudice ironically guarantees the deadly truth about that impassability, a truth to which the corpses of Gerard, Marney, and many others on Mowbray Moor attest.

The necessity of using the words "many others" here to refer to those members of the masses who do not occupy center stage in Disraeli's narrative points to a problem inherent in a novel that purports to have as its subject "the condition of the people."[29] Sybil Gerard, Walter Gerard, and Stephen Morley are the primary characters who perceive themselves (and are perceived by others) as belonging to "the People"; however, each of these three bears a singular relation to the masses, and their lives could not be considered representative of the quotidian.[30] Thus, if the narrative seeks to represent the condition of labor as afflicted with suffering and degradation, Sybil, Gerard, and Morley can support this position only through their rhetoric; their everyday lives do not reflect those conditions.

Of those characters whose lives are, presumably, meant to be representative of "the condition of the people," none plays a major role in any of the novel's various plot lines. The weaver Warner and his family, the women who are subject to the cruelty of the tommy-shop owner Diggs and his son, the colliers who talk of "going to play," the inhabitants of Hell-House Yard—all are offered as examples drawn from the reality of working-class experience, yet each remains marginal and peripheral. Often, we are introduced to certain working-class scenes and characters only because one of the main characters happens to be passing through: Sybil visits the Warners on a mission of mercy and survives "scenes of terror" in Seven Dials, while Morley discourses with the miners, and attends to an injured boy at Diggs's tommy shop, on his way to Wodgate. As Louis Cazamian has remarked, "*Sybil* tells us everything about working-class life that one would expect a highly intelligent and politically well-informed tourist to bring away from a quick survey of the situation."[31]

And indeed, one gets the impression that Disraeli is taking us through these scenes like a tour guide, perhaps the inevitable result of Disraeli's own mediated relation to the everyday lives of the suffering masses. Claiming to rely on "the authority of his own observation," as well as on "the authentic evidence which has been received by Royal Commissions and Parliamentary committees" (*Sybil*, 24), Disraeli depended far more heavily on the latter than the former.[32] Even so, if Disraeli devoted more time to appropriating the descriptions and testimonies of the conditions of the working class from Blue Books than he did to actually investigating those conditions in person, that choice reflects, presumably, his intent to remain relatively remote from the experience of the working class. As a result, his representation of the working class mirrors that remoteness; the descriptions, characters, and events, though drawn from actual interviews and eyewitness accounts, function in the narrative as representative of an utterly alien "other" with respect to Disraeli and his political world, as well as to the bourgeois and aristocratic worlds of his readership. As Sybil and her cabdriver enter the slums of Seven Dials, for example, the narrator tells us that "[t]he houses, the population, the costume, the manners, the language through which they whirled their way, were of a different state and nation to those with which the dwellers in the dainty quarters of this city are acquainted" (376).

This assertion of an essential cultural difference between the classes forms the core of the Two Nations perspective. While such a difference would mean, at least theoretically, that each class perceives its opposite as "other," Disraeli's narrative consistently ascribes the quality of "foreignness" exclusively to the poorest class. Indeed, the very fact that Sybil, a self-proclaimed "daughter of the People," finds herself venturing into Seven Dials as if into a foreign (and therefore threatening) environment, dramatically deepens the sense of "otherness" Disraeli associates with the working class in order to demonstrate conclusively its need for redemption "from above." And nowhere is this otherness more strikingly displayed than in the two chapters in Book 3 concerning the inhabitants of Hell-House Yard.

Hell-House Yard, or Wodgate, we are told, is populated by "swarming thousands, lodged in the most miserable tenements in the most hideous burgh in the ugliest country in the world" (203). What distinguishes Wodgate from other communities in the north of England, apart from its "hideous" appearance, is the utter absence of infrastructure: "There are no landlords, head-lessees, main-masters, or butties in Wodgate. No church there has yet raised its spire. There is no municipality, no magistrate, no local acts, no vestries, no schools of any kind" (203). To borrow Ure's phrase, Wodgate is devoid of "moral machinery," and although the inhabitants are renowned for their workmanship, Wodgate lacks central manufacturing as well; there are no factories. Instead, as the narrator tells us, "Here Labour reigns supreme" (203).

This description of the condition of the Wodgate inhabitants, derived primarily from actual accounts of the town of Willenhall detailed in part 2 of the appendix to the *Second Report of the Children's Employment Commission* (1842), is not intended merely to illustrate their moral depravity, but to demonstrate conclusively their utter helplessness in the face of their degraded social condition.[33] As the narrator asserts: "It is not that the people are immoral, for immorality implies some forethought; or ignorant, for ignorance is relative; but they are animals; unconscious; their minds a blank; and their worst actions only the impulse of a gross or savage instinct" (204). These, then, are the people about whom Stephen Morley reflects "'Ah me . . . and could not they spare one Missionary from Tahiti for their fellow countrymen at Wodgate!'" (208). Morley's thoughts foreground the irony inherent in the "otherness" of Wodgate itself; as an island of remoteness within England, Wodgate is more foreign, seemingly, than the most distant lands imaginable. Were it only perceived as such, Morley muses, the "backwardness" of the people might be attended to in the way colonizing missionaries attend to the lowly ignorance of other "savages."[34]

Morley's thoughts here underscore not only the degradation of the people, but also the utter necessity of an imperial, redemptive force to deliver them from their "animal-like" and "savage" condition.[35]

However, it is not the church (established or otherwise) that the narrative turns to in an attempt to address the redemption of people such as those who reside at Wodgate; instead, the second Wodgate chapter, in which Morley witnesses the brutality of Bishop Hatton's workshop, contrasts with the following chapter, in which Trafford's factory is offered as a model of a "kinder and gentler" organization of labor. Here, labor does not "reign supreme," but its needs are provided for and its members are consequently "elevated."

Mr. Trafford, we are told, "imbibed, at an early period of his career, a correct conception of the relations which should subsist between the employer and the employed. He felt that between them there should be ties other than the payment and receipt of wages" (224). This description echoes, of course, Carlyle's indictment of "cash-payment" as the "nexus" of social relations in industrial society, and the character of Trafford has been interpreted, subsequently, as representative of Carlyle's "captain of industry."[36] Although the basis for this interpretation is usually limited to this echo of Carlyle, a further connection is evident in the organization of Trafford's factory. Ivan Melada has argued that the physical structure of the building itself—essentially a very large, open, well-ventilated room—addresses criticisms leveled at factory architecture by Cobbett, Engels, and others,[37] but the infrastructure of the workplace directly mirrors Carlyle's ideal organization of labor. The narrator tells us that "the moral advantages resulting from superior inspection and general observation are not less important" than the physical structure of the building, and these moral advantages are based on the following specific organization: "the child works under the eye of the parent, the parent under that of the superior workman; the inspector or employer at a glance can behold all" (225).[38] As we have seen, the structure of this hierarchy is based on what Carlyle refers to in *Past and Present* as the "Great Taskmaster's eye," a centralized authority that orders the surrounding chaos by virtue of its "all-penetrating" gaze.[39]

As we have also seen, for Carlyle, the "captains of industry" are best-equipped to carry out this divine-like task of organizing labor because they "stand practically in the middle of it" (*PP*, 267). Trafford, however, deploys this logic of the Taskmaster's Eye not only in the organization of his factory, but also in the geography of the village that houses his workers: "In the midst of this village, surrounded by beautiful gardens . . . was the house of Trafford himself, who comprehended his position too well to withdraw himself with vulgar exclusiveness from his real dependents" (226). The centrality of Trafford's residence reproduces geographically the hierarchical organization of the factory itself; the force of Foucauldian "discipline," as it were, is thus exerted, deliberately, across the boundary between work and domesticity.

The primary goal of this method of structuring both the work and leisure life of the laboring class through a hierarchy that simulates "closeness" is the improvement of their moral character. As the narrator explains, "Proximity to the employer brings cleanliness and order, because it brings observation and encouragement" (226). Trafford reiterates this goal in his conversation with Lord de Mowbray, describing his desire "to improve the condition of my work people," and "to elevate their character," as one of his "hobbies" (230). We are not, presumably, supposed to read Trafford's remark as that of a condescending paternalist. After all, Trafford is an industrialist, and need not exert energy for the benefit of the people; he does so only out of an innate sense of moral duty.[40] Indeed, when Egremont claims, after visiting Trafford's factory and village, "If all men acted like Mr. Trafford, the condition of the people would be changed," Morley replies, "But all men will not act like Mr. Trafford. . . . It requires a sacrifice of self which cannot be expected, which is unnatural" (237). Trafford himself, though, earlier revealed this sacrifice to be not so much "unnatural" as eminently practical. When Lord de Mowbray expresses concern that Trafford's effort to improve the condition of his workers must come at a great financial expense, Trafford replies: "I should find an ample reward in the moral tone and material happiness of this community; but really viewing it in a pecuniary point of view, the investment of capital has been one of the most profitable I ever made" (230).

Trafford's investment is thus doubly profitable; his workers profit through their elevation, and Trafford profits financially. And this profitability, on both fronts, distinguishes Trafford's factory and village from the town of Wodgate. While the people of Wodgate work ably, and produce commodities of unparalleled quality, their perpetual state of degradation attests to the fact that labor itself is not enough to redeem the masses. Their elevation depends on Ure's moral machinery, and that moral machinery, whether of the cross or the model employer, is itself dependent on a scrutinizing central authority whose seemingly sacrifical expenditure "raises up" those who subject themselves to its logic. Those who refuse this logic, such as the mobilized and radicalized inhabitants of Wodgate known as the Hell-cats, condemn themselves to their own destruction.

As we have seen, the narrative has established the town of Wodgate as utterly devoid of capitalist relations of production; there is no Shuffle and Screw here, no butties, doggies or tommy shops, no factories or mines of any kind. Given the absence of the usual infrastructure, then, the fact that Wodgate proves to be the most easily radicalized of populations in the north, willing to lead a massive general strike in the name of the People's Charter, seems unlikely at best. To be sure, part of the answer lies in the economy; economic suffering increases significantly over the course of the novel—in Mowbray, in the mining communities nearby, and even in Wodgate itself, where the population was "suffering and half-starving" (442). Beyond this similarity among members of the working-class population, however, there lies an important difference with respect to Wodgate, one we have already mentioned: its extreme otherness. As Parama Roy has noted, Wodgate "assumes the role of the antagonistic *Other* to the governing class, and upon it is projected all the aristocratic horrors of 'mob rule' and social destabilization."[41] This perception of Wodgate as "other," however, is not limited to the landed gentry; the miners who live between Mowbray and Wodgate also perceive the people of Hell-house Yard as significantly different from themselves. They tell Morley, for example, that the people of Wodgate are "a very queer lot even in sunshine" and liken their town to a "divils carnal" (184). This alien otherness, as we have noted, functions as a sign of the extreme depth of Wodgate's degradation, and thus of the degree to which the town's inhabitants stand in need of elevation. Although Morley's comment at the end of the first Wodgate chapter makes this circumstance clear, Wodgate remains in Book 3 a reality *separate* from the rest of England, rich or poor. Wodgate's geographic separation underscores this otherness, and even those who live relatively close, like the miners, express strong reservations about going there, especially at night.

What, then, motivates the isolated, separate, heterogeneous reality of Wodgate to mobilize and direct its energy outward, as a destructive force? The narrator claims that "this had been brought about, as most of the great events of history, by the unexpected and unobserved influence of individual character" (442). The reference here is to the Chartist agitator Field, the "pale young man" who conspired with Gerard at the secret meeting of the Chartist leadership in Seven Dials, and who has now persuaded the "natural leader" of Wodgate, Bishop Hatton, to take up the Chartist banner and force the cessation of labor everywhere "until the Charter was the law of the land" (444). Field's role is clearly that of a catalyst; his agency transforms potential energy into violent force. With suffering throughout the country, the narrator tells us, "All that was required was the first move, and the Chartist emissary had long fixed upon Wodgate as the spring of the explosion" (443).[42]

Already reduced to an animal-like, "unconscious" state, their behavior governed by "the impulse of a gross or savage instinct" (204), the denizens of Wodgate are more predisposed to radical action than the rest of the population because their everyday lives already embody an absolute unwillingness to be governed by the logic that determines social relations elsewhere.[43] Thus, as they transform themselves from the isolated inhabitants of Hell-house Yard to the aggressive, politicized "Hell-cats," their significance as "other" shifts from that of a relatively self-contained society to that of a subversive force that threatens the entire terrain. And that threat exerts itself, interestingly, not only as a force for violent destruction, but also as a force for ideological conversion, as a kind of parody of the hegemonic consent solicited by Egremont.[44] Above all, the Hell-cats represent the absolute denial of capitalist productive relations, and the absolute refusal of consent to symbolic representation, to the ordering logic of redemption.

Using "absolute" here may be problematic, given the ostensible goal of the Hell-cats' activity—the adoption of the People's Charter—which would, of course, legitimate the political representation of the working class, and thus terminate the mass strike. However, Disraeli's text makes clear that Chartism means little if anything to Bishop Hatton, who "embraced the Charter, without having a definite idea what it meant" (443), or to the Hell-cats in general, whose destructive tendencies exceed the limits of Chartist ideology, and thus also call into question the Hell-cats' commitment to any sort of "end," in both senses of that word, to their activity.

Still, the Hell-cats do pay lip service, at least, to a long-range objective, namely their own redemption, and they have devised their own means to that redemption—by severing all work relations with the rest of society, through the mass *cessation* of labor:

> Every trade of every kind and description was to be stopped: tailor and cobbler, brushmaker and sweep, tinker and carter, mason and builder, all, all; for all an enormous Sabbath that was to compensate for any incidental suffering that it induced by the increased means and the elevated condition it ultimately would insure—that paradise of artizans [*sic*], that Utopia of Toil, embalmed in those ringing words, sounds cheerful to the Saxon race—'A fair days wage for a fair day's work.' (444)

Here, the general work stoppage is situated within a redemptive economy that reverses the logic of the one advocated elsewhere in the novel by Egremont and Sybil. Instead of a sacrifice from above initiating the redemption (the new generation of aristocracy expending their political energy in the direction of "saving" the masses, or the Trafford-like captains of industry expending their financial capital in the same direction), here that sacrifice comes *from below,* in the form of a strategic withdrawal from productive activity (and thus from the very means to survival) in exchange for a future, "elevated" state of existence. As the finer points of this passage suggest, those who subscribe to this particular redemptive economy represent whatever suffering ensues as merely "incidental." Suffering, in fact, appears to be rather subtly deemphasized, with the general strike termed "an enormous Sabbath" or a "national holiday" (423), both of which foreground, by implication, the association of the general work stoppage with *rest*, and even with a kind of solemn festivity. This foregrounding of rest and leisure, rather than sacrifice and suffering, is ironically reiterated in Disraeli's use of the infinitive "to play" to denote "to strike." In an author's footnote at the beginning of Book 3, Disraeli informs his readers that "[w]hen miners and colliers strike they term it, 'going to play'" (181). As Martin Fido notes, Disraeli discovered the use of this phrase in *The First Report from the Midland Mining Commissioners, South Staffordshire* (1843); however, as Fido also notes, Disraeli "defines 'play' as striking, although he had read it used to mean suffering victimization through a refusal of employment."[45] Though Fido attributes this discrepancy (and others) to confusion or misunderstanding on Disraeli's part, the use of the phrase "going to play" (and its assorted variations) among working-class characters in *Sybil* transforms the word from its normally passive sense (to be played by an employer) to an active one; in other words, the miners and colliers now "go to play" themselves, rather than suffer the indignity of "being played." As the working-class characters, especially the Hell-cats, "go to play," then, they become the very embodiment of the irrational other, "playing" completely outside the boundaries of *Sybil*'s redemptive economy. Although the Hell-cats purport, in theory, to be willing to exchange the cessation of labor for the legislative adoption of the People's Charter, in practice, their methods exceed that proposal, as their anarchic, destructive force targets anything in its immediate path, including ordinary homes (446).

In an effort to highlight this wanton destructiveness, Disraeli contrasts the Hell-cats' methods with those employed by a group of two thousand Lancashire workers. At a time when the strike "began to be severely felt," this group of two thousand sufferers entreated a local aristocrat for food, which they received in return for their promise "to maintain order and conduct themselves with decorum" (445). Afterward, the two thousand then requested permission to walk through the estate's gardens:

> The permission was granted: the multitude in order, each file under a chief and each commander of the files obedient to a

> superior officer, then made a progress through the beautiful gardens of their beautiful hostess. They even passed through the forcing houses and vineries. Not a border was trampled on, not a grape plucked; and when they quitted the domain, they gave three cheers for the fair castellan. (446)

This "self-organised discipline" on the part of the Lancashire strikers precisely imitates, of course, the organization of labor within Trafford's factory. Each functions according to an internally homogenizing, centralized hierarchy that places each person under scrutiny, with the desired orderly effect contingent on obedience to that hierarchy. Moreover, the specific exchange enacted here between the strikers and the aristocrat (food for obedience) functions in the narrative as a miniature allegory of the larger, "proper" social relations the novel endorses. In return for their respect of the "borders" of propriety and property (represented literally by the workers' self-organised method of keeping their bodies "in line"), the masses will be supplied with the means to their survival.

The respect for "borders" that such a "self-organised discipline" invokes also implies, clearly, that the "trampling" of such borders constitutes a transgression not just of the boundaries of property and class, but of the very boundaries between rationality and irrationality, between homogeneity and heterogeneity—the very boundaries, in short, that structure the social order. The Hell-cats, all bodily excess, "cheering and laughing amid flames and rapine" (446), are the literary embodiment of this transgression, truly a "divils carnal," as one of the colliers puts it. Indeed, during the Hell-cat-led attack on Diggs's tommy shop, "Men, women and children were alike at work with the eagerness and energy of fiends" (450) as they burn down the shop, consuming Master Joseph inside, at whose fate "the mob gave an infernal cheer" (450). This metaphorical association of the Hell-cats with evil signifies the extremity of their transgressive status as *beyond* redemption—outside of, even excluded from, the redemptive logic to which the narrative insists labor must subscribe, if that logic is to "work."

This is not to say, however, that the Hell-cats ultimately represent a substantial threat to that redemptive order; although the sacking of

Mowbray castle is serious enough to merit the intervention of regional troops, the demise of the Hell-cats itself suggests that their excessive, physical, destructive activity, though directed at "the enemies of the people," leads only to their *own* obliteration. Because the Hell-cats embody transgression from *below*—from the most degraded, hellish, unconscious state—it is not surprising that the scene of the Hell-cats' destruction takes place in the cellars of Mowbray castle, where the Bishop and his cohorts lay in a drunken stupor, while the rest of the mob continue "their debauch" in the upper rooms of the castle "by the destruction of everything around them" (486). In the lower rooms, "from heedlessness or insane intention," the Hell-cats allow the castle to catch fire, and it begins to burn from the bottom up. While the motivation is left undetermined, the agency of this destruction could not be made clearer: "the funeral pile of the children of Woden," we are told, "was prepared and lighted by themselves" (491). The ultimate "end" of the Hell-cats proves to be a self-destructive one, as they are literally consumed by their own excessiveness.

The Hell-cats' demise thus differs somewhat in its significance from the deaths of Gerard and Morley, who also meet their ends at the conclusion of the novel. While Gerard's and Morley's deaths prepare the way for the resolution of the Sybil/Egremont plot line (Gerard's death eliminates his claim to the Mowbray estate, and Morley's death disposes of his threat to Sybil and Egremont), the Hell-cats' self-immolation represents the inherently self-destructive character of *any* effort to purchase redemption transgressively. In this way, the logic of a redemptive, moral economy, based as it is on the respect for boundaries of class, property, rationality, and homogeneity, is shown to be unassailable; the integrity of its borders is guaranteed by the fate that awaits those who dare transgress them. In *Sybil*, therefore, as far as the "lower" orders are concerned, any pursuit of self-representation, by definition, falls outside of the "legitimate" redemptive economy and will result, ironically, in self-destruction.

In his chapter on the industrial novel in *Culture and Society*, Raymond Williams asserts that, apart from their shared critique of industrialism and a generally sympathetic attitude toward the plight of the suffering masses, works like *Alton Locke*, *Mary Barton*, and *Felix Holt* exhibit a strong fear of working-class social action, especially violent action, coupled with a fear that the sympathizing observer may be consumed by such violence:

> [T]he basic pattern is a dramatization of the fear of being involved in violence: a dramatization made possible by the saving clause of innocence and mistaken motive, and so capable of redemption. What is really interesting is that the conclusion of this kind of dramatization is then taken as proof of the rightness of the author's original reservations. The people are indeed dangerous, in their constant tendency to blind disorder. Anyone sympathizing with them is likely to become involved. Therefore (a most ratifying word), it can be sincerely held that the popular movements actually under way are foolish and inadequate, and that the only wise course is dissociation from them.[46]

Williams is thinking here of "dramatizations" that include "redeemable" characters like Alton Locke and Felix Holt, both mistakenly accused of leading riots and subsequently imprisoned, and Jem Wilson, wrongly accused of the murder committed by John Barton. *Sybil,* though, contains no such "innocent" working-class characters among its major players. Though the novel intends to investigate the "condition of the People" by directly embodying their subjectivity, in the end the narrative calls for the cessation of their voices and the destruction of their bodies. In fact, few of the working-class characters manage even to survive the plot; those directly involved in violent action—Gerard, Morley, Bishop Hatton, and the Hell-cats—are all killed.[47] As Daniel Bivona observes, the violent conclusion of the novel "precipitates . . . a new symbolic 'sorting out' of . . . barbarian from civilized, the truly alien from those who only temporarily appear so, 'Bishop' Hatton from Dandy Mick."[48] Indeed, such a symbolic "sorting out" is signified by a kind of literal redemption in the case of minor characters like Dandy Mick Radley and Devilsdust. Though complicit with the violence at Mowbray Castle (especially Devilsdust, who fought the yeomanry and was wounded), each sheds his class affiliation thanks to Egremont, who repays Radley's efforts "in the service of Sybil" by "establish[ing] him in business" (495).[49] Mick then takes Devilsdust on as a partner, and "having thus obtained a position in society and become a capitalist," Devilsdust erases his name, adopting a more appropriately "decorous appellation"—Mowbray (495).[50]

Unlike most of the industrial novels published in the mid-nineteenth century, then, the end of *Sybil* thus also means the "end" of the working class.[51] The narrative conjures "the People" through literary representation in an effort to attest to their *real* conditions, to body forth their subjectivity, and to emplot a trajectory for their (fictional) redemption. But while Cobbett's historiography and social criticism focus on the material reformation of the working-class body, and Carlyle's social criticism seeks to scrutinize and discipline those bodies, in Disraeli's narrative, those working-class elements represented as exceeding the boundaries of his homogenizing trajectory are summarily eradicated, condemned to the realm of the unredeemable. And those who manage to survive and earn "redemption" do so only by casting off their working-class affiliation and jettisoning their political convictions. For the rest of the working class—the masses—the final chapter proves unable to represent the "end" of the redemptive process; its melodramatic resolution of the romantic plot line, coupled with its facile appeal to the magic of economic recovery, leaves the promise of redemption unfulfilled. As Parama Roy has noted, "the People conveniently melt away once [Sybil's] inheritance issue is resolved."[52] *Sybil* thus ends without "the People"; their fictional redemption is deferred and displaced—exchanged for a future improved state. Though purporting to address, in part, the fact that "the Multitude" has been "blotted out of the history of England" because "the privileges of the People have disappeared" (497), the narrative itself is thus forced, ironically, to reproduce this disappearance of the People as well.

It would be relatively easy, given this "conclusion," to claim that the novel fails in its "end." Disraeli, after all, offers no specific plan for the utilization of the redemptive power assigned to the younger generation of aristocrats, providing, it seems, only melodramatic symbolic gestures. As Catherine Gallagher has argued, Disraeli finds himself in a peculiar bind in *Sybil,* having created a "political novel in which politics is always in the process of dissolving into a representation of something else—the social (ironically) or the sacred (symbolically)—and itself goes unrepresented."[53] Yet the "end" of *Sybil* (its final chapter in particular) *does*, perhaps, convey Disraeli's vision of an England governed by a new generation, precisely because it depicts an England in which politics itself *appears to disappear.* If the "end" of *Sybil* fails to represent, fully, the politics of redemption, then this failure may well be a product of the novel's overriding interest in the redemption of politics, in the erasure of political representation and the rise of a new moral representation that simulates the recovery of the past and the redemption of the present, a simulation to be governed by a new generation of signifiers.

Conclusion

"But what are we to do?"

"BUT WHAT ARE WE TO DO?" EXCLAIMS the practical man, impatiently on every side: "Descend from speculation and the safe pulpit, down into the rough market-place, and say what can be done!"—O practical man, there seem very many things which practice and true manlike effort, in Parliament and out of it, might actually avail to do. But the first of all things, as already said, is to gird thyself up for actual doing; to know that thou actually either must do, or, as the Irish say, 'come out of that!'[1]

Thus begins the last section of Carlyle's essay *Chartism* (1839). Though, ironically, the essay itself ends with a rather weak gesture toward just such a "practical" solution, the passage above asserts accurately the essay's primary function—to establish the urgency of addressing the "Condition-of-England question" as a crisis with social, political, and historical implications.[2] As Carlyle describes it in his opening paragraph, the condition of England appears to him "to be the most ominous of all practical matters whatever; a matter in regard to which if something be not done, something will *do* itself one day, and in a fashion that will please nobody."[3]

It is in response to precisely this sense of crisis that Cobbett, Carlyle, and Disraeli all seek to account for the condition of England historically, in an attempt "to gird themselves (and others) up for the actual doing." In this respect, we have seen how each writer views the present times in the context of a historical shift away from a world order dependent on fixed referents and stable meanings, toward a destabilized world marked by Carlylean "indirectness" and the erosion of guaranteed referentiality. In addition, each writer tracks the effects on the forms and functions of labor and the laboring body within that historical shift, offering both a descriptive account of the conditions of contemporary labor and a means (practical or not) for the amelioration of that condition.

In this way, the efforts of Cobbett, Carlyle, and Disraeli might be described as endeavoring to resituate the condition of England as an object of labor, as something that can be directly addressed and reformed, rather than as a "condition" or "symptom" that itself affects the practice of labor, and ultimately threatens England's social stability. To put it another way, each of these three authors shares the implicit assumption that the "condition" of England is best understood and measured in relation to the condition of England's workers. If the material conditions of rural and urban laborers are, on the whole, degraded (or worse, if able-bodied men and women are denied the very opportunity to engage in "a fair day's work"), the origin of that degradation lies in a historical shift toward a capitalist mode of production within which the condition of labor (and thus the condition of England itself) figures as a mere by-product of the productive process. Such a marginal side-effect may be regrettable on an individual level, but it remains ultimately acceptable on the social level, as the inevitable "price" of economic progress.

In turning the condition of England into an object of labor rather than a symptom of the productive process, Cobbett, Carlyle, and Disraeli seek, in a sense, to "restore" the relation between honest work and material comfort, between the physical energy expended in labor, and the equitable "return" on that expenditure. That this project might be charged with nostalgia for an idealized, even imaginary, vision of a past social structure is hardly surprising, and to a certain extent justified. Such a charge, however, deemphasizes the degree to which this project fixes its attention on the analysis of present circumstances, an analysis that seeks to discern and reform that perplexing present. The shared strategy of these writers, in fact, is to assert that the condition of England is a product of a specific historical situation—the rise of industrial capitalism—and that this condition is having not only a palpable effect on the material lives and bodies of England's working and unworking poor, but a cultural effect on the significance and meaningfulness of work itself. Their analysis is offered not as a mere resistance to change (though it does express regret at the direction in which Cobbett's "Thing" has been moving), but as an active force *for* change—an attempt, through writing, to influence and shape the course of English social history.

In this respect, Carlyle's gesture toward a "practical" solution at the end of his essay *Chartism* is rather ironical, given the extent to which the essay as a whole obviously exists in the world to exert some amount of force, no matter how imperceptible, toward "real" change in the "condition" of everyday life. That Carlyle would acknowledge the pressure to *do* something beyond "mere" social critique, to present (or at least advocate) a plan or strategy for palpable reform, suggests that he felt keenly the potential separation between the practice of writing and the practical world of living—the relation, in short, between textual representation and lived experience. Both Cobbett and Disraeli, like Carlyle, were self-conscious in regard to this relation, foregrounding the engagement of their texts with the material conditions of everyday life, and regarding their own works as attempting to represent and redress those conditions.

In taking up the material world in this way, of course, all three writers foreground the textuality of the condition of England itself, as each reads and writes the "signs of the times." And taking as its subject the condition of England, their own labor—their writing—struggles within and against "the times" in an attempt to analyze and shape the very context within which those writings appear. Thus, that labor, like Michel de Certeau's historiographic enterprise, remains inherently paradoxical, desiring at once a clear articulation of the relation between signifier and signified, between past and present, between the textual and the material, but also recognizing that such borders are always provisional and negotiable, capable of being reimagined and redrawn. Indeed, as I hope to have shown, their own texts engage the discourse of the condition-of-England question in an attempt to negotiate, rearticulate and re-form those very borders in order to conserve the possibility of social meaning, which they believed was in danger of disappearing.

Notes

Introduction

1. Thomas Carlyle, "Signs of the Times," in *The Works of Thomas Carlyle in Thirty Volumes* (1899; reprint, New York: AMS, 1969), 27:59.

2. Raymond Williams, *Culture and Society, 1780–1950* (New York: Columbia University Press, 1983), 71–72.

3. For a nuanced reading of the way "Signs of the Times" seeks to redress this shift by striking a balance of sorts between the physical and the spiritual, the material and the metaphoric, see Ralph Jessop, *Carlyle and Scottish Thought* (New York: St. Martin's Press, 1997), 150–54.

4. In fact, in "Signs of the Times" Carlyle considers the outer, material conditions of the people of England to be improving: "how much better fed, clothed, lodged and, in all outward respects, accommodated men now are, or might be, by a given quantity of labour, is a grateful reflection which forces itself on every one" (60). Even in 1829, however, Carlyle's assessment of the effect of this relative prosperity was not an unqualified one. Although "wealth has more and more increased," writes Carlyle, that wealth has "at the same time gathered itself more and more into masses . . . increasing the distance between the rich and the poor" (60)

5. While his diagnosis that the times are "sick and out of joint" remains viable from "Signs of the Times" (1829) through *Latter-Day Pamphlets* (1850), Carlyle's prognosis for those times actually worsens.

6. Williams, *Culture and Society*, 75.

7. Thomas Carlyle, *Past and Present*, edited by Richard Altick (Boston: Houghton Mifflin, 1965), 146.

8. This has been more often the case in the study of Cobbett and Disraeli than it has for Carlyle, whose complex understanding of history has generated thoughtful commentary from a variety of critics, especially in the last twenty-five years.

9. George Levine, "Victorian Studies," in *Redrawing the Boundaries: The Transformation of English and American Literary Studies*, ed. Stephen Greenblatt and Giles Gunn (New York: MLA, 1992), 150.

10. Gareth Stedman Jones's essay "Rethinking Chartism" (in *Languages of Class: Studies in English Working Class History, 1832–1982* [New York: Cambridge University Press, 1983], 90–178), for example, situates Chartism firmly within the tradition of radical discourse dating back to the last quarter of the eighteenth century, and accounts for Chartism's rise and fall as a function of the efficacy of that discourse, its ability to persuade people across class boundaries of the credibility and relevance of the Chartist political platform. Gallagher's influential study examines the impact of the condition-of-England discourse on the formal structures of industrial fiction published between the two Reform Bills, with an emphasis on the resulting formal paradoxes and contradictions within the industrial novel, which led, Gallagher argues, to the formation of a "politics of culture" and the emergence of new literary realism in the latter part of the nineteenth century (see Catherine Gallagher, *The Industrial Reformation of English Fiction: Social Discourse and Narrative Form, 1832–1867* [Chicago: University of Chicago Press, 1985]). Poovey's book, while certainly acknowledging the multiplicity of competing discourses from 1830 to 1864, focuses on the building of an overarching, homogenizing discourse that sought to regulate and merge various heterogeneous elements into one unified "social body" (see Mary Poovey, *Making a Social Body: British Cultural Formation, 1830–1864* [Chicago: University of Chicago Press, 1995], 1–24). Gilmartin's study of the radical press during the first half of the nineteenth century is an impressively detailed, materialist account of the way various radical writers and publishers articulated the cause of reform by generating a "counter public sphere," within which their discourses circulated in a wide variety of print media (see Kevin Gilmartin, *Print Politics: The Press and Radical Opposition in Early Nineteenth-Century England* [New York: Cambridge University Press, 1997]).

11. Joan Scott, in her critique of both Stedman Jones's "Rethinking Chartism" and E. P. Thompson's *The Making of the English Working Class*, argues that class and gender are mutually constructed. Indeed, Scott contends that "[g]ender becomes so implicated in concepts of class that there is no way to analyze one without the other" (Joan Wallach Scott, *Gender and the Politics of History*, rev. ed. [New York: Columbia University Press, 1999], 60). Scott's work is an important source of influence and inspiration for Crosby's volume, which articulates how the Victorian fascination with history is interwoven with the Victorian obsession with the "Woman Question," that is, woman as "other," as that which lies outside history (Christina Crosby, *The Ends of History: Victorians and "the Woman Question"* [New York: Routledge, 1991], 1–11). As Linda Shires states, the essays collected in *Rewriting the Victorians* are specifically "concerned with analyzing the power relations between men and women in the Victorian period" (Linda M. Shires, ed., *Rewriting the Victorians: Theory, History, and the Politics of Gender* [New York: Routledge, 1992], x). Drawing on feminist, Marxist, and post-structuralist theories, among others, the essays range across a wide variety of texts, examining, for example, articles in the *Edinburgh Review*, George Eliot's *The Mill on the Floss*, Charles Eastlake's *Hints on Household Taste*, and Elizabeth Gaskell's *My Lady Ludlow*.

12. As Stedman Jones has noted, this "foregrounding of representation" (in the

sense of political representation) was especially true of radical discourse, in which "the dividing line between classes was not that between employer and employed, but between the represented and the unrepresented" (106). As early as 1818, for example, the radical writer and publisher T. J. Wooler published an "Address to the Unrepresented Part of the Community," arguing in part that the marginalized, disenfranchized portion of the populace signified nothing in the context of electoral politics. (See Gilmartin, *Print Politics*, 22–24.)

13. A certain kind of singularity is detectable in Gallagher's book as well, where the discussion of *Sybil* (as Gallagher herself acknowledges) disrupts the narrative chronology of her argument. While parts 1 and 2 of *The Industrial Reformation of English Fiction* trace the progression of industrial narratives from their primary concern with the tension between free will and determinism in the 1830s and 1840s to their subsequent focus in the 1850s on the relationship between the public and private spheres, part 3 discusses those works that emphasize the connection between political and literary representation: *Sybil* and *Felix Holt*. Articulating (convincingly) the key affinities and differences between the way these two novels grapple with the issue of political representation, Gallagher demonstrates that *Sybil* (1845) has more in common with *Felix Holt* (1866), published twenty-one years later, than with *Alton Locke* (1850), *Mary Barton* (1848), or *Hard Times* (1854).

14. Shires, 188.

15. Michel de Certeau, *The Writing of History*, translated by Tom Conley (New York: Columbia University Press, 1988), 5.

16. Jean Baudrillard, *Simulations*, translated by Philip Beitchman, Paul Foss, and Paul Patton (New York: Semiotext[e], 1983), 4.

17. Shires, 185.

Chapter 1

1. William Cobbett, *A History of the Protestant "Reformation," in England and Ireland; Showing how that event has impoverished and degraded the main body of the People in those Countries. In a series of letters, addressed to all sensible and just Englishmen* (London: Charles Clement, 1824–26), XII:369. All references are to the first edition, which contains no pagination; citations will be given as above, with letter number in Roman numerals, followed by paragraph number. Citations may be easily cross-referenced with the more readily available Gasquet edition (William Cobbett, *A History of the Protestant Reformation in England and Ireland*, revised and edited by Francis Cardinal Gasquet [Rockford, Ill: Tan Books, 1988]); letter numbers are equivalent to chapter numbers, and paragraph numbers remain the same, at least up to paragraph 284. In the first edition of Cobbett's *A History*, due to printer error, there are *two* paragraphs numbered 284; Gasquet has corrected this error, so the paragraphs after the first 284 in the initial printing appear in the Gasquet edition with the assigned number one digit higher (e.g., first edition paragraph 297 = Gasquet 298 and so on). I have avoided the Gasquet

edition here, though, primarily because of his intrusive changes to Cobbett's original emphases, as well as his outright omissions and "revisions" of portions of the text.

2. Cobbett is not the only historian to criticize the monument's inscription. David Hume, in his *History of England* (a text Cobbett sets his own *History* over and against), agrees that "[n]o proof . . . or even presumption, after the strictest inquiry by a committee of Parliament, ever appeared to authorize such a calumny" (*The History of England from the Invasion of Julius Caesar to the Abdication of James the Second, 1688* [Philadelphia: Porter and Coates, n.d.], 5:108). Although acknowledging that the city authorities designed the inscription "in order to give countenance to the popular prejudice," Hume, unlike Cobbett, ultimately lays much of the blame on the people themselves: "So credulous, as well as obstinate, are the people in believing everything which flatters their prevailing passion!" (5:108). The monument itself, designed by Christopher Wren, did not originally carry the inscription attributing the fire to a Catholic conspiracy; that statement was added later, in 1681, during a reprise of anti-Catholic activity (Walter George Bell, *The Great Fire of London in 1666* [London: The Bodley Head, 1951], 208–9).

3. As Gasquet notes, the inscription was eventually erased again, and for the last time, in 1830 (*A History of the Protestant Reformation*, Gasquet edition, 308 n. 12). See also Bell, 209.

4. On this point, Disraeli's view of history is entirely in agreement with Cobbett's; they also share, as a consequence, a desire to recover marginalized players and suppressed facts. In discussing the occasion of Parliament's petition to Queen Mary and King Philip (in November 1554) proffering "*sincere repentance for their past transgressions*" (VIII:228) and seeking the sovereigns' intercession with the Pope "for their [Parliament's] forgiveness, and for their re-admission into the fold of Christ" (VIII:230), Cobbett remarks: "Are the people of England aware of this? No: not one man out of fifty thousand" (VIII:228). As we will see in Chapter Five, Disraeli expresses a similar astonishment at the absence of John Wildman from the pages of English history: "Not one man in a thousand . . . has ever heard of Major Wildman" (Benjamin Disraeli, *Sybil; or, The Two Nations*, edited by Thom Braun [New York: Penguin, 1985], 40). But if Cobbett was influential in shaping Disraeli's view of history as largely a misrepresentation of the truth, their perspectives diverge when it comes to refashioning historical representation to suit their particular visions of social and political reform. In contrast to Cobbett's project, Disraeli's view of history underwrites his larger attempt at a simulated "re-covery" that purports to offer direct embodiment and the restoration of lost rights, but that in fact seeks only a hegemonic consent toward the leadership of a "natural" aristocracy. Cobbett instead, as we will see, attempts to return history to the material body, seeking, in the process, both a re-formation of the condition of labor, and a re-formation of historical representation.

5. A. M. D. Hughes, ed., *Cobbett Selections* (Oxford: Clarendon, 1961), 147.

6. This assertion that the Protestant Reformation "has impoverished and degraded

the main body of the People" appears in the subtitle of Cobbett's first edition of his *History*, and the phrase reappears, refrain-like, throughout his text.

7. Raymond Williams, for example, credits Cobbett with a "surprising share of the responsibility for that idealization of the Middle Ages which is so characteristic of nineteenth-century social criticism" (*Culture and Society*, 19).

8. Cobbett is usually accused of idealizing at least one of *two* pasts, either the "old England" of his boyhood (the 1760s–1770s) or the considerably more remote medieval past—and sometimes he is accused of idealizing both (see, for example, Alice Chandler, *A Dream of Order: The Medieval Ideal in Nineteenth-Century English Literature* [Lincoln: University of Nebraska Press, 1971], 61, 79). In an interesting and valuable counter-argument, Ian Dyck approaches the concept of "old England" as a "construction of class experience" rather than a merely nostalgic notion, and persuasively links Cobbett's representation of the past to representations already in circulation among the agrarian laborers of the time (*William Cobbett and Rural Popular Culture* [New York: Cambridge University Press, 1992], 125–51, esp. 138).

9. As R. J. Smith notes, Cobbett's "firm approval of the monasteries" first appears in his *Political Register* in 1822, though he had been "appeal[ing] regularly to the social record of the Middle Ages" since 1817 ("Cobbett, Catholic History, and the Middle Ages," *Studies in Medievalism* 4 [1992]: 127, 122). After 1822, writes Smith, in both his *Political Register* and in *A History of the Protestant "Reformation,"* Cobbett's "medievalist polemic had a double purpose: to advance the Emancipation case, and to resist Poor Law Reform" (127).

10. See also II:57 and V:150 for similar assertions. An adaptation of this passage also appears in William Cobbett, *Rural Rides*, edited by G. D. H. and Margaret Cole, 3 vols. (London: Peter Davies, 1930), 2:494.

11. In his initial conversation with Walter Gerard on the grounds of the ruins of Marney Abbey, Egremont asks, referring to the monks who once lived there, "do you really think they were easier landlords than the present ones?" Gerard replies: "Human nature would tell us that, even if history did not confess it. The Monastics could possess no private property; they lived, received and expended in common" (Disraeli, *Sybil*, 92).

12. For a discussion of Carlyle's panoptic model of workplace organization, see chapter 4. Disraeli's depiction of Trafford's factory is discussed in chapter 6.

13. This is especially true of Ireland, writes Cobbett, where the degradation of the people is primarily due to "'*absenteeship*'; that is to say, the absence of the land-owners, who draw away the revenues of the country, and expend them in other countries" (V:151).

14. See also VII:206. Accordingly, when Cobbett metaphorizes the dispossession of the Catholic Church, he does so in terms of a figurative body. Subsequent to an act of Parliament that rendered all church property in the possession of Henry VIII legally his, and with "the carcass thus being laid prostrate, the rapacious vultures, who had as-

sisted in the work, flew on it, and began to tear it in pieces" (VI:173). Later in the same letter Cobbett remarks, "The monasteries were now plundered, sacked, gutted; for, this last is the proper word whereby to describe the deed" (VI:181).

15. This quotation appears toward the end of a paragraph in which Cobbett lists the locations of various abbeys and priories in his native county of Surrey that were seized or destroyed during the Reformation. A complete cataloging of the dispossession of the abbeys, priories, and other Catholic Church properties in England, Wales, and Ireland appears in the second part of Cobbett's *History of the "Reformation,"* published as a separate volume in 1827. (See William Cobbett, *The Protestant "Reformation," Part Second; Containing a List of the Abbeys, Priories, Nunneries, Hospitals, and other Religious Foundations, in England and Wales, and in Ireland, confiscated, seized on, or alienated, by the Protestant "Reformation" Sovereigns and Parliaments* [London: Cobbett, 1827].)

16. Cobbett makes a similar statement in *Cottage Economy*: "The old sayings about English roast beef and plum-pudding, and about English hospitality, had not their foundation in *nothing*" ([London: Davies, 1926], 4).

17. Derek Attridge, Geoff Bennington, and Robert Young, eds., *Post-structuralism and the Question of History* (New York: Cambridge University Press, 1987), 188.

18. Ibid.

19. As Cobbett writes in his *Advice to Young Men*, "a young man should bestow his time upon no book the contents of which he cannot apply to some useful purpose" (Hughes, 147).

20. Elaine Scarry, ed., *Literature and the Body: Essays on Populations and Persons* (Baltimore: Johns Hopkins University Press, 1990), xxii.

21. Ibid.

22. As a partial solution to this question, the materialist project must attempt, Scarry states, "to extend [the] referential capacities" of language, even if such an attempt falls short of its aspirations (xx). Cobbett's effort at "reforming" historical representation may be understood as just such an attempt at extending the referential capacities of language, as evidenced, in particular, by his treatment of the term *reformation*.

23. Inexplicably, Gasquet's edition drops the quotation marks from the word "reformation" in the volume's title.

24. Raymond Williams, *Cobbett* (New York: Oxford University Press, 1983), 50.

25. As Dyck puts it, "Cobbett did not seek to restore the past for the past's sake; what he wanted was radical reform, and by that he meant not nostalgia but simply '*a change for the better*', whether that meant going forward or backward" (147).

26. *Rural Rides* and *A History of the Protestant "Reformation"* overlap in the dates of their composition; the original edition of *Rural Rides* includes entries from the years 1822–26, while the "letters" that make up the first volume of *A History of the Protestant "Reformation"* were written between 1824 and 1826.

27. Clearly, Cobbett intended the second volume of his *History* to function as just

such a handbook, whereby anyone seeking information about property of the Catholic Church that was seized during the Reformation may easily determine "*what it was*, and when *it arose*, how it was *put down*, and *who got it*" (see the introduction to William Cobbett, *The Protestant "Reformation," Part Second*, paragraph 6).

28. Chandler, 75. In an untypically blunt assessment, Chandler asserts that "[a]s history, Cobbett's study of the Reformation is often nonsense and his analysis of its effects as ridiculous in some ways as it is profound in others" (74). See also Cole, for whom Cobbett's *History* is, rather understatedly, "not among the best of his books" (G. D. H. Cole, *The Life of William Cobbett* [Westport, Conn.: Greenwood Press, 1971], 286). Despite this judgment, Cole defends Cobbett from those commentators "who have abused the book for its historical inadequacy and its one-sided presentation of facts. . . . It is not a history, in the academic sense; it is a brilliant philippic" (289).

29. Williams, *Cobbett*, 25.

30. Ibid.

31. Ibid., 56.

32. Cole, 289. As Cole also notes, and it is worth remembering here, Cobbett's *History of the Protestant "Reformation"* reached a large audience, not just in England, but in Europe and America (289). Spater puts the sales figure in England alone at 700,000 by 1828, with more than 100,000 copies sold in the United States (George Spater, *William Cobbett: The Poor Man's Friend*, 2 vols. [New York: Cambridge University Press, 1982], 2:445).

33. See Dyck's chapter, "Old England: Nostalgia and Experience," in his *William Cobbett and Rural Popular Culture*, 125–51. Subsequent references to this text will be noted parenthetically.

34. Significantly, Cobbett makes this assertion not with reference to accounts that he dismisses, like Burnet's *History of the Reformation* (which he calls "a mass of the most base falsehoods and misrepresentations that ever were put on paper" [XIV:405]), but to those texts, like Fortescue's, with which he already largely sympathizes.

35. Gilmartin, *Print Politics*, 177.

Chapter 2

1. Thomas Carlyle, "Sir Walter Scott," in *The Works of Thomas Carlyle in Thirty Volumes* (1899; reprint, New York: AMS, 1969), 29:38. Subsequent page references are noted parethetically within the text, with the abbreviation SWS.

2. Carlyle was not the first to make a connection between Scott and Cobbett with regard to their "health." Nearly a decade earlier, William Hazlitt remarked that Walter Scott "put me in mind of Cobbett, with his florid face and scarlet gown, which were just like the other's red face and scarlet waistcoat. The one is like an English farmer, the other like a Scotch laird. Both are large, robust men with great strength and composure of features" (*The Complete Works of William Hazlitt*, ed. P. P. Howe, 21 vols. [New York:

AMS Press, 1967], 11:276). However, Hazlitt stopped short of acknowledging a more profound connection; indeed, if anything, he found them equally lacking in transcendent quality: "I saw nothing of the *ideal* character in the romance-writer any more than I looked for it in the politician" (11:276).

3. Carlyle's statement echoes Coleridge's 1820 assessment of Cobbett as a "political Rhinoceros, with his Coat-armour of dry and wet Mud and his one Horn of brutal strength on the Nose of Scorn and Hate—not to forget the fleaing Rasp of his Tongue!" (E. L. Griggs, ed., *The Collected Letters of Samuel Taylor Coleridge*, 6 vols. [London: Oxford University Press, 1956–71], 5:115).

4. William Cobbett, *Rural Rides*, ed. G. D. H. and Margaret Cole, 3:520. All subsequent citations refer to the Cole edition unless otherwise noted, and will be abbreviated *RR*.

5. For an overview of the Carlylean perspective on health and the nation, see Bruce Haley, *The Healthy Body and Victorian Culture* (Cambridge: Harvard University Press, 1978), 69–83.

6. Hazlitt, again commenting on both Scott and Cobbett, writes: "They have a strong, vivid, bodily perception (so to speak), a material intuition of what they write about. All their ideas are concrete, not abstracted" (*Complete Works*, 19:96). For more recent investigations of the materiality of Cobbett's rhetoric see Lionel Basney, "How the Matter Stood: Cobbett's Moral and Political Ecology," *Sewanee Review* 101 (summer 1993): 354–74, and Kevin Gilmartin, "'This Is Very Material': William Cobbett and the Rhetoric of Radical Opposition," *Studies in Romanticism* 34 (spring 1995): 81–101.

7. To be sure, such a correlation is not new. As Catherine Gallagher observes, eighteenth-century writers like Adam Smith and David Hume "maintained a two-millennia-old tradition of seeing the individual body as sign—both as metaphor and source—of the health or infirmity of the larger social body" ("The Body versus the Social Body in the Works of Thomas Malthus and Henry Mayhew," in *The Making of the Modern Body: Sexuality and Society in the Nineteenth Century*, ed. Catherine Gallagher and Thomas Lacqueur [Berkeley: University of California Press, 1987], 83). In contrast to Smith and Hume, Gallagher locates Thomas Malthus's population theory in particular as intervening in this tradition by problematizing "the possibility of using the healthy body to signify the healthy society" (85). Nevertheless, "by making the body absolutely problematic," writes Gallagher, Malthus "helps place it in the very center of social discourse" (85). Malthus, of course, was one of Cobbett's favorite targets. Cobbett considered the primary tenet of his population theory (that human population growth will inevitably exceed the means to sustain it), to be "a mixture of madness and blasphemy" (*RR*, 2:361), and never would have accepted Malthus's subversion of the healthy body/healthy state equation.

8. For an account of the rise of the "social body" metaphor as an ambiguous successor to the "body politic" and the "great body of the people," see Mary Poovey, *Making a Social Body*, esp. 7–8.

9. As Poovey notes, while the bourgeois version of the social body was used by some to call for the political enfranchisement of the poor, it was also used to underwrite the bureaucratic inspection and control of the working class (77–78).

10. Gilmartin, *Print Politics*, 187.

11. G. K. Chesterton, *William Cobbett* (London: Hodder and Stoughton, n.d.), 204.

12. See George Spater, *William Cobbett: The Poor Man's Friend*, 2:442–43. As Raymond Williams has noted, this particular designation of London was not invented by Cobbett, though he undoubtedly popularized its use (*The Country and the City* [New York: Oxford University Press, 1973], 145–46). See also William Cobbett, *Rural Rides*, 2 vols. (1912; reprint, New York: Dutton, 1966), 2:301 n. 43.

13. Cobbett's anti-Semitism is evident throughout *Rural Rides* (see, for example, *RR*, 1:88, 90, 104, and 2:440), and he even refers to the capitalist enterprise as the "Jew-system" (*RR*, 2:441). Cobbett's anti-Semitism, however, was not limited to his association of Jews with what he considered to be unproductive occupations. As Spater notes, Cobbett's "dislike" of Jews also derived from his xenophobia, and from his belief that the practice of Judaism blasphemes Christianity (*William Cobbett*, 2:441). Daniel Green puts the case more strongly, describing Cobbett's anti-Semitism as "violent hatred" (*Great Cobbett: The Noblest Agitator* [Toronto: Hodder and Stoughton, 1983], 321), and asserting that Cobbett "was voicing . . . an ancient, deep-rooted, popular prejudice that had been recently reinforced by the growing hatred the working classes felt for the new capitalism" (323). In this context, we might say that Cobbett "capitalizes" on his own racism, as well as on that of his audience, in an effort to rally his readers to his anticapitalist cause. In her *William Cobbett: The Politics of Style* (New York: Cambridge University Press, 1995), Leonora Nattrass advances this view, arguing that Cobbett's anti-Semitism (among other examples of bigotry) is the product of a "highly-wrought self-consciousness" that is "always striving for a calculated effect" (13). See also Kevin Binfield, "Demonology, Ethos, and Community in Cobbett and Shelley," in *Romanticism, Radicalism, and the Press*, ed. Stephen Behrendt (Detroit: Wayne State University Press, 1997), 157–69, for a similar view of Cobbett as a "moral entrepreneur" (160). Cobbett's anti-Semitism is thus part and parcel of his rhetorical strategy, but it also remains, according to Karl W. Schweitzer and John W. Osborne, "an integral part of his personality" (*Cobbett in His Times* [London: Leicester University Press, 1990], 75). Both aspects together reveal that Cobbett's vision of a healthy nation is built with the aid of exclusionary and racist ideology, far from the consistently "humane" and "compassionate" Cobbett his biographers often portray.

14. See Jan B. Gordon, "'Booked for Passage' on Cobbett's *Rural Rides*: Ecology as Revolution," *Nineteenth-Century Prose* 19, no. 3 (1992): 60–84, for a brief discussion of both "tax-eaters" and "dead weight" as constituting a single "parasitical organism" (63–64).

15. The vague and abstract connotations of the term were, of course, deliberate on Cobbett's part, reflecting well his sense of the way in which the political, the economic, and the social combined into a large, interdependent but amorphous mass of institu-

tions and policies. As W. J. Keith notes, Cobbett's use of the term "the THING" (especially in the form "the accursed THING") has its source in the Old Testament (see W. J. Keith, *The Rural Tradition: A Study of the Non-Fiction Prose Writers of the English Countryside* [Toronto: University of Toronto Press, 1974], 77 and 268 n. 41).

16. Gilmartin, "'This Is Very Material,'" 97. Gilmartin cites as his example Cobbett's self-proclaimed desire to hold his nose while riding through Cheltenham. For a slightly reworded version of Gilmartin's comment see his *Print Politics*, 179.

17. Robert Southey, *Sir Thomas More; or, Colloquies on the Progress and Prospects of Society*, 2nd ed., 2 vols. (London: John Murray, 1831), 1:171.

18. As Gilmartin notes, this problem is not unique to Cobbett, but is symptomatic of radical discourse in general, in which "[a] 'system' of corruption was grasped as a dense metaphor or sequence of metaphors (chain, net, web, knot, nest), and any prospect of termination or escape was cut off by the insistence upon categorical absolutes (all, every, never, not)" (*Print Politics*, 15). Mary Poovey notes a similar problem with the use of the term "social body" in the 1830s: "because scientific medicine had yet to provide guidelines for when a doctor should intervene in the operations of organs still imperfectly understood, the image of the social body could not help reformers address the issues of when and how to interfere in a social process that seemed increasingly out of control" (75; see also 40–41).

19. William Cobbett, *Cottage Economy*, 1–2. Subsequent citations are abbreviated *CE*.

20. For this discussion of sign-value I am indebted to Jean Baudrillard's essay "Sign Function and Class Logic" in his *For a Critique of the Political Economy of the Sign*, translated by Charles Levin (St. Louis: Telos Press, 1981), 29–62.

21. Significantly, Cobbett finds himself "reflecting on the thousands of scores of bacon and thousands of bushels of bread that had been eaten from the long oak-table," and fearing its appropriation by a "stock-jobber" who might use the wood to construct a bridge "over an artificial river in his cockney-garden," he instructs a friend to purchase the table, so he can "keep it for the good it has done in the world" (*RR*, 1:278). With this strangely sentimental gesture, Cobbett redeems the table's sign-value, if not its use-value, and thus, in a small but self-satisfying way, once again sees himself as thwarting the progress of the "accursed system."

22. On this point, Cobbett says that the hypothetical forebear of the farmer Charington likely took "a cup of *strong beer* to himself, when they [the farm laborers] had none; but that was pretty nearly all the difference in their manner of living" (*RR*, 1:277).

23. Tim Fulford, *Romanticism and Masculinity* (New York: St. Martin's, 1999): 163.

24. *RR*, 1:160. See also *CE*, 173, of which this section of *Rural Rides* is an elaboration.

25. Indeed, as Catherine Hall has noted, Cobbett's restriction of women to the domestic sphere is but one example of the way radical discourse continued to express socially conservative ideals with respect to sexual difference. See Catherine Hall, *White*,

Male and Middle Class: Explorations in Feminism and History (New York: Routledge, 1992), 138–41.

26. Of the suffering poor, Cobbett writes: "I know that they are in rags, and that they have not a belly-full; and I know that the way to make them good, to make them honest, to make them dutiful, to make them kind to one another, is to enable them to live well; and I also know that none of these things will ever be accomplished by Methodist sermons, and by those stupid, at once stupid and malignant things, and roguish things, called Religious Tracts" (*RR*, 1:176).

27. This is not to say, of course, that Cobbett's own "charity" occurs without a context. Indeed, that context might be understood as a kind of "exchange" as well—usually a brief conversation regarding the living circumstances of the laborer and the relation of those circumstances to the policies of government. In the instance regarding the parish-work laborers, Cobbett gives the workers some money during a discussion about their low wages, and he reports that "I told them that the farmers and hop-planters were as much objects of compassion as themselves, which they acknowledged" (*RR*, 1:94).

28. Dyck, 109.

29. Williams, *Cobbett*, 38.

30. Ibid., 41–42.

31. E. P. Thompson, *The Making of the English Working Class* (New York: Vintage, 1966), 759, 761. See also Gilmartin, *Print Politics*, 34–35.

32. Williams, *Cobbett*, 44.

33. For a brief discussion of Cobbett's use of the machine as a metaphor for the corrupt political system, see Gilmartin, *Print Politics*, 161–62.

34. See Gordon, "Booked for Passage," 67.

35. Quoted in Dyck, 196.

36. Ibid. During this time (before and after the passage of the Reform Bill) Cobbett also supported the annual election of Parliament, the secret ballot, and the ten-hour work day (see Williams, *Cobbett*, 27 and 42; Cole, 358). As an anti-Semite, however, Cobbett was opposed to Jews serving in Parliament (see John Osborne, "William Cobbett's Anti-Semitism," *Historian* 47 [November 1984]: 90).

37. As Dyck points out, opposition to the Reform Bill "was manifestly unpopular among rural labourers and freeholders" (197). Thus, if Cobbett were to oppose the Bill, he might jeopardize his own chances of being elected to Parliament.

38. Both elections were marred by corruption, and violence disrupted the voting in the 1820 election at Coventry. Gilmartin notes that after his loss in the Coventry election, Cobbett "produced anecdotal evidence of popular 'acclamations' in order to claim the 'representative' status denied him at the polls" (*Print Politics*, 32). For accounts of Cobbett's experiences in these two elections see Spater, 2:392–98 and 457–63.

39. Cobbett ran for election in Oldham at the invitation of John Fielden, also a candidate for Oldham and a popular and progressive manufacturer. Fielden made his

offer (indeed his very candidacy) contingent on Cobbett standing with him as a team (Spater, 2:504). As Dyck notes, this situation resulted in Cobbett being "regarded locally as the running-mate of John Fielden" (199). Cobbett was reelected in 1835; he died in June of that year. For more on the rather unusual alliance between Fielden and Cobbett, see Dyck, 199–201.

40. Gilmartin goes so far as to explicitly link Cobbett's call for parliamentary reform and his desire for election: "Cobbett ruthlessly attacked a corrupt parliament only because he so fervently believed in a reformed one, and longed for the authority that awaited him there" (*Print Politics*, 31).

41. See Cobbett, *Cottage Economy*, 12–48.

42. See, for example, Green, 456; Cole, 392–94; and Briggs, who describes Cobbett as "one of the few 'curiosities'" in a House otherwise very similar in appearance to the one that convened before the passage of the Reform Bill (Asa Briggs, *William Cobbett* [Oxford: Oxford University Press, 1967], 57).

43. Quoted in Spater, 2:522. The quotation is from Macaulay's personal journal. As Spater notes, Macaulay served in the House with Cobbett in 1833.

44. Quoted in Green, 464.

45. See, for example, *RR*, 2:486 and 520–21.

46. Williams, *Cobbett*, 81.

47. Ibid., 1. The image is drawn from an altercation in 1822 that began, not incidentally, with a proposal to toast Cobbett's health (see *RR*, 1:65).

48. "Radical egotism," as Gilmartin points out, is also "a central feature of the language and practice of a radical counterpublic sphere," and thus not a self-representation unique to Cobbett (*Print Politics*, 39).

49. Hazlitt, 8:53. For more discussion of Hazlitt's perception of Cobbett as "an example of literary masculinity," see Fulford, 238, and especially 224–25.

50. Gilmartin, *Print Politics*, 167. "One firm and united body" is Cobbett's phrase, from his *Political Register* in 1817 (see Gilmartin, 166).

51. Cobbett lost his farm in Botley as a result of filing for bankruptcy in 1820 (see Cole, 242–43). Gilmartin argues that "if the *Rides* helped Cobbett overcome a sense of exile by returning him to the land and to his readers, they were also the deepest symptom of his dislocation, since they put his body as well as his prose in circulation, and forced him again and again to depart from the 'land of promise' he had rediscovered" (*Print Politics*, 192–93).

Chapter 3

1. Thomas Carlyle and Jane Welsh Carlyle, *The Collected Letters of Thomas and Jane Welsh Carlyle*, edited by Charles Richard Sanders, Kenneth J. Fielding, Clyde de L. Ryals, et al., 28 vols. (Durham: Duke University Press, 1970–2000), 3:218–19. Hereafter cited parenthetically and abbreviated as *CL*. In his letters to his family written

from London in late 1824, Carlyle refers to London as a "wen" on at least two other occasions; see *CL*, 3:166 and 232.

2. Fred Kaplan, *Thomas Carlyle: A Biography* (Ithaca: Cornell University Press, 1983), 207.

3. Thomas Carlyle, *Past and Present*, edited by Richard Altick, 45. All further references to this text will be cited parenthetically and cited as *PP*.

4. In his introduction to the Riverside edition of *Past and Present*, for example, Richard Altick states that *Past and Present* "can hardly be said to have been planned; it grew spontaneously out of Carlyle's experiences in the late summer of 1842" (xii). In his *Carlyle and the Burden of History*, John D. Rosenberg echoes Altick's statement: "In the late summer of 1842, outward accident and inner necessity led Carlyle on a journey that resulted in the publication of *Past and Present* the following spring" ([Oxford: Clarendon Press, 1985], 118). See also Chandler, 138. For the precise week of Carlyle's trip see Kaplan, 294.

5. Kaplan, 295.

6. William Baker, "The London Library Borrowings of Thomas Carlyle, 1841–1844," *Library Review* 30 (summer 1981): 93. Baker himself subscribes to the thesis that Carlyle's trip to East Anglia marks the moment *Past and Present* was "conceived," and consigns the role of Jocelin's text to one of "profound influence" (93). See, however, Joel J. Brattin, "New Manuscript Evidence about the Origin of 'Past and Present,'" *Nineteenth-Century Prose* 31 (spring 1996): 13–24, for a discussion of manuscript evidence that appears to indicate a portion of Book 4 was drafted as early as 1841.

7. For a typical chronological summary of the revival of literary and antiquarian interest in the medieval see Sir Kenneth Clark's 1928 study, *The Gothic Revival: An Essay in the History of Taste* (New York: Scribner's, 1950), 91–93. Clark's rendering of the progression of revivalist works is still the standard one; similar versions appear in Joanna Banham and Jennifer Harris, eds., *William Morris and the Middle Ages* (Dover, N.H.: Manchester University Press, 1984), 18–31; Chandler, 16–25; and Mark Girouard, *The Return to Camelot: Chivalry and the English Gentleman* (New Haven: Yale University Press, 1981), 20–22.

8. Oliver Elton, *A Survey of English Literature, 1780–1880*, 4 vols. (New York: Macmillan, 1920), 3:240. Elton's remark is cited in Chandler, 138, and in Grace Calder, *The Writing of* Past and Present (New Haven: Yale University Press, 1949), 32.

9. Indeed, the seminal work on this medievalist phenomenon, Sir Kenneth Clark's *Gothic Revival* (1928, revised 1949) makes no mention of Carlyle at all. Nor is there any mention of Carlyle in the work that Clark's study superseded—Sir Charles Eastlake's 1872 *A History of the Gothic Revival* (New York: Humanities Press, 1970). The second chapter of Grace Calder's *Writing of* Past and Present (1949) contains a section promisingly titled "*Past and Present* and the Medieval Revival," but she explicitly avoids situating Carlyle's book in relation to the revivalist literary tradition, and instead contextualizes the Camden Society's publication of Jocelin's *Chronicle* within the

surge of interest in medieval historiography that occurred after 1830 (23–33). Another mid-twentieth-century scholar, Emery Neff, asserts that *Past and Present* bears only an "accidental" relationship to the literature of the Gothic revival, "the result of coincidence with the great stream of reaction against modern tendencies and toward the Middle Ages" (*Carlyle* [1932; reprint, New York: Russell and Russell, 1968], 207). For more recent accounts that group *Past and Present* with the literature of the medieval revival see Banham and Harris, 4–5; Chandler, 122–51; Raymond Chapman, *The Sense of the Past in Victorian Literature* (London: Croom Helm, 1986), 60–64; Girouard, who groups *Past and Present* into a canon of "textbooks of chivalry" (263–64); and Rosemary Jann, who identifies *Past and Present* as "an especially interesting document of the medieval revival (of which it is a part) for not only does it illustrate the key values and beliefs implicit in the nineteenth-century's idealization of the Middle Ages, but it also provides a classic example of how that medieval ideal was put to use in the Victorian period" ("The Condition of England Past and Present: Thomas Carlyle and the Middle Ages," *Studies in Medievalism* 1 [spring 1979]: 15). For a dissenting view see J. W. Burrow, "The Sense of the Past," in *The Victorians*, edited by Laurence Lerner (New York: Holmes and Meier, 1978), 120–38.

10. For example, in her 1984 essay, "William Morris and the Middle Ages," Jennifer Harris acknowledges the relative heterogeneity of the revival of interest in medievalism, but asserts that the different manifestations of this revival are unified by "the desire to return to an ordered yet organically vital society in the face of great social change," and thus the "Middle Ages were viewed increasingly as a golden age of faith, stability and creativity, with which the present day compared most unfavourably" (Banham and Harris, 2). Similarly, R. J. Smith's *The Gothic Bequest* notes that the Gothic revival turned the Enlightenment's otherwise "neutral recognition" of the distinct stages of English society's development into an "active nostalgia" for the past (*The Gothic Bequest: Medieval Institutions in British Thought, 1688–1863* [New York: Cambridge University Press, 1987], 156).

11. Chandler, 1.

12. For example, the anonymous reviewer of *Past and Present* in the journal *Athenaeum* asks, "Is it philosophy to idly invoke an irrevocable past, and to imagine that effects can be revived in the absence of their causes? No: Mr. Carlyle's admirers would perhaps admit that such is not the truth, and they would tell us it is—poetry; we say it is childishness and absurdity" (*Athenaeum* [20 May 1843]: 481). Similarly, W. H. Smith, writing in *Blackwood's*, remarks: "what must strike everyone is the manifest partiality Mr. Carlyle shows to the past, and the unfair preference he gives it over the present. The whole parallel which he runs between past and present is false—whimsically false" (see Jules Paul Seigel, ed., *Thomas Carlyle: The Critical Heritage* [New York: Barnes and Noble, 1971], 215–17).

13. Thomas Carlyle, "On History," in *The Works of Thomas Carlyle in Thirty Volumes* (1899; reprint, New York: AMS, 1969), 27:89–90.

14. See Suzy Anger, "Carlyle: Between Biblical Exegesis and Romantic

Hermeneutics," *Texas Studies in Literature and Language* 40 (spring 1998): 78–96, for a discussion of how Carlyle's "Prophetic Manuscript" metaphor is deeply indebted to (but also significantly deviates from) "Calvinist exegesis" (82).

15. Jonathan Loesberg has answered this question by affirming both poles of the opposition, asserting that Carlyle's epistemology is itself contradictory, positing "a univocal truth that is the aim and object of consciousness, its only proper goal," but at the same time valuing "the workings of consciousness as it interprets nature," rather than as it contemplates its "univocal goal" (*Fictions of Consciousness: Mill, Newman and the Reading of Victorian Prose* [New Brunswick: Rutgers University Press, 1986], 186). This contradiction thus leads Carlyle to invent "strange and idiosyncratic narrative histories" (204) which function as an "embodiment and expression of an epistemology for which Carlyle can find no other embodiment, no other expression" (304). Though Loesberg's analysis is sharply original and compelling, I think the contradiction is mainly a product of the limitations of that embodiment, that the "truth" for Carlyle, historical or philosophical, is always under erasure as a hypothesis that authorizes or underwrites the process of interpretation.

16. As Suzy Anger explains: "Carlyle sets forth a theory of interpretation that is at once intentionalist and relativistic, simultaneously grounded in intuitionism and in aesthetic subjectivism. The text is determinate and objective, meaning is grounded in intention, but intention is never realizable in its entirety. Yet Carlyle insists that there is a transcendent ground beyond history that guarantees determinate meaning" (84). See also Ann Rigney's essay, "The Untenanted Places of the Past: Thomas Carlyle and the Varieties of Historical Ignorance," *History and Theory* 35, no.3 (1996): 338–58.

17. See, for example, Eastlake, 113; Clark, 94–95 (though Clark feels the overall influence of the Waverley novels has been overrated); Chandler, 51; and Banham and Harris, 25.

18. See Lowell T. Frye's essay, "Romancing the Past: Walter Scott and Thomas Carlyle," *Carlyle Studies Annual* 16 (1996): 37–49, for a full and persuasive account of Carlyle's complicated relationship with Scott. Frye argues for the significance of Carlyle's essay on Scott as "an important document in Carlyle's career, a gateway through which Carlyle passed to reach his social criticism of the next decade" (42), because it reveals the degree to which Carlyle is indebted to Scott's method of resurrecting the past, but also, and more important, because it marks Carlyle's definitive break with Scott. Thus, whereas Scott's novels are essentially romances of the past, Carlyle's essays are, as Frye astutely puts it, "historical narratives that offer the romance of *absence*, not *presence*" (45).

19. Hayden White, *Metahistory: The Historical Imagination in Nineteenth-Century Europe* (Baltimore: Johns Hopkins University Press, 1973), 15.

20. White eventually comes to an analogous conclusion, noting that while Carlyle's project is one of "palingenesis, the pious reconstruction of the past in its integrity" (146), his "conception of history" remains "more resistant to nostalgic self-indulgence than the historical philosophies of the early Romantics" (147).

21. See especially James Kerr's *Fiction against History: Scott as Storyteller* (New York: Cambridge University Press, 1989), which rejects Lukács's claim for the "historical veracity" (2) of Scott's fiction, in favor of Hayden White's notion of the "re-emplotment" of history (4–5).

22. See Kaplan, 111–14. For a provocative and enlightening discussion of Carlyle's conflicted relationship to his own body, and of the profound impact of that relationship on his language and thought, see George Levine, "Carlyle, Descartes, and Objectivity," *Raritan: A Quarterly Review* 17 (summer 1997): 45–58.

23. Thomas Carlyle, *Reminiscences*, edited by J. A. Froude (New York: Scribner's, 1881), 526.

24. Robert Southey, *Sir Thomas More: or, Colloquies on the Progress and Prospects of Society*, 2nd ed., 2 vols. (London: John Murray, 1831), 1:79. Hereafter cited parenthetically as *STM*.

25. Joseph Childers, "Carlyle's *Past and Present*, History and a Question of Hermeneutics," *CLIO* 13 (spring 1984): 248.

26. Gordon Hirsch, "History Writing in Carlyle's *Past and Present*," *Prose Studies* 7 (December 1984): 225.

27. See "Speculum," *The Oxford English Dictionary*, 2nd ed. C. Malone has also noted this dual meaning of "speculum": Carlyle "invites his reader to look into a 'magical speculum,' a speculum that both mirrors and opens an orifice, opening into the twelfth century to reflect not his image or ours, but the image of its bearer" (C. Malone, "Voices of the Ages: The Editor and His Texts in *Past and Present*," *Carlyle Annual* 10 [1989]: 45).

28. See Jocelin of Brakelond, *The Chronicle of Jocelin of Brakelond, Monk of St. Edmundsbury*, translated by L. C. Jane (New York: Cooper Square, 1966), 174–81.

29. *Chronicle*, 166. This event is only briefly mentioned by Carlyle, who notes only Abbot Samson's interpretation of the fire as a judgment against the monks "for murmuring about their meat and drink" (122).

30. As Carol T. Christ has noted concerning Carlyle's gendered concept of the heroic, "In this world of heroic masculinity, women have almost no place" ("'The Hero as Man of Letters': Masculinity and Victorian Nonfiction Prose," in *Victorian Sages and Cultural Discourse: Renegotiating Gender and Power*, edited by Thais E. Morgan [New Brunswick: Rutgers University Press, 1990], 20). Indeed, St. Edmundsbury itself seems to embody this masculinity, given its concentric concentration of male-centeredness (as a monastic-centered community focused geographically, historically and spiritually on the corpse of a dead male saint). For a fine and full analysis of the Carlylean representation of masculinity as it pertains to Abbot Samson in particular and Carlyle's early works in general, see Herbert Sussman, *Victorian Masculinities: Manhood and Masculine Poetics in Early Victorian Literature and Art* (Cambridge: Cambridge University Press, 1995), 16–72.

31. Such a violation of the decorum of reverence would also disrupt Abbot Samson's status as a Carlylean masculine hero. As Sussman observes, Samson "exemplifies manliness by exemplifying reserve" (28).

32. The most common error among scholars who comment on this passage is the acknowledgement, on the one hand, that the corpse of St. Edmund is not literally unwrapped to the bare remains of flesh and bones, accompanied by a gloss that, on the other hand, takes this moment to be one of unmediated physical contact. Chandler, for instance, repeats the phrase about Samson "not daring to behold the sacred flesh" but then refers to the scene as the "unveiling of the body of Landlord Edmund" anyway (144). A more recent example is Richard Schoch's essay, "'We Do Nothing But Enact History': Thomas Carlyle Stages the Past" (*Nineteenth-Century Literature* 54 [June 1999]: 27–52), which compellingly establishes the extent to which "Carlyle relied upon theatrical codes and conventions as the surest means of providing his readers with the vibrant, animated, and enacted history he promised them" (33). However, Schoch's overemphasis on the specular aspects of Carlyle's images leads him to conclude that, for Carlyle, "[i]n order to reveal the moral content of history . . . the past had to be resurrected in the flesh" (52). Although he does quote the passage from *Past and Present* stating that Abbot Samson dare not "look at the sacred flesh naked," Schoch overlooks the significance of what *must not be seen*, in favor of stressing the sole importance of the body's "wholeness." Whereas Schoch, then, asserts that "Carlyle performs history as the exhibition of a body, whole and unblemished," I am insisting instead on the specular limit of that performance, on the fact that the body is not, must not, cannot be revealed. Only in this latter way can the body function as an embodiment of the past. A significant exception to this misreading is W. David Shaw's chapter on Carlyle in his *Victorians and Mystery* (Ithaca: Cornell University Press, 1990). Shaw links, as I do, "Saint Edmund's voluminously wrapped body" to "Carlyle's many-layered narrative," and suggests that the "shroud within shroud of protective garments conspires to hold more than is ever revealed," and that "some ultimate meaning, or absence of meaning, must be held in reserve" (84).

33. H. Aram Veeser, ed., *The New Historicism* (New York: Routledge, 1989).

34. Compare also Schoch, who argues that "both Carlyle and stage impresarios such as Charles Kean engaged in a process of historical recovery and restoration that gave pronounced emphasis to liveness, physical presence, and performance" (50).

35. Indeed, this appeal to a metaphorics of conjuring and spiritualism, particularly with respect to the *desire* of the writer/historian, appears to be part of the new historicism's allure for some critics. Stephen Greenblatt's *Shakespearean Negotiations* opens with the sentence "I began with the desire to speak with the dead" (*Shakespearean Negotiations: The Circulation of Social Energy in Renaissance England* [Berkeley: University of California Press, 1988], 1), and Veeser asserts that this sentence encapsulates "a good part of the New Historicism's appeal" (1), but only, he feels, because it references the subjectivity of the writer, and not because it articulates, as I am suggesting, a desire that has since become thematic (and axiomatic) of some "new" approaches to history.

36. I am in agreement here with Peter Keating, who has also argued that "[t]he full force of the book [*Past and Present*] is centred on the present, not on the past; on an emergent, industrial, democratic society, not on a monastic, Catholic, agrarian society" ("Backward or Forward? Carlyle's *Past and Present*," in *Thomas Carlyle 1981: Papers*

Given at the International Thomas Carlyle Centenary Symposium, edited by Horst W. Drescher [Frankfurt: Verlag Peter Lang, 1981], 210).

Chapter 4

1. This language may be indebted to *Chartism* (published four years earlier), in which Carlyle maps a similar terrain of disease from "symptoms on the surface" (Chartist activity, for example), to their source "deep within" the social body (120). For an insightful discussion of these metaphors in the context of Carlyle's effort to appropriate and rearticulate Chartist discourse, see John Plotz, *The Crowd: British Literature and Public Politics* (Berkeley: University of California Press, 2000), 127–53, esp. 144–45.

2. Although Carlyle was no doubt unaware of the work of the much younger Marx and Engels in 1843 (they were both contributing to the *Deutsch-französische Jahrbucher*, and Marx's most substantial writing in the following year, *The Economic and Philosophic Manuscripts*, was not published in Carlyle's, or Marx's, lifetime), Engels was, of course, living in England from November 1842 to August 1844, and was very much aware of Carlyle. Georg Lukács has remarked that *Past and Present* in particular "received the approval and in part the enthusiastic admiration of the young Engels" (see *History and Class Consciousness: Studies in Marxist Dialectics*, translated by Rodney Livingstone [Cambridge: MIT Press, 1971], 190). Indeed, in a review of *Past and Present* from 1844, Engels proclaimed that "[o]f all the fat books and thin pamphlets which have appeared in the past year . . . the above work is the only one which is worth reading" (see Frederick Engels, "The Condition of England: *Past and Present* by Thomas Carlyle, London, 1843," in *Karl Marx, Frederick Engels: Collected Works* [New York: International Publishers, 1975], 3:445). First published in German in the *Deutsch-französische Jahrbucher*, 1844.

3. Relevant to our discussion here is Marx's very early association of a mystified consciousness with the unconscious and therefore unrealized desires of the past: "Our motto must therefore be: Reform of consciousness not through dogmas, but through analyzing the mystical consciousness, the consciousness which is unclear to itself, whether it appears in religious or political form. Then it will transpire that the world has long been dreaming of something that it can acquire if only it becomes conscious of it. It will transpire that it is not a matter of drawing a great dividing line between past and future, but of carrying out the thoughts of the past." The quotation appears in a letter written in 1843, the year *Past and Present* was published. See Robert C. Tucker, ed., *The Marx-Engels Reader* (New York: Norton, 1978), 15.

4. Engels, "The Condition of England: *Past and Present* by Thomas Carlyle, London, 1843," 463.

5. For accounts of the Midas myths see Ovid, *Metamorphoses*, translated by Rolfe Humphries (Bloomington: Indiana University Press, 1955), 261–65; and Robert

Graves, *The Greek Myths 1* (New York: Penguin, 1985), 281–85. As Richard Altick has noted, Carlyle appears to "fuse" the two Midas tales—his wish for the golden touch and Apollo's curse of the jackass's ears—into a single narrative about the transgression of divine law (*PP,* 12 n. 13). Because Carlyle introduces his account here as "the secret of *gold* Midas" (my emphasis), I presume the matter of Midas's misguided desire for wealth is foremost in Carlyle's mind, and that he includes the "long ears" merely to accent Midas's foolishness.

6. Louis Althusser, *Lenin and Philosophy* (New York: Monthly Review Press, 1971), 162.

7. The words are Jean Baudrillard's; see *Simulations*, 25.

8. Thomas Carlyle, *Chartism*, in *The Works of Thomas Carlyle in Thirty Volumes* (1899; reprint, New York: AMS, 1969), 29:151.

9. Ibid., 137.

10. Baudrillard, *Simulations*, 4.

11. Rosenberg, 130.

12. Baudrillard, *Simulations*, 10–11.

13. Jean-Joseph Goux, *Symbolic Economies: After Marx and Freud*, translated by Jennifer Curtiss Gage (Ithaca: Cornell University Press, 1990), 44.

14. Thomas Richards, *The Commodity Culture of Victorian England: Advertising and Spectacle, 1851–1914* (Stanford: Stanford University Press, 1990), 48.

15. In *The Commodity Culture of Victorian England,* Thomas Richards notes that this particular method of advertising commodities began in the 1830s and became so popular a gimmick that "by the 1840's the streets of London were clogged with the effigies of things" (48).

16. Compare Teufelsdröckh's rhetorical question in *Sartor Resartus*, where it is not the spirit that reforms the body, but a re-formed body that houses and nourishes the spirit: "Wilt thou help us to embody the divine Spirit of that [Christian] religion in a new Mythus, in a new vehicle and vesture, that our Souls, otherwise too like perishing, may live?" (Thomas Carlyle, *Sartor Resartus*, in *The Works of Thomas Carlyle in Thirty Volumes* [1899; reprint, New York: AMS, 1969], 1:154).

17. Indeed, in *Sartor Resartus* Carlyle declares this process of reinscription itself to be a divine task: "A Hierarch, therefore, and Pontiff of the World will we call him, the Poet and inspired Maker; who, Prometheus-like, can shape new Symbols, and bring new Fire from Heaven to fix it there" (179).

18. This sacrificial aspect of labor received its most famous elaboration (though in a more narrow context than Carlyle's) in John Ruskin's *The Seven Lamps of Architecture* (1849), most notably, of course, in "The Lamp of Sacrifice." Typical of Ruskin's conception of the value of labor is the following: "It is not the church we want, but the sacrifice; not the emotion of admiration, but the act of adoration; not the gift, but the giving" (*The Seven Lamps of Architecture* [New York: Dover, 1989], 19).

19. Georges Bataille, *Visions of Excess: Selected Writings, 1927–1939*, edited and

translated by Allan Stoekl (Minneapolis: University of Minnesota Press, 1985), 242. See also Bataille's short report titled "The College of Sociology," in which he states, "I am now ready to say of the 'sacred' that it is communication between beings" (in Denis Hollier, ed., *The College of Sociology (1937–1939)*, translated by Betsy Wing [Minneapolis: University of Minnesota Press, 1988], 338).

20. Walter Houghton, *The Victorian Frame of Mind, 1830–1870* (New Haven: Yale University Press, 1957), 256. For Houghton, the religious context in which Carlyle situates work is offered in the spirit of intellectual compromise, and "could be adopted or ignored or held in willing suspension of disbelief" (256).

21. See part 3 of the *Communist Manifesto* (Tucker, The *Marx-Engels Reader*, 491). Engels in particular, though, was always careful to distinguish Carlyle's project from that of "Young England." In a footnote to *The Condition of the Working Class in England*, for example, Engels asserts that Carlyle merits serious consideration precisely because of his interest in the *organization of labor*: "The hope of 'Young England' is a restoration of the old 'merry England' with its brilliant features and its romantic feudalism. This object is of course unattainable and ridiculous, a satire upon all historic development; but the good intention, the courage to resist the existing state of things and prevalent prejudices, and to recognise the vileness of our present condition, is worth something anyhow. Wholly isolated is the half-German Englishman, Thomas Carlyle, who, originally a Tory, goes beyond all those hitherto mentioned. He has sounded the social disorder more deeply than any other English bourgeois, and demands the organisation of labour. I hope that Carlyle, who has found the right path, will be capable of following it. He has my best wishes and those of many other Germans" (in *Karl Marx, Frederick Engels: Collected Works*, 4:578–79). Engels revised his opinion of Carlyle subsequent to the revolutions of 1848, which made Carlyle "an out-and-out reactionary . . . grumbling at the tide of history that cast him ashore" (*Collected Works*, 4:579 [note to the 1892 German edition of *The Condition of the Working Class*]).

22. See, for example: Chapman, 38; Chandler, 152; Girouard, 130–131; and Houghton, 318–19.

23. Perhaps the most concise statement of Carlyle's critique of Bentham occurs in an 1831 letter to Macvey Napier, then the editor of the *Edinburgh Review*: "Bentham is a denyer, he denies with a loud and universally convincing voice: his fault is that he can *affirm* nothing, except that money is pleasant in the purse and food in the stomach, and that by this simplest of all Beliefs he can reorganize Society" (Kaplan, 158, original emphasis).

24. Gallagher, *Industrial Reformation*, 196.

25. Quoted in Chandler, 130. Carlyle's remarks on chivalry are from his unfinished history of German literature.

26. Frederick William Roe, *The Social Philosophy of Carlyle and Ruskin* (New York: Gordian Press, 1970), 106–7.

27. Michel Foucault, *Discipline and Punish: The Birth of the Prison*, translated by Alan Sheridan (New York: Vintage, 1979), 202–3.

28. Ibid., 201.

29. Sharon Aronofsky Weltman, "Female and Maelstrom: The Gender Vortex in Carlyle and Ruskin," *Carlyle Studies Annual* 17 (1997): 91. Weltman also notes, though, that Carlyle's metaphoric use of whirlpools and maelstroms are not consistently gendered, and are sometimes figured as masculine (see especially 91, 93, and 98 n. 6).

30. On this point see also Sussman, who identifies "Samson's mental force" as "equally innate, penetrative, [and] male, able to bring order to the fluid formlessness of the psyche as well as the social order of the monastery" (32–33).

31. As in the case of Cobbett, Carlyle's anti-Semitism also rears its ugly head within his condition-of-England discourse, leading him to effuse over Abbot Samson's banishment of Jewish creditors from St. Edmundsbury, in a passage that rhetorically implicates the reader in Carlyle's enthusiastic approval: "the harpy Jews not only settled with, but banished, bag and baggage, out of the *Bannaleuca* (Liberties, *Banlieue*) of St. Edmundsbury,—so has the King's Majesty been persuaded to permit. Farewell to *you*, at any rate; let us, in no extremity, apply again to you! Armed men march them over the borders, dismiss them under stern penalties,—sentence of excommunication on all that shall again harbour them here: there were many dry eyes at their departure" (*PP*, 96). Carlyle does not mention the Christian creditors; one presumes that they were not accorded a similar fate.

32. Sussman, 53.

33. As James Eli Adams has observed, "These all male societies . . . depended on not one but two models of heroism: that of the charismatic leader, and that of the devoted followers who strive to embody his imperatives in a systematic discipline" (*Dandies and Desert Saints: Styles of Victorian Masculinity* [Ithaca: Cornell University Press, 1995], 39).

34. Thomas Carlyle, *Latter-Day Pamphlets*, in *The Works of Thomas Carlyle in Thirty Volumes* (1899; reprint, New York: AMS, 1969), 20:54. Subsequent references are cited parenthetically as *LDP*.

35. Froude identifies the prison as the Millbank Penitentiary; see James Anthony Froude, *Thomas Carlyle: A History of His Life in London, 1834–1881* (New York: Scribner's, 1884), 2:25.

36. Thomas Carlyle, *On Heroes and Hero-Worship and the Heroic in History*, in *The Works of Thomas Carlyle in Thirty Volumes* (1899; reprint, New York: AMS, 1969), 5:172–73. Subsequent references are cited parenthetically as *OH*.

37. See E. P. Thompson, *The Making of the English Working Class*, 61; and Roe, 107–27.

38. See John B. Lamb's essay, "Carlyle's 'Chartism,' the Rhetoric of Revolution, and the Dream of Empire" (*VIJ: Victorians Institute Journal* 23 [1995]: 129–50), for an extended analysis of Carlyle's imperialist rhetoric, especially as it is deployed in *Chartism*. Lamb argues that Carlyle turns to a "new mythus of empire" in *Chartism* in his search for "a credible replacement for the idea of revolution he proposed in the *French Revolution*" (137). Also significant is the connection between Carlyle's "Captains of In-

dustry" and the imperialist project itself. As Chris R. Vanden Bossche has noted, "Carlyle's representations of the 'Captain of Industry' owe a great deal to his enthusiasm for the men who were leading 'poor starving drudges' out to found new colonies, to settle new lands" (*Carlyle and the Search for Authority* [Columbus: Ohio State University Press, 1991], 114).

Chapter 5

1. Raymond Williams will serve as a typical example: "The heroically drawn Samson, like the figures celebrated in *Heroes and Hero-Worship*, underlines the steady withdrawal from genuinely social thinking into the preoccupations with personal power. In the *Latter-Day Pamphlets* the decisive shift has taken place. . . . By the time of *Shooting Niagara* this call [for power] has become a contemptuous absolutism, and the elements which made the former criticism humane have virtually disappeared" (*Culture and Society*, 82–83).

2. Monypenny seems to have deliberately distorted the quotation by taking it out of context, perhaps to create the impression that Disraeli himself might seem to be soliciting, albeit posthumously, purchase of the multivolume set. Evidence that Monypenny knew perfectly well the contextual meaning of the quotation may be found later in volume 1 of *The Life of Benjamin Disraeli*. In the chapter on *Contarini Fleming* and *Alroy*, Monypenny quotes Baron Fleming's imperative to "Read no history" in its full context, and refers to that passage as a prime example of the Baron's "Polonius-like advice" (William Flavelle Monypenny and George Earle Buckle, *The Life of Benjamin Disraeli Earl of Beaconsfield*, 4 vols. [1929; reprint, New York: Russell and Russell, 1968], 1:193). For a similar, and more recent, out-of-context quotation of this particular text, see Jane Ridley, *Young Disraeli, 1804–1846* (New York: Crown, 1995), 1.

3. Napoleon is also one of Carlyle's "great men"—"our last Great Man!" says Carlyle (*OH*, 243).

4. Benjamin Disraeli, *Contarini Fleming: A Psychological Romance*, in *The Bradenham Edition of the Novels and Tales of Benjamin Disraeli, 1st Earl of Beaconsfield* (New York: Knopf, n.d.), 4:111.

5. Richard G. Weeks, Jr., "Disraeli as Political Egoist: A Literary and Historical Investigation," *Journal of British Studies* 28 (October 1989): 387.

6. Peter Jupp, "Disraeli's Interpretation of English History," in *The Self-Fashioning of Disraeli, 1818–1851*, edited by Charles Richmond and Paul Smith (Cambridge: Cambridge University Press, 1998), 131.

7. See Gary Handwerk, "Behind Sybil's Veil: Disraeli's Mix of Ideological Messages," *Modern Language Quarterly* 49 (December 1988): 321 and 321 n. 1.

8. Robert O'Kell, "Two Nations, or One? Disraeli's Allegorical Romance," *Victorian Studies* 30 (winter 1987): 215.

9. Benjamin Disraeli, *Sybil; or, The Two Nations*, edited by Thom Braun (New York: Penguin, 1980, repr. 1985), 501. Subsequent references to this edition of *Sybil*

will be noted parenthetically. Braun reiterates his position in his *Disraeli the Novelist*, asserting that the Disraelian version of history in *Sybil* is "distorted" and "rarely becomes more than inconsequential" ([London: George Allen and Unwin, 1981], 92). See also Jupp, who notes that most historians and biographers hold the position "that Disraeli's interpretation [of history] is not to be taken too seriously, either as history or as a means by which Disraeli established a purpose for himself and a role in the eyes of the public" (132). As Jupp's essay clearly demonstrates, though, Disraeli's interpretation was not ill-informed or idiosyncratic, but in fact a product of "very extensive reading and a careful synthesis of contemporary conceptual approaches to the past" (151).

10. Monypenny detected at least a "note" of irony in Disraeli's theory of history, an irony in the service of making "a travesty of the rival Whig theory that held the field" (Monypenny and Buckle, 1:693). While Monypenny does take Disraeli's theory quite seriously, he warns "against the temptation of taking him too literally" (1:694).

11. Gallagher, *Industrial Reformation*, 207.

12. Unfortunately, in her attempt to differentiate Carlyle's project from Disraeli's, Gallagher herself "simply juxtaposes" *Past and Present* and *Sybil*, and in the process offers an uncharacteristically reductive assessment of Carlyle's work. As I've argued in chapter 3, far from "simply juxtaposing" the two terms, Carlyle positions the past in *Past and Present* as stabilizer of meaning, a point of reference around which meaning may be organized, but ultimately as something utterly remote and other that may be only represented, not resurrected, restored, or embraced.

13. Richard A. Levine, *Benjamin Disraeli* (New York: Twayne, 1968), 89.

14. Levine identifies this center of the "spiraling motion" as the "laws and principles of the Hebraeo-Christian Church," though he labels that center somewhat inaccurately, at least in terms of the metaphor, as a base. More importantly, Levine sees Disraeli as offering this "spiraling" view of history as an improvement on the cyclical models offered by Comte and Saint-Simon; Levine is thus able to package neatly (though somewhat tautologically) Disraeli's own view of history as an element of its forward progress. See Levine, 88–89.

15. Gallagher, *Industrial Reformation*, 206.

16. See G. P. Gooch, *History and Historians in the Nineteenth Century* (Boston: Beacon Press, 1959), 14–23, and Louise Merwin Young, who writes in her *Thomas Carlyle and the Art of History* that by 1811, "Niebuhr had laid the foundations for the science of historical criticism" ([New York: Octagon Books, 1971], 3).

17. White, 146. Among the "palingenetic" group of historians, as we have seen in chapter 3, White also includes Carlyle.

18. Wildman was a prominent, though relatively short-term, member of the Levellers (from 1647 to 1649) and "one of the most diligent of the intermediaries between the London Levellers and the Army Agitators" (Joseph Frank, *The Levellers* [New York: Russell and Russell, 1955], 112). He was also the primary author of "The Case of the Armie truly stated" (October 1647), a Leveller pamphlet that set the stage for the debates at Putney late that year, where Wildman was the Leveller's "leading spokesman"

(Frank, 135). Christopher Hill identifies Wildman as leading, along with Lilburne, "a moderate constitutional wing of the Levellers," focusing on issues of constitutional reform, rather than advocating (for example) the abolition of private property, as was the case with the Diggers (*The World Turned Upside Down* [New York: Viking Press, 1972], 91–93). Even so, says Hill, "the constitutional Levellers were a very radical left wing of the revolutionary party" (99).

19. Frank, 225–26. Indeed, when Wildman does appear in the accounts of the second half of the seventeenth century by historians of Disraeli's time, it is only as a prolific, seemingly perpetual conspirator. Macaulay, for example, in his *History of England* (1849), labels Wildman upon his exile in 1685 as one of many "outlaws" marked by "fiery temper and weak judgment," and of Wildman's years as a Leveller leader Macaulay states only that "Wildman had served forty years before in the parliamentary army, but had been more distinguished there as an agitator than as a soldier, and had early quitted the profession of arms for pursuits better suited to his temper" (Thomas Babington Macaulay, *The History of England from the Accession of James II*, 3 vols. [New York: Dutton, 1906], 1:401–2). Macaulay attributes Wildman's post-Leveller activity to his "hatred of monarchy," rendered all the more loathsome by his "tender care for his own safety" (402). See Edward Hyde Clarendon, *The History of the Rebellion and Civil Wars in England*, 6 vols. (Oxford: Clarendon Press, 1958), 5:303–5, for the still-standard account of Wildman's plot against Cromwell, subsequent arrest, and imprisonment.

20. Thomas Carlyle, *Oliver Cromwell's Letters and Speeches with Elucidations*, 5 vols. (London: Chapman and Hall, 1893), 4:112. Wildman was arrested in 1655 while in the process of drafting a call to arms against Cromwell (Carlyle, *Cromwell*, 4:111; Clarendon, 304). Carlyle writes that Wildman "has been the centre of an extensive world of Plots this winter [1654–55], as his wont from of old was: the mainspring of royalist Anabaptistry, what we call the *frantic* form of Republicanism, which hopes to attain its object by assisting even Charles Stuart against the Tyrant Oliver" (*Cromwell*, 4:112). Wildman was subsequently (and rather promptly) released from prison, an event Carlyle attributes to Cromwell's magnanimity, but one that others have seen as evidence of Wildman's status as a double agent (Clarendon, 305; Wilbur Cortez Abbott, *The Writings and Speeches of Oliver Cromwell*, 4 vols. [1937–47; reprint, New York: Russell and Russell, 1970], 4:199).

21. Benjamin Disraeli, "GENERAL PREFACE by the Author, to the collected edition of his Novels published in 1870, and known as the Hughenden Edition," in *The Bradenham Edition of the Novels and Tales of Benjamin Disraeli, 1st Earl of Beaconsfield* (New York: Knopf, n.d.), x. As Peter Jupp has noted, Disraeli was metaphorically "born" in his father Isaac's 25,000-volume library, "much of which appears to have contained works of history" (143).

22. Disraeli, "General Preface," xii-xiii. Disraeli makes a similar statement about his positions—among them, that "the written history of our country for the last ten reigns has been a mere phantasma" (496)—in *Sybil*'s penultimate paragraph: "It is

nearly fourteen years ago, in the popular frenzy of a mean and selfish revolution which neither emancipated the Crown nor the People, that I first took the occasion to intimate and then to develope [*sic*] to the first assembly of my countrymen that I ever had the honour to address, these convictions. They have been misunderstood as is ever for a season the fate of Truth, and they have obtained for their promulgator much misrepresentation as must ever be the lot of those who will not follow the beaten track of a fallacious custom" (497).

23. Robert Blake, *Disraeli* (New York: St. Martin's, 1967), 167.

24. M. G. Wiebe, J. B. Conacher, John Matthews, and Mary S. Millar, eds., *Benjamin Disraeli Letters: Volume Four, 1842–1847* (Toronto: University of Toronto Press, 1989), xv.

25. *CL*, 17:311–12. Engels held a similar opinion of Young England (see chapter 4, note 22).

26. Blake, 167 and 183. For an account of Disraeli's petitioning of Peel and Peel's response, see Monypenny and Buckle, 1:515–20; Blake, 164–66; and Ridley, 253–56. Disraeli's outsider status, of course, precedes this particular event in his political career. His middle-class origin, his lack of the typical privileged public school education, and especially his Jewish heritage all marked Disraeli as an alien presence within the Tory party. For an excellent discussion of how others perceived Disraeli and how he perceived himself with regard to his Jewish identity, see Todd M. Endelman, "'A Hebrew to the End': The Emergence of Disraeli's Jewishness," in *The Self-Fashioning of Disraeli, 1818–1851*, edited by Charles Richmond and Paul Smith (Cambridge: Cambridge University Press, 1998), 106–30.

27. Blake, 167.

28. Monypenny and Buckle, 1:595. At least one contemporary critic agrees; see Weeks, 394.

29. In a letter to his wife a little more than five months after Peel's reply to his letter of solicitation, Disraeli writes: "You cannot conceive how solitary I feel: utterly isolated. Before the change of Government, political party was a tie among men, but now it is only a tie among men who are in office. The supporter of administration, who is not in place and power himself, is a solitary animal. He has neither hope nor fear" (Monypenny and Buckle, 1:523).

30. Paul Smith, "Disraeli's Politics," in *The Self-Fashioning of Disraeli, 1818–1851*, edited by Charles Richmond and Paul Smith (Cambridge: Cambridge University Press, 1998), 164–65.

31. Weeks, 388.

32. As Braun remarks, after the publication of *Coningsby* in particular, "[a]dvancement for Disraeli *within* a Peelite Administration would now have been unacceptable, or, more likely, just impossible. The only course of action was really to reinforce an ideological independence by a concentration of criticism of the government" (84).

33. Monypenny and Buckle, 1:643–44.

34. As Blake notes, Disraeli's *Sybil* wasn't exactly consumed by "the masses," even though Disraeli would announce retroactively (in the 1849 preface to *Coningsby*) that he chose "to adopt the form of fiction" to embody his ideas because it "offered the best chance of influencing opinion." Although the book "sold briskly, going through three editions (2500 copies) during the summer" (Ridley, 309), its readership consisted mainly of those who traveled in "society and parliamentary circles" (Blake, 192–93). Still, such an audience is precisely the right target for "influence" if one is seeking "recognition."

35. Paul Smith, introduction to *The Self-Fashioning of Disraeli, 1818–1851*, edited by Charles Richmond and Paul Smith (Cambridge: Cambridge University Press, 1998), 5. Smith is referring here primarily to Disraeli's novels of the 1820s and 1830s, but the statement applies equally well to the *Coningsby*, *Sybil*, *Tancred* trilogy.

36. Williams, *Culture and Society*, 97. Repeating the deceptiveness with which Monypenny's epigraph began this chapter, I have taken Williams' words somewhat out of context. In describing Disraeli's tone as "the generalized anger of an outsider making his way," Williams is referring specifically to Disraeli's portrayal of the physical and economic suffering of the urban and rural poor, an experience from which Disraeli's own life was very much separated.

37. The words are Carlyle's (*Chartism*, 151).

38. Much has been made of the authenticity of Disraeli's claim to have, as an authority, his "own observation." As Raymond Williams has warned, "[a]nyone who is prepared to give credit to Disraeli's unsupported authority on any matter of social fact has of course mistaken his man" (*Culture and Society*, 97). Although it is only as a "generalizing rhetorician of human suffering" (97) that Williams finds Disraeli valuable, both Martin Fido and Sheila Smith have firmly established much of the specific source material (mostly Blue Books) for Disraeli's portrayal of urban and agrarian life. Disraeli dramatized some of the written reports he encountered; parts of others were appropriated verbatim. One might cite Disraeli's plagiarism as evidence of his weakness as a writer, but at the very least it does demonstrate the accuracy of much of his detail. Fido even judiciously acknowledges that "one cannot overrule the possibility that Disraeli had actually visited some of the places he describes in other people's words, whether their accounts first drew his attention to the existence of the locations, or whether he later backed up cursory inspections with library research" ("'From His Own Observation': Sources of Working Class Passages in Disraeli's *Sybil*," *Modern Language Review* 72 [1977]: 276. See also Sheila M. Smith, "Willenhall and Wodgate: Disraeli's Use of Blue Book Evidence," *Review of English Studies* 13 [1962]: 368–84).

39. The process of producing false, or at least dubious, claims to medieval titles and land rights became increasingly common in the eighteenth and nineteenth centuries. According to Girouard, the revival of interest in establishing familial linkage to medieval titles through genealogical and heraldic research, particularly through the revival of baronies formerly in abeyance, reached its peak in the 1830s (Girouard, 40).

40. Gallagher, *Industrial Reformation*, 206.

41. *Sybil*'s narrator offers an explanation in a later chapter for the effect these ruins have upon the mind of Egremont and others: "One of the reasons urged for the destruction of the monasteries after the dispersion of their inhabitants, was the pernicious influence of their solemn and stately forms on the memories and imagination of those that beheld them. It was impossible to connect systematic crime with the creators of such divine fabrics" (*Sybil*, 141).

42. Here is Cobbett: "The Monastics could possess no private property, they could save no money, they could bequeath nothing. They had a life interest in their estate, and no more. The lived, received and expended *in common*" (*History of the Protestant "Reformation,"* V:151). For a more detailed discussion of the close relation between Gerard's statements and Cobbett's *History of the Protestant "Reformation,"* see Chandler, 178–80. In addition, Morley's observation that English society is not a community but an "aggregation," one that operates on a "dissociating, rather than a uniting, principle," mirrors a similar observation in Carlyle's *Past and Present*: "We call it a Society; and go about professing openly the totalest separation, isolation. Our life is not a mutual helpfulness; but rather . . . a mutual hostility" (148).

43. It is perhaps indicative of Walter Gerard's aristocratic character that after the death of his father, and without financial resources of his own, he left the land that once belonged to his forebears, because, he says, "I would not sink to be a labourer on the soil that had once been our own" (115).

44. Gerard seeks the papers in order to bolster the legal proceedings he has already initiated against Lord de Mowbray; Morley seeks the papers out of his fanatical devotion to Sybil; and Hatton himself seeks the papers in order to fulfill his own aristocratic fantasies, with Sybil as his wife and link to the "old blood."

45. Egremont later reiterates this impression when he unexpectedly encounters Sybil in yet another sacred place—Westminster Abbey. There, the "soft radiance" of the church appears to form "a kind of halo" around her head (283–84). Egremont is not alone in this visionary experience of Sybil's presence; Baptist Hatton also describes her as "that seraphic being whose lustre even now haunts my vision" (309).

46. This effect is reinforced rather lightheartedly in Book 3. As Sybil walks through the village near the Trafford factory, "beautiful children" greet her with cries of "the queen, the queen," to which Sybil replies, laughingly, "My subjects" (226). For a full analysis of the symbolic connection between Sybil and Victoria, see Jennifer Sampson, "*Sybil*, or the Two Monarchs," *Studies in Philology* 95 (winter 98): 97–119.

47. Gallagher, *Industrial Reformation*, 214–15.

48. Part of what "sells" Sybil on the integrity of Egremont's character is his pronouncement in Parliament "that the rights of labour were as sacred as those of property" (350).

49. O'Kell, for example, reads Sybil's significance allegorically, as representative of "the spirit of piety and devotion" that provides "a divine sanction" of Egremont's

agenda (216). For a similar reading, see also Daniel Schwarz, *Disraeli's Fiction* (New York: Harper and Row, 1979), 114. Jennifer Sampson's insightful essay "*Sybil,* or the Two Monarchs" argues for reading Sybil as a figure for Victoria, and her marriage to Egremont as a symbolic recasting of the relationship between the monarchy and Parliament (97–119).

50. Michael McCully, "Beyond 'The Convent and the Cottage': A Reconsideration of Disraeli's *Sybil,*" *College Language Association Journal* 29 (March 1986): 324.

51. Crosby, 6.

52. Similarly, Gary Handwerk has also asserted that "*Sybil*'s main interest is political legitimacy as reached by a process of consensus" (325). Contrary to my own argument, though, Handwerk believes "that the text's underlying theme is that politics revolves around persons rather than principles, and is more attuned to pragmatic issues of persuasion and power than to abstract political concepts" (322). Although he does refer once to Sybil's "conversion" (333), Handwerk seems to use this word to mean "the state of being fully persuaded." In contrast, I am deliberately using the word "conversion" to draw out both its religious and passive connotations, in the sense of being "converted to" an ideology.

53. Crosby, 146.

54. Other critics have also read the Sybil/Egremont relationship as representative of the relation between the masses and the "new" aristocracy, usually characterizing this relationship as a *union* of the two classes. Patrick Brantlinger, for example, sees the union as belonging to "the standard Victorian fictional strategy of an interclass marriage," albeit ironized (and undermined) by Sybil's aristocratic heritage ("Tory-Radicalism and 'The Two Nations' in Disraeli's *Sybil,*" *Victorian Newsletter* 41 [spring 1972]: 13, and *The Spirit of Reform: British Literature and Politics, 1832–1867* [Cambridge: Harvard University Press, 1977], 97). Clare Simmons downplays the irony of Sybil's heritage, asserting that her symbolism "maintains at least a tenuous hold on a romantic theory of natural aristocracy" and that "Sybil deserves to be the natural leader of her people" (*Reversing the Conquest: History and Myth in Nineteenth-Century British Literature* [New Brunswick: Rutgers University Press, 1990], 106). In contrast, I hope to have shown that their relation is not so much a union, as yet another displacement (this time of Sybil herself) through "consent."

55. The word "restoration" is used with reference to Sybil's inheritance in the novel's final chapter. After revealing that Sybil is now Countess Marney, the narrator tells us that although Egremont's presence prevented Baptist Hatton from completely realizing his designs on Sybil, "there was nothing he desired more ardently than to see her restored to her rights, and to be instrumental in that restoration. How successful he was in pursuing her claim, the reader has already learnt" (495).

56. Rosemarie Bodenheimer, in her chapter "Politics and the Recovery of Story," stresses Disraeli's overarching interest in establishing historical continuity through the "recovery" of marginalized narratives. This continuity is achieved, she argues, only through a paradoxical disruption of the present (i.e., the violent conflict on Mowbray

Moor and in Mowbray Castle) that allows for the desired connection between past and future (Sybil and Egremont). While I have also been using the term "recovery" to designate Disraeli's interest in re-presenting the historically marginalized and dispossessed, I'm arguing here that what purports to be "continuity" is itself, in the end, only a further disruption or displacement, a "recovery" that "covers over" the claims of the past, cloaking them under the textual fabric of a new generation of terms and conditions. Thus my use of the term "recovery" is more self-consciously ironic (and more directly revealing of its ideological purpose) than the term appears to be in Bodenheimer's chapter. See Rosemarie Bodenheimer, *The Politics of Story in Victorian Social Fiction* (Ithaca: Cornell University Press, 1988), 166–88.

Chapter 6

1. Carlyle, *Chartism*, 151.

2. As Trygve Tholfson has noted in his *Working Class Radicalism in Mid-Victorian England* (New York: Columbia University Press, 1977), this rhetoric of individual improvement has at its source, generally speaking, the Enlightenment and Evangelicalism of the eighteenth century (61ff.). E. P. Thompson's *The Making of the English Working Class* also attests to this relation. See Thompson's chapter "The Transforming Power of the Cross" (350–400) for a revealing analysis of the relationship between Methodism in particular and working-class radicalism, including Chartism.

3. Andrew Ure, *The Philosophy of Manufactures; or, an Exposition of the Scientific, Moral, and Commercial Economy of the Factory System of Great Britain* (London: Charles Knight, 1835), 417.

4. Thompson, 361.

5. Ure, 423.

6. Ibid., 15. In addition, as Karl Marx has noted, Ure represents the factory system "not only as an automaton, but as an autocrat. 'In these spacious halls [writes Ure] the benignant power of steam summons around him his myriad of willing menials'" (*Capital: A Critique of Political Economy*, translated by Samuel Moore and Edward Aveling [New York: International Publishers, 1967], 396).

7. John Francis Bray, *Labour's Wrongs and Labour's Remedy; or The Age of Might and the Age of Right* (1839; reprint, New York: Kelley, 1968), vi.

8. Ibid., 7. Bray's allusion to the Christian redemption is of a piece with the rhetoric adopted by Owenite working-class groups in the mid- to late 1840s, like the Leeds Redemption Society, which were formed (in the words of James Hole) "to enable the Working Classes to work out their own Redemption by union amongst themselves" (qtd. in Tholfson, 254). Tholfson identifies Hole as one of the "founding members" of the Leeds Redemption Society, which formed in 1845, the same year *Sybil* was published (254).

9. Bray, 7.

10. See Sheila Smith and Martin Fido for useful and detailed comparisons of *Sybil*

and Disraeli's source material. For my own purposes, I am less interested in the question of the novel's accuracy (or the accuracy of the source material, for that matter) than I am in the effect Disraeli wishes to produce: that the representation of the conditions of labor in *Sybil* correspond to the conditions that exist in reality. See Disraeli's "Advertisement" (*Sybil*, 24) for his most direct assertion of that relation.

11. Brantlinger, *The Spirit of Reform*, 100.

12. Ibid., 99.

13. "For there is a perennial nobleness, and even sacredness, in Work. Were he never so benighted, forgetful of his high calling, there is always hope in a man that actually and earnestly works: in Idleness alone is there perpetual despair" (Carlyle, *Past and Present*, 196).

14. An appeal to the same motto appears also in *Past and Present*, of course, in the chapter titled "Reward." Carlyle writes, "Admirable was that of the old monks, '*Laborare est Orare*, Work is Worship'" (201).

15. Thompson, 364–65.

16. I have suggested in the previous chapter that this realization of Sybil's leads her to offer her consent, both personal and political, to Egremont as a representative of that "body" which will both govern the people and "guide" Sybil herself. It is important to note here, in addition, the extent to which that consent is predicated on Sybil's revised estimation of the utter degradation of the laboring class, the extent to which the terms of that revision had already been established in Book 3, and the implications of that revision for her own identity as a "daughter of the People."

17. In addition to the physical and ideological separation from her father, Sybil also becomes estranged, shortly thereafter, from the trusted family friend Stephen Morley. The revelation of Morley's moral corruption (he attempts to blackmail Sybil into marrying him) is intended, of course, to invalidate Morley's political rhetoric, and to ironize his platitudes concerning the value of "community." While he did participate in the Chartist Convention as a delegate, Morley admits that it was only because of his love for Sybil that he "embarked in a cause with which I have little sympathy" (*Sybil*, 266).

18. Brantlinger, *The Spirit of Reform*, 99–100.

19. O'Kell, 231.

20. Monypenny and Buckle, 1:654. See also Chandler, 177.

21. Sampson, 110.

22. Compare, by way of contrast, the riot scene in *North and South*, in which Margaret Hale embraces the threatened body of John Thornton, making "her body into a shield from the fierce people beyond," and suffering a stone to the head from the angry crowd as a result (Elizabeth Gaskell, *North and South*, edited by Dorothy Collin [New York: Penguin, 1986], 234–35).

23. Quoted in Benjamin Disraeli, *Benjamin Disraeli Letters: Volume Three, 1838–1841*, edited by M. G. Wiebe, J. B. Conacher, John Matthews, and Mary S. Millar (Toronto: University of Toronto Press, 1987), 272.

24. Ibid.

25. Handwerk, 328.

26. Compare Gerard's earlier, more sympathetic portrayal of Morley (215). Gerard's and Morley's increased separation over the course of the novel is a product not only of their differing interpretations of historical circumstance, but also of Morley's betrayal of his friendship with the Gerards by conspiring to blackmail Sybil. Though Gerard never learns of this side of Morley, he does note that the "intimacy" between Sybil and Morley "had entirely died away," and detects a certain "reserve" in Morley's behavior toward him (434).

27. Sybil's assertion here reiterates Egremont's words to her at the end of Book 4, just prior to Sybil's "conversion": "The People are not strong; the People never can be strong. Their attempts at self-vindication will end only in their suffering and confusion" (334). The views of Sybil and Egremont both reflect contemporary views of Chartism in the early 1840s; as Gareth Stedman Jones has noted, most observers (Carlyle included) emphasized the social, rather than the political, aspect of Chartist agitation, "projecting onto it deeper, unavowed motives and sentiments" (*Languages of Class*, 90–91). After being arrested, tried and imprisoned, Gerard (with hindsight) agrees with Sybil that it was "a mistake . . . to have moved in –39" (434). But true to the consistency of his political convictions and his commitment to physical force, Gerard insists that only the timing, not the theory or method, was in error: "We should have waited three years" (434).

28. Although Gerard's primarily defensive participation is less blamable than Marney's, it should be noted that Marney's misinterpretation of the crowd on Mowbray Moor is not entirely due to his usual supercilious and obnoxious inanity, but also to an "alarming and exaggerated report" he received "of the insurrection and the havoc that was probably impending" (488).

29. Disraeli, "General Preface," xiv.

30. As we have seen, Sybil stands apart because of her unassailable virtue, and Gerard because of his unimpeachable integrity. Morley's radical utopian convictions (including a disparaging view of the family), undermined by the revelation of his obsessive (and ultimately villainous) relationship with Sybil, do not set him "above" the masses, as with the Gerards, but rather to the side, as a behind-the-scenes player whose primary interest is self-serving.

31. Louis Cazamian, *The Social Novel in England, 1830–1850*, translated by Martin Fido (Boston: Routledge, 1973),192.

32. See Fido, 268.

33. See Sheila Smith, 23–24, for more about the Commission's First and Second Reports. Smith's article irrefutably demonstrates Disraeli's indebtedness to the appendix of the Second Report. Although many critics cite Smith's article when making the point that Disraeli "exaggerated" the material he found in the report (see O'Kell, 227 n. 20; and Braun, *Disraeli the Novelist*, 98), this is not the thesis of Smith's article. She concedes that "Disraeli is not entirely guiltless of exaggeration," usually in "the form of

significant omissions" (380), but contends that "concerning his descriptions of Wodgate's material conditions; of the appearance, customs, and nature of its inhabitants; and of the hard treatment received by its apprentices, Disraeli's claim, in the Advertisement to the first edition of *Sybil*, that he has not exaggerated but has relied on 'the authentic evidence which has been received by Royal Commissions and Parliamentary Committees,' is just" (372–73). In fact, writes Smith, "sometimes he does not make his narrative as lurid as it might well be with full support from [the appendix's] evidence" (373).

34. Morley's sentiment also carries with it the implication that "ministering" to foreigners comes at the expense of the needy but neglected masses at home. The narrator echoes this view in another context in Book 3; when discussing the inhumane working conditions of the mines near Wodgate, the narrator comments that these conditions "seem to have escaped the notice of the Society for the Abolition of Negro Slavery" (178). One of the most vocal critics of this alleged hypocrisy, of course, was Carlyle (see *Past and Present*, 274–75), but such comparisons may be found throughout radical discourse in the early nineteenth century, including the works of Cobbett. As Catherine Gallagher has made clear, the worker/slave metaphor has its origins in late-eighteenth-century pro-slavery rhetoric. She identifies Cobbett, in fact, as a key figure in the transmission of this metaphor to radical discourse; while retaining his antiabolitionist stance, Cobbett used the worker/slave comparison to rail against the economic condition of laborers in England. (See Gallagher, *Industrial Reformation*, 6–10).

35. As Daniel Bivona has argued, the novels *Coningsby*, *Sybil*, and *Tancred*, when read together as a discourse on English political desire, clearly demonstrate that "Disraeli saw the mission to colonize alien cultures as an imperative of the same form as the mission to 'colonize' the middle and working classes in England. England's duty is defined as one of expanding by appropriating and reshaping the alien to suit its purposes, but it must do so under the guise of restoring an ancient unity" ("Disraeli's Political Trilogy and the Antinomic Structure of Imperial Desire," *Novel: A Forum on Fiction* 22 [spring 1989]: 306).

36. See Carlyle, *Past and Present*, 148. For a typical reading of Trafford as a captain of industry, see Ivan Melada, *The Captain of Industry in English Fiction, 1821–1871* (Albuquerque: University of New Mexico Press, 1970), 127–28.

37. Melada, 127. See also Parama Roy, who suggests that Trafford's factory represents "a contemporary, nineteeth-century version of the medieval country house" (Parama Roy, "*Sybil:* The Two Nations and the Manorial Ideal," *VIJ: Victorians Institute Journal* 17 [1989]: 70).

38. Interestingly, given this centralized hierarchy, Gerard (the inspector) and Trafford (the employer) occupy nearly identical positions, further reinforcing the perception that Gerard, though "belonging" to the People, remains "above" them.

39. Carlyle, *Past and Present*, 207, 95. As Altick notes, Carlyle appropriates the term "Great Taskmaster's eye" from Milton (207 n. 22).

40. Several other characteristics round out Trafford's sense of duty. Though an in-

dustrialist, Trafford is not of the middle class, but is the younger son of an aristocratic family (like Egremont), and seems to have an affinity for lost social relations: he has "old English feelings," the narrator tells us (224). Conveniently, though a younger son, Trafford inherited a huge sum of money from a distant relative, just at the right moment to invest in manufacturing.

41. Roy, 70.

42. The events of Book 6 allude to the Plug Plot riots in the summer of 1842 (see Cazamian, 205). Unlike the Hell-cat activity, however, the Plug Plot riots initially arose solely from economic suffering. Chartist leaders grafted their cause onto the movement shortly thereafter, and strikers passed "resolutions in favour of remaining out of employment until the People's Charter became the law of the land" (Briggs, ed., *Chartist Studies* [London: MacMillan, 1959], 385; see also 53–55).

43. This unwillingness, of course, remains qualified and ironized by their willingness to follow Bishop Hatton, whose own movements are largely orchestrated by the Chartist Field.

44. Bishop Hatton's alliance with the Chartist cause is compared satirically to Constantine's conversion (443), and Field is referred to as the "Chartist Apostle" (460). See O'Kell, 232.

45. Fido, 280.

46. Williams, *Culture and Society*, 104–5.

47. In response to John Manners's criticism of the series of disasters "crowded at the end" of the novel, Disraeli writes: "I agree with you as to the catastrophe: it is a decided but almost an inevitable, fault. We call up the spirits from the vasty deep, but they are sometimes too vital to get rid of at the end of the third volume" (*Benjamin Disraeli Letters: Volume Four, 1842–1847*, 167 and 167 n. 2).

48. Bivona, 317. See also Roy, who describes the immolation of the Hell-cats in Mowbray Castle as "a ritual of exorcism" (72), and Bodenheimer, who concludes that the only way "to get from the past to the future" in *Sybil* is through "a final disruption, a tear in the social fabric which admits the redemptive beings" (188).

49. Radley successfully delivered to Sybil the box of papers that legitimize the Gerard claim to the Mowbray estate.

50. "The firm of Radley, Mowbray, and Co.," we are told, "is a rising one; and will probably furnish in time a crop of members of Parliament and Peers of the realm" (495).

51. Parama Roy aptly contrasts *Sybil*'s conclusion with the endings of *Silas Marner* and *Felix Holt* (75 n. 1). In the latter novel, for example, Esther Lyon renounces her inheritance and rejects Harold Transome, clearing the way for her marriage to Felix Holt, who maintains his working-class affiliation. Her "union" with Holt is thus not at all like the "enrapturing" assimilation of Sybil to Egremont; when Felix cautions Esther about the working-class people she will now live among, she replies, "I know it is serious. Since I have been at Transome Court I have seen many things seriously. If I had not, I should not have left what I did leave. I made a deliberate choice" (George Eliot,

Felix Holt, The Radical, edited by Peter Coveney [New York: Penguin, 1972], 601–2). Roy's point is that "it would never occur to Sybil . . . to renounce the station to which Providence has restored her" (73); to this I would add that a character like Felix Holt—redeemed by the end, but still staunchly self-identified as working class—is also inconceivable in Disraeli's symbolic economy. It is worth remembering, though, that Felix Holt does manage to disappear in Eliot's epilogue, moving to a town the narrator determines to "keep . . . a secret, lest he should be troubled by any visitor having the insufferable motive of curiosity" (606).

52. Roy, 72.

53. Gallagher, *Industrial Reformation*, 218. See also Bodenheimer, who offers a fine analysis of the way in which Disraeli's narrative technique consistently focuses only on the "before" and "after" of a sequence of events, leaving the present unrepresented or "excised" (186–88, esp. 187).

Conclusion

1. Carlyle, *Chartism*, 190.

2. Carlyle's essay ends with a call for national education and emigration; Carlyle offers the former as necessary for the "self-regulation" of the working class (*Chartism*, 194), and the latter as an almost self-evident means for that class to regain the productivity that has been stripped from them (see esp. 203–4).

3. Carlyle, *Chartism*, 118.

Works Cited

Abbott, Wilbur Cortez. *The Writings and Speeches of Oliver Cromwell*. 4 vols. 1937–47. Reprint, New York: Russell and Russell, 1970.

Adams, James Eli. *Dandies and Desert Saints: Styles of Victorian Masculinity*. Ithaca: Cornell University Press, 1995.

Althusser, Louis. *Lenin and Philosophy*. New York: Monthly Review Press, 1971.

Anger, Suzy. "Carlyle: Between Biblical Exegesis and Romantic Hermeneutics." *Texas Studies in Language and Literature* 40 (spring 1998): 78–96.

Attridge, Derek, Geoff Bennington, and Robert Young, eds. *Post-structuralism and the Question of History*. New York: Cambridge University Press, 1987.

Baker, William. "The London Library Borrowings of Thomas Carlyle, 1841–1844." *Library Review* 30 (summer 1981): 89–95.

Banham, Joanna, and Jennifer Harris, eds. *William Morris and the Middle Ages*. Dover: Manchester University Press, 1984.

Basney, Lionel. "How the Matter Stood: Cobbett's Moral and Political Ecology." *The Sewanee Review* 101 (summer 1993): 354–74.

Bataille, Georges. *Visions of Excess: Selected Writings, 1927–1939*. Edited and translated by Allan Stoekl. Minneapolis: University of Minnesota Press, 1985.

Baudrillard, Jean. *For a Critique of the Political Economy of the Sign*. Translated by Charles Levin. St. Louis: Telos Press, 1981.

———. *Simulations*. Translated by Philip Beitchman, Paul Foss, and Paul Patton. New York: Semiotext(e), 1983.

Bell, Walter George. *The Great Fire of London in 1666*. 1923. Reprint, London: The Bodley Head, 1951.

Binfield, Kevin. "Demonology, Ethos, and Community in Cobbett and Shelley." In *Romanticism, Radicalism, and the Press*, edited by Stephen C. Behrendt. Detroit: Wayne State University Press, 1997.

Bivona, Daniel. "Disraeli's Political Trilogy and the Antinomic Structure of Imperial Desire." *Novel: A Forum on Fiction* 22 (spring 1989): 305–25.

Blake, Robert. *Disraeli*. New York: St. Martin's, 1967.

Bodenheimer, Rosemarie. *The Politics of Story in Victorian Social Fiction*. Ithaca: Cornell University Press, 1988.

Brantlinger, Patrick. *The Spirit of Reform: British Literature and Politics, 1832–1867*. Cambridge: Harvard University Press, 1977.

———. "Tory-Radicalism and 'The Two Nations' in Disraeli's *Sybil*." *Victorian Newsletter* 41 (spring 1972): 13–17.

Brattin, Joel J. "New Manuscript Evidence about the Origin of 'Past and Present.'" *Nineteenth-Century Prose* 31 (spring 1996): 13–24.

Braun, Thom. *Disraeli the Novelist*. London: George Allen and Unwin, 1981.

Bray, John Francis. *Labour's Wrongs and Labour's Remedy; or The Age of Might and the Age of Right*. 1839. Reprint, New York: Kelley, 1968.

Briggs, Asa. *William Cobbett*. Oxford: Oxford University Press, 1967.

———, ed. *Chartist Studies*. London: MacMillan, 1959.

Burrow, J. W. "The Sense of the Past." In *The Victorians*, edited by Laurence Lerner. New York: Holmes and Meier, 1978.

Calder, Grace. *The Writing of* Past and Present. New Haven: Yale University Press, 1949.

Carlyle, Thomas. *Chartism*. In vol. 29 of *The Works of Thomas Carlyle in Thirty Volumes*. 1899. Reprint, New York: AMS, 1969.

———. *Latter-Day Pamphlets*. Vol. 20 of *The Works of Thomas Carlyle in Thirty Volumes*. 1899. Reprint, New York: AMS, 1969.

———. *Oliver Cromwell's Letters and Speeches With Elucidations*. 5 vols. London: Chapman and Hall, 1893.

———. *On Heroes, Hero-Worship, and the Heroic in History*. Vol. 5 of *The Works of Thomas Carlyle in Thirty Volumes*. 1899. Reprint, New York: AMS, 1969.

———. "On History." In vol. 27 of *The Works of Thomas Carlyle in Thirty Volumes*. 1899. Reprint, New York: AMS, 1969.

———. *Past and Present*. 1843. Edited by Richard Altick. Boston: Houghton Mifflin, 1965.

———. *Reminiscences*. Edited by J. A. Froude. New York: Scribner's, 1881.

———. *Sartor Resartus*. Vol. 1 of *The Works of Thomas Carlyle in Thirty Volumes*. 1899. Reprint, New York: AMS, 1969.

———. "Signs of the Times." In vol. 27 of *The Works of Thomas Carlyle in Thirty Volumes*. 1899. Reprint, New York: AMS, 1969.

———. "Sir Walter Scott." In vol. 29 of *The Works of Thomas Carlyle in Thirty Volumes*. 1899. Reprint, New York: AMS, 1969.

Carlyle, Thomas, and Jane Welsh Carlyle. *The Collected Letters of Thomas and Jane Welsh Carlyle*. Edited by Charles Richard Sanders, Kenneth J. Fielding, Clyde de Ryals, et al. 28 vols. Durham: Duke University Press, 1970–2000.

Cazamian, Louis. *The Social Novel in England, 1830–1850*. Translated by Martin Fido. Boston: Routledge, 1973.

Certeau, Michel de. *The Writing of History*. Translated by Tom Conley. New York: Columbia University Press, 1988.

Chandler, Alice. *A Dream of Order: The Medieval Ideal in Nineteenth-Century English Literature*. Lincoln: University of Nebraska Press, 1971.

Chapman, Raymond. *The Sense of the Past in Victorian Literature*. London: Croom Helm, 1986.

Chesterton, G. K. *William Cobbett*. London: Hodder and Stoughton, n.d.

Childers, Joseph. "Carlyle's *Past and Present*, History and a Question of Hermeneutics." *CLIO* 13 (spring 1984): 247–58.

Christ, Carol T. "'The Hero as Man of Letters': Masculinity and Victorian Nonfiction Prose." In *Victorian Sages and Cultural Discourse: Renegotiating Gender and Power*, edited by Thais E. Morgan. New Brunswick: Rutgers University Press, 1990.

Clarendon, Edward Hyde. *The History of the Rebellion and Civil Wars in England*. 6 vols. Oxford: Clarendon Press, 1958.

Clark, Sir Kenneth. *The Gothic Revival: An Essay in the History of Taste*. New York: Scribner's, 1950.

Cobbett, William. *Cottage Economy*. London: Davies, 1926.

———. *A History of the Protestant "Reformation," in England and Ireland; Showing how that event has impoverished and degraded the main body of the People in those Countries. In a series of letters, addressed to all sensible and just Englishmen*. London: Charles Clement, 1824–26.

———. *A History of the Protestant Reformation in England and Ireland*. 1824–26. Revised and edited by Francis Cardinal Gasquet. 1896. Reprint, Rockford, Ill.: Tan Books, 1988.

———. *The Protestant "Reformation," Part Second; Containing a List of the Abbeys, Priories, Nunneries, Hospitals, and other Religious Foundations, in England and Wales, and in Ireland, confiscated, seized on, or alienated, by the Protestant "Reformation" Sovereigns and Parliaments*. London: Cobbett, 1827.

———. *Rural Rides*. 2 vols. 1912. Reprint, New York: Dutton, 1966.

———. *Rural Rides*. 3 vols. Edited by G. D. H. and Margaret Cole. London: Peter Davies, 1930.

Cole, G. D. H. *The Life of William Cobbett*. Westport, Conn.: Greenwood Press, 1971.

Crosby, Christina. *The Ends of History: Victorians and "the Woman Question."* New York: Routledge, 1991.

Disraeli, Benjamin. *Benjamin Disraeli Letters: Volume Three, 1838–1841*. Edited by M. G. Wiebe, J. B. Conacher, John Matthews, and Mary S. Millar. Toronto: University of Toronto Press, 1987.

———. *Benjamin Disraeli Letters: Volume Four, 1842–1841*. Edited by M. G. Wiebe, J. B. Conacher, John Matthews, and Mary S. Millar. Toronto: University of Toronto Press, 1989.

———. *Contarini Fleming: A Psychological Romance*. Vol. 4 of *The Bradenham Edition of the Novels and Tales of Benjamin Disraeli, 1st Earl of Beaconsfield*. New York: Knopf, n.d.

———. "GENERAL PREFACE by the Author, to the collected edition of his Novels published in 1870, and known as the Hughenden Edition." In vol. 1 of *The Bradenham*

Edition of the Novels and Tales of Benjamin Disraeli, 1st Earl of Beaconsfield. New York: Knopf, n.d.

———. *Sybil; or, The Two Nations*. Edited by Thom Braun. New York: Penguin, 1985.

Dyck, Ian. *William Cobbett and Rural Popular Culture*. New York: Cambridge University Press, 1992.

Eastlake, Sir Charles. *A History of the Gothic Revival*. Edited by J. Mordaunt Crook. 1872. Reprint, New York: Humanities Press, 1970.

Eliot, George. *Felix Holt, The Radical*. Edited by Peter Coveney. New York: Penguin, 1972.

Elton, Oliver. *A Survey of English Literature, 1780–1880*. 4 vols. New York: Macmillan, 1920.

Endelman, Todd M. "'A Hebrew to the End': The Emergence of Disraeli's Jewishness." In *The Self-Fashioning of Disraeli, 1818–1851*, edited by Charles Richmond and Paul Smith. Cambridge: Cambridge University Press, 1998.

Engels, Frederick. "The Condition of England: *Past and Present* by Thomas Carlyle, London, 1843." In vol. 3 of *Karl Marx, Frederick Engels: Collected Works*. New York: International Publishers, 1975.

———. *The Condition of the Working Class in England*. Vol. 4 of *Karl Marx, Frederick Engels: Collected Works*. New York: International Publishers, 1975.

Fido, Martin. "'From His Own Observation': Sources of Working Class Passages in Disraeli's *Sybil*." *Modern Language Review* 72 (1977): 268–284.

Foucault, Michel. *Discipline and Punish: The Birth of the Prison*. Translated by Alan Sheridan. New York: Vintage, 1979.

Frank, Joseph. *The Levellers*. New York: Russell and Russell, 1955.

Froude, James Anthony. *Thomas Carlyle: A History of His Life in London, 1834–1881*. 2 vols. New York: Scribner's, 1884.

Frye, Lowell T. "Romancing the Past: Walter Scott and Thomas Carlyle." *Carlyle Studies Annual* 16 (1996): 37–49.

Fulford, Tim. *Romanticism and Masculinity: Gender, Politics and Poetics in the Writings of Burke, Coleridge, Cobbett, Wordsworth, DeQuincey and Hazlitt*. New York: St. Martin's, 1999.

Gallagher, Catherine. "The Body versus the Social Body in the Works of Thomas Malthus and Henry Mayhew." In *The Making of the Modern Body: Sexuality and Society in the Nineteenth Century*, edited by Catherine Gallagher and Thomas Lacqueur. Berkeley: University of California Press, 1987.

———. *The Industrial Reformation of English Fiction: Social Discourse and Narrative Form, 1832–1867*. Chicago: University of Chicago Press, 1985.

Gaskell, Elizabeth. *North and South*. Edited by Dorothy Collin. New York: Penguin, 1986.

Gilmartin, Kevin. *Print Politics: The Press and Radical Opposition in Early Nineteenth-Century England*. New York: Cambridge University Press, 1997.

———. "'This Is Very Material': William Cobbett and the Rhetoric of Radical Opposition." *Studies in Romanticism* 34 (spring 1995): 81–101.

Girouard, Mark. *The Return to Camelot: Chivalry and the English Gentleman.* New Haven: Yale University Press, 1981.

Gooch, G. P. *History and Historians in the Nineteenth Century.* Boston: Beacon Press, 1959.

Gordon, Jan B. "'Booked for Passage' on Cobbett's *Rural Rides:* Ecology as Revolution." *Nineteenth-Century Prose* 19, no. 3 (1992): 60–84.

Goux, Jean-Joseph. *Symbolic Economies: After Marx and Freud.* Translated by Jennifer Curtiss Gage. Ithaca: Cornell University Press, 1990.

Graves, Robert. *The Greek Myths: 1.* New York: Penguin, 1985.

Green, Daniel. *Great Cobbett: The Noblest Agitator.* Toronto: Hodder and Stoughton, 1983.

Greenblatt, Stephen. *Shakespearian Negotiations: The Circulation of Social Energy in Renaissance England.* Berkeley: University of California Press, 1988.

Griggs, E. L. *The Collected Letters of Samuel Taylor Coleridge.* 6 vols. London: Oxford University Press, 1956–71.

Haley, Bruce. *The Healthy Body and Victorian Culture.* Cambridge: Harvard University Press, 1978.

Hall, Catherine. *White, Male and Middle Class: Explorations in Feminism and History.* New York: Routledge, 1992.

Handwerk, Gary. "Behind Sybil's Veil: Disraeli's Mix of Ideological Messages." *Modern Language Quarterly* 49 (December 1988): 321–41.

Hazlitt, William. *The Complete Works of William Hazlitt.* 21 vols. Edited by P. P. Howe. New York: AMS Press, 1967.

Hill, Christopher. *The World Turned Upside Down.* New York: Viking Press, 1972.

Hirsch, Gordon. "History Writing in Carlyle's *Past and Present.*" *Prose Studies* 7 (December 1984): 225–31.

Hollier, Denis, ed. *The College of Sociology (1937–39).* Translated by Betsy Wing. Minneapolis: University of Minnesota Press, 1988.

Houghton, Walter E. *The Victorian Frame of Mind, 1830–1870.* New Haven: Yale University Press, 1957.

Hughes, A. M. D., ed. *Cobbett Selections.* Oxford: Clarendon, 1961.

Hume, David. *The History of England from the Invasion of Julius Caesar to the Abdication of James the Second, 1688.* 5 vols. Philadelphia: Porter and Coates, n.d.

Jann, Rosemary. "The Condition of England Past and Present: Thomas Carlyle and the Middle Ages." *Studies in Medievalism* 1 (spring 1979): 15–31.

Jessop, Ralph. *Carlyle and Scottish Thought.* New York: St. Martin's Press, 1997.

Jocelin of Brakelond. *The Chronicle of Jocelin of Brakelond, Monk of St. Edmundsbury.* Translated by L. C. Jane. New York: Cooper Square, 1966.

Jupp, Peter. "Disraeli's Interpretation of English History." In *The Self-Fashioning of Disraeli, 1818–1851,* edited by Charles Richmond and Paul Smith. Cambridge: Cambridge University Press, 1998.

Kaplan, Fred. *Thomas Carlyle: A Biography.* Ithaca: Cornell University Press, 1983.

Keating, Peter. "Backward or Forward? Carlyle's *Past and Present.*" In *Thomas Carlyle*

1981: Papers Given at the International Thomas Carlyle Centenary Symposium, edited by Horst W. Drescher. Frankfurt: Peter Lang, 1981.

Keith, W. J. *The Rural Tradition: A Study of the Non-Fiction Prose Writers of the English Countryside*. Toronto: University of Toronto Press, 1974.

Kerr, James. *Fiction against History: Scott as Storyteller*. New York: Cambridge University Press, 1989.

Lamb, John B. "Carlyle's 'Chartism,' the Rhetoric of Revolution, and the Dream of Empire." *VIJ: Victorians Institute Journal* 23 (1995): 129–50.

Levine, George. "Carlyle, Descartes, and Objectivity." *Raritan: A Quarterly Review* 17 (summer 1997): 45–58.

———. "Victorian Studies." In *Redrawing the Boundaries: The Transformation of English and American Literary Studies*. Edited by Stephen Greenblatt and Giles Gunn. New York: MLA, 1992.

Levine, Richard A. *Benjamin Disraeli*. New York: Twayne, 1968.

Loesberg, Jonathan. *Fictions of Consciousness: Mill, Newman and the Reading of Victorian Prose*. New Brunswick: Rutgers University Press, 1986.

Lukács, Georg. *History and Class Consciousness: Studies in Marxist Dialectics*. Translated by Rodney Livingstone. Cambridge: MIT Press, 1971.

Macaulay, Thomas Babington. *The History of England from the Accession of James II*. 3 vols. New York: Dutton, 1906.

Malone, C. "Voices of the Ages: The Editor and His Texts in *Past and Present*." *Carlyle Annual* 10 (1989): 41–49.

Marx, Karl. *Capital: A Critique of Political Economy*. Vol 1. Edited by Frederick Engels. Translated by Samuel Moore and Edward Aveling. New York: International Publishers, 1967.

McCully, Michael. "Beyond 'The Convent and the Cottage': A Reconsideration of Disraeli's *Sybil*." *College Language Association Journal* 29 (March 1986): 318–35.

Melada, Ivan. *The Captain of Industry in English Fiction, 1821–1871*. Albuquerque: University of New Mexico Press, 1970.

Monypenny, William Flavelle, and George Earle Buckle. *The Life of Benjamin Disraeli Earl of Beaconsfield*. 4 vols. 1929. Reprint, New York: Russell and Russell, 1968.

Nattrass, Leonora. *William Cobbett: The Politics of Style*. New York: Cambridge University Press, 1995.

Neff, Emery. *Carlyle*. 1932. Reprint, New York: Russell and Russell, 1968.

O'Kell, Robert. "Two Nations, or One? Disraeli's Allegorical Romance." *Victorian Studies* 30 (winter 1987): 211–34.

Osborne, John. "William Cobbett's Anti-Semitism." *Historian* 47 (November 1984): 90.

Ovid. *Metamorphoses*. Translated by Rolfe Humphries. Bloomington: Indiana University Press, 1955.

Plotz, John. *The Crowd: British Literature and Public Politics*. Berkeley: University of California Press, 2000.

Poovey, Mary. *Making a Social Body: British Cultural Formation, 1830–1864*. Chicago: University of Chicago Press, 1995.

Review of *Past and Present*, by Thomas Carlyle. *The Athenaeum* (20 May 1843): 480–81.

Richards, Thomas. *The Commodity Culture of Victorian England: Advertising and Spectacle, 1851–1914*. Stanford: Stanford University Press, 1990.

Ridley, Jane. *Young Disraeli, 1804–1846*. New York: Crown, 1995.

Rigney, Ann. "The Untenanted Places of the Past: Thomas Carlyle and the Varieties of Historical Ignorance." *History and Theory* 35, no. 3 (1996): 338–58.

Roe, Frederick William. *The Social Philosophy of Carlyle and Ruskin*. New York: Gordian Press, 1970.

Rosenberg, John D. *Carlyle and the Burden of History*. Oxford: Clarendon Press, 1985.

Roy, Parama. "*Sybil*: The Two Nations and the Manorial Ideal." *VIJ: Victorians Institute Journal* 17 (1989): 63–75.

Ruskin, John. *The Seven Lamps of Architecture*. New York: Dover, 1989.

Sampson, Jennifer. "Sybil, or the Two Monarchs." *Studies in Philology* 95 (winter 1998): 97–119.

Scarry, Elaine, ed. *Literature and the Body: Essays on Populations and Persons*. Baltimore: Johns Hopkins University Press, 1990.

Schoch, Richard W. "'We Do Nothing But Enact History': Thomas Carlyle Stages the Past." *Nineteenth-Century Literature* 54 (June 1999): 27–52.

Schwarz, Daniel. *Disraeli's Fiction*. New York: Harper and Row, 1979.

Schweitzer, Karl W., and John W. Osborne. *Cobbett in His Times*. London: Leicester University Press, 1990.

Scott, Joan Wallach. *Gender and the Politics of History*. Rev. ed. New York: Columbia University Press, 1999.

Seigel, Jules Paul, ed. *Thomas Carlyle: The Critical Heritage*. New York: Barnes and Noble, 1971.

Shaw, W. David. *Victorians and Mystery: Crises of Representation*. Ithaca: Cornell University Press, 1990.

Shires, Linda M., ed. *Rewriting the Victorians: Theory, History, and the Politics of Gender*. New York: Routledge, 1992.

Simmons, Clare. *Reversing the Conquest: History and Myth in Nineteenth-Century British Literature*. New Brunswick: Rutgers University Press, 1990.

Smith, Paul. "Disraeli's Politics." In *The Self-Fashioning of Disraeli, 1818–1851*, edited by Charles Richmond and Paul Smith. Cambridge: Cambridge University Press, 1998.

———. Introduction to *The Self-Fashioning of Disraeli, 1818–1851*, edited by Charles Richmond and Paul Smith. Cambridge: Cambridge University Press, 1998.

Smith, R. J. "Cobbett, Catholic History, and the Middle Ages." *Studies in Medievalism* 4 (1992): 113–42.

———. *The Gothic Bequest: Medieval Institutions in British Thought, 1688–1863*. New York: Cambridge University Press, 1987.

Smith, Sheila M. "Willenhall and Wodgate: Disraeli's Use of Blue Book Evidence." *Review of English Studies* 13 (1962): 368–84.

Southey, Robert. *Sir Thomas More; or, Colloquies on the Progress and Prospects of Society*. 2nd ed. 2 vols. London: John Murray, 1831.

Spater, George. *William Cobbett: The Poor Man's Friend*. 2 vols. New York: Cambridge University Press, 1982.

"Speculum." *The Oxford English Dictionary*. 2nd ed.

Stedman Jones, Gareth. *Languages of Class: Studies in English Working Class History 1832–1982*. New York: Cambridge University Press, 1983.

Sussman, Herbert. *Victorian Masculinities: Manhood and Masculine Poetics in Early Victorian Literature and Art*. Cambridge: Cambridge University Press, 1995.

Tholfson, Trygve. *Working Class Radicalism in Mid-Victorian England*. New York: Columbia University Press, 1977.

Thompson, E. P. *The Making of the English Working Class*. New York: Vintage, 1966.

Tucker, Robert C., ed. *The Marx-Engels Reader*. New York: Norton, 1978.

Ure, Andrew. *The Philosophy of Manufactures; or, an Exposition of the Scientific, Moral, and Commercial Economy of the Factory System of Great Britain*. London: Charles Knight, 1835.

Vanden Bossche, Chris R. *Carlyle and the Search for Authority*. Columbus: Ohio State University Press, 1991.

Veeser, H. Aram, ed. *The New Historicism*. New York: Routledge, 1989.

Weeks, Richard G. Jr. "Disraeli as Political Egoist: A Literary and Historical Investigation." *Journal of British Studies* 28 (October 1989): 387–410.

Weltman, Sharon Aronofsky. "Female and Maelstrom: The Gender Vortex in Carlyle and Ruskin." *Carlyle Studies Annual* 17 (1997): 91–99.

White, Hayden. *Metahistory: The Historical Imagination in Nineteenth-Century Europe*. Baltimore: Johns Hopkins University Press, 1973.

Williams, Raymond. *Cobbett*. New York: Oxford University Press, 1983.

———. *The Country and the City*. New York: Oxford University Press, 1973.

———. *Culture and Society, 1780–1950*. New York: Columbia University Press, 1983.

Young, Louise Merwin. *Thomas Carlyle and the Art of History*. New York: Octagon Books, 1971.

Index